Twaar't Naars

A Flatlander's guide to Cowboy Hunting

By Dale E. Wagman

Copyright © 2010 by Dale E. Wagman

All rights reserved. No part of this book may be reproduced in any form or by any electronic or mechanical means, including information storage and retrieval systems, without permission in writing from the publisher.

ISBN 978-0-578-07633-1

Thanks Dick

CONTENTS

1) **Introduction**
   - Introduction
   - What is Cowboy Hunting?
   - Million dollar cowboys

2) **Getting There**
   - To Go Or Not To Go
     - Bar talk X
   - Timing
     - The Fastest Elk in The West
   - Species
     - Cornucopia
   - Where to go
   - The Land of the Cowboys
   - Licensing
   - Draw Partner
   - The Kingdom
   - Combos
   - One is good two is better

3) **Options a Plenty**
   - Options
   - Empty Men
   - Options

4) **Outfitters**
   - Finding a reputable outfitter
   - The bad the worse and the really ugly
   - The good the better…and Dick

Finding Outfitters II

5) Guides

Joe Menji

More Guide Stuff

Mile Marker # 8

Need more proof

Wranglers – Worth their weight in work

Dinner – you didn't think of this one?

Costs

6) Homework

Getting ready

Training

A scent on the wind

Packing

Bad weather

Really bad weather

Horrible weather

Doing it right

What to bring

Guns

Gentlemen Choose your Weapons

7) Finally – you're there

Now what?

Normal Camps

Un-normal Camps

8) Horse Stories

No Lakers no Dallas

Airborne

What would ray Charles do?

Wild Strawberries

What Kind of Goofy Horse is That?

Smarter Than They Look

9) Danger

Danger

Hunters Beware

Blind man Walking

Hypothermia

Moving to Jamaica

Dehydration

Brain Storm

Orientation Disabilities

Lost Boys

Cliffs

On… or off the edge

Lions, Tigers and Bears and Wolves too!

Getting out of Dodge

Horse Wrecks and Rodeos

Royal Oak Rodeo

Rock Pile Rodeo

Twenty Mule Team Stomp

10) Truck hunting

Cowboy Lite

No Horse Hunting – Still Fun (sort of)

Roarin' Roger

11) Getting them out

Liquid Sheep

Dead deer walking

12) Going Home

Going Home

Processing

Shipping etc

Taxidermy

Tipping guides and outfitters

INTRODUCTION

We were college kids in the late '60s and lucky that the war in Vietnam passed us by. Yep, bell bottoms, long hair, flower power, protest marches - the '60s - what a great time! The best part – since we had no money – was that we could hitch-hike without fear of death or worse. Hitch-hiking was an absolute hoot! Not only could you get from one place to another for almost nothing, but it was an excellent inroad to adventure.

While some people in New York were having a party of sorts – Woodstock – some of our friends were having a party of sorts of their own, in a small town in Colorado - Aspen. In those days, Aspen was just a couple of dirt roads, not yet overrun by the rich and famous. We'd never been to Colorado. It was only a couple of thousand miles away and, a party is a party. We stuck out our thumbs and in a few days, found a whole new world in the west.

But, things are what they are and, for myriad reasons, I have lived all of my life in Michigan and have lost touch with most of my old traveling buddies. The west, however, has remained an ever-present lure – a lure, which calls me back two or three times each year. I have made thirty or so auto trips from Michigan along highways I-80, I-70 and I-90 to the Rockies. I have made another thirty or so along the same routes by plane. My wife and I have spent every July hiking, camping and exploring the high peaks and pristine meadows of that wonderland. I have changed baby diapers in the moonlight under the Tetons, melted countless S'mores along the banks of the Colorado River and had many a snowball war on small un-melted glaciers, high up in Rocky Mountain, Yellowstone and Glacier National Parks. I have taken part in just about every possible tourist activity, from white-water rafting to fourteen thousand foot climbs to sideways rooms at the Mystery Spot. I have also had the good fortune to have made many fall trips to the west, to hunt Elk and Mule Deer.

None of this, of course, qualifies me to discuss living in the west, but it darn sure has made me an expert at getting to and from it and having fun once we get there – especially if we're going hunting.

I own a high-traffic business in Michigan and several head mounts of Deer and Elk adorn our lobby. I am constantly fielding questions about big game hunting trips in the Rockies. They come from hundreds of guys who wish they could hunt out west and from hundreds more who are actually planning a trip and want to ask logistical questions: How to get there? What to bring? What about outfitters? Where to go? How much will it cost? What kind of gun?

I have asked all those questions myself to outfitters and guides with whom I have hunted, as well as to many others with whom I have not yet had the pleasure. I have learned much more myself, by actually having done it many many times. This book is an attempt to answer all of those uninitiated wannabes who have asked.

Each year thousands of hunters migrate to the west from all over the country. But, for every one who does, there are ten who would love to and plan to. This book is for them.

The events depicted in the hunts are true. Of course, they are all suitably embellished, as any good hunting story should be. They all may not have happened on the same hunt, nor happened exactly as described, but, they did happen – not always to me, but to someone with whom I have hunted. The characters are real people and although names have been changed to protect the guilty, they will still know who they are. The horses are real horses. The trails do exist. The hunts, or something similar, can be booked today. And the mountains? They remain one of planet earth's most treasured attributes.

WHAT IS COWBOY HUNTING?

Cowboy hunting is stepping back into time. It is losing, for a while, whatever it is that defines your days-crawling-by-like-a-slow-freight-train life. It's something different. It's something exciting. It's something truly difficult and sometimes even dangerous. Cowboy hunting scratches an itch down deep in some primitive brain crease. Cowboy hunting is one hell of an adventure and in the end, adventure is what life is really about.

MILLION DOLLAR COWBOYS

Gabriel lifts a stubby finger into the air and spits a garbled knot of twangy words through weathered, scabby lips. He's speaking, of course, but I might as well be listening to a fourteen-year-old girl, on a cell phone, in a crowded restaurant. All I hear is "twartnaars." Admittedly, my hearing has been a little cloudy in recent years. It helps if I can read lips while I listen. He's ten windy yards ahead on his horse. The bull-tough wilderness we're riding through punches the middles out of words spoken even at close range, so comprehension is hopeless. Our altitude doesn't help. Nothing makes much sense above ten thousand feet.

Actually, I gave up trying to understand the big man yesterday sometime. We speak different languages – me; Eastern Standard English, him; deep-in-the-holler West Virginian. Except, he has some sort of speech impediment to go with it.

He slips out of the saddle nimbly, like a spring cat – my signal to dismount. After two full days on a saddle as hard as Mars, various body parts are failing. I, more or less, fall off the horse, praying all the while my feet will land somewhat simultaneously and on something relatively flat. Pain squishes from every joint. I take a few triple breaths to make up for oxygen debt.

My horse casts a giant, brown eye at me as I slide down his flank. He does not need words to express his delight at my dismounting. It has been a very hard climb. Air whooshes through his baseball-size nostrils and his chest heaves, expanding ten inches with every breath. At several points on the climb, I thought the poor thing's heart was about to attack him. I could feel it slapping the insides of my thighs through his ribs and the hard leather saddle.

The trail Gabe has chosen to get here is barely a trail at all. It's more like a vertical obstacle course, delineated by an occasional bent blade of grass or a conspicuous flat spot.

"I didn't catch that," I say, remembering my vow not to say "what" anymore.

Gabe leads his horse back to mine. He takes my reigns in his haystack paw. I notice someone has inked my name in the center of his palm. He points to some refugee pine trees, which cling desperately to the rocks - progeny of luckless seeds. His BB eyes are wet and red. I can barely see them, through his perpetual squint. Cruel weather and cruel genes have ridden his fleshy face hard. Another flight of words pours through his large gap-toothed smile. Most of what he says passes through my head like polished pebbles. I catch "hitch, critters, trees, yonder, trieeal" and "twaar't naars." I screw up my face and send him my best puzzled-look.

Gabe cocks his head toward a large talus field a few-hundred yards to our right. I spin. The field slopes up at about a 60-degree angle and then terminates abruptly at a solid wall of granite. The sun hammers through the frozen air and blisters the rock. A small Pica casts an eye skyward in search of death on the wing and then gives me a quick stare. Concluding I'm no threat, he goes back to stashing grass in rock holes. Apparently my poor condition is obvious - even to Rodents.

"What?" I drop my arms to my sides and flash open palms Gabe's way – the universal signal of confusion. I hope he is not thinking about climbing that wall. It's well worth breaking my no "what" rule.

It seems like no one is actually from the west. Everyone comes here from somewhere else. Gabriel spent twenty years flat on his back with an Appalachian coal seam a couple of feet from his face. Most everyone he knew had lung disease. It is rumored that even he has had a piece of lung removed. One day he said goodbye to all his "kin," trailered up his mule and headed for the "purdiest heels" he'd ever seen in Wyoming's Teton County. He is a living legend. His exploits are fodder for many an evening yarn-telling war. He is respected by guides and hated by horses for as far as the eye can see - which at this altitude is quite far. He sleeps only an hour or two a night. It is said that he walked thirty-two miles, one day, mostly after dark, when his chronically failing truck broke an axle out on some two-track, in the Wind Rivers. He has climbed more un-climbable peaks than most of Wyoming's resident Mountain Sheep. He almost never rides anything but a horse or a mule considered difficult and then takes it to places considered impossible. And when the hunting is rat stinky, Gabe always comes in with an Elk or a Wall-hanger deer. He is relentless, obsessive, compulsive and tougher than day-old bagels on most hunters. (Some, I'm told, negotiate with the boss to get paired up with one of the other guides thereby reducing their abuse levels. I didn't know you could do that.)

If you take a close look though, you can see it in his Oak-bark face. This isn't a job for Gabe. He loves this. He would rather do this than anything. Being born somewhere other than here was a miscalculation by nature – one, which he has managed to correct. It is said that even on his days off, he comes up into these "hee-els" to make trails, string ropes and scout for the next hunt.

String ropes?

He repeats the litany of garble, slowly this time as though he is talking to an idiot. "Fixin ta, hitch, horses, trees, git up tri ee al, t' waar, it naars."

I stand for a minute, face blank, mind blank - dead like my computer screen when the "please wait a minute" sign is on. I have a numb spot in my back just west of my right shoulder blade. A bee or something buzzes near my leg – a miniature helicopter. It's too cold up here for bugs. My mind drifts. I remember my last tee shot at Marion Oaks. Actually hit the fairway. I love my new driver. And, then suddenly, I get it – most of it anyway.

"Okay okay, I got it. You want to leave the horses here in these trees and head up the trail to where it does something. I am sorry Gabe, but I just can't make out that last word."

"Naars," he says, gesturing with his bulbous hands as though measuring a fish.

My head drains - all thoughts gone, blue sky empty.

"Narrows." After an embarrassingly long pause, it hits me.

"To where it narrows," I say, feeling as sharp as a pumpkin.

I triple breathe again from the exertion of all that thinking.

"We can't go up there, Gabe."

His eyes bulge. His ruddy face puckers. "Sho nuff can."

Some friends and I had flown out from the lowlands of Michigan the day before our hunt. Rather than suffer airplane food, we drove the rental car straight to the Million Dollar Cowboy bar in Jackson for lunch. The bar has saddles for bar stools. We always start and finish our hunting trips there. Over the years, we've tossed back countless toasts to the Million Dollar Cowboys, and wondered who they are. Wealthy ranchers? Movie stars?

We drove from the bar to a ranch at about seven thousand feet and spent the night. We had "hunted in" to the high camp yesterday, which meant that we turned a sixteen-mile normally dude-pleasant horse ride into a forty-mile agony, by wandering around in the mountains all day and then a furlong or two past supper - far into the black night.

Gabe cannot feel pain or the effects of the altitude, but they are both killing me. I have had no time to acclimatize. This is just day two in the mountains. Any movement at all, even fighting to get my fly open, leaves me gasping for air. Taking the three quick breaths is not voluntary. It just happens. I've been through this before. It'll take four or five days for me to adjust - just in time to go home.

Gabe ties the horses to the skinny trees, and I wrangle my rifle from its scabbard.

"I don't see a trail, Gabe." He is already forty yards ahead of me.

"Reckon it's a deer tri-ee-al," he yells back.

"It's a mouse trail," I say, gasping. "A deer could never get his foot on this. In fact, it's so damn vertical; it's probably a bird trail."

The mountains are full of big rocks with cracks in them - something left over from Volcanoes or up-thrusts or cooling lava or all of the above. From time to time, over a few million years, ice forms in the cracks and peels large slabs of rock free. The slabs splinter into zillions of pieces when they hit ground. Over the years, the relentless cycle of water and ice continues to chop the pieces finer and finer. They call this collection of small busted rocks, talus. Walking on talus is no easy task. With each step, one or the other of my ankles twists and new monsters of pain romp up my spine. Walking on this particular talus is the stuff Circus acts are made of.

"What are you planning to do when we get to the wall, " I ask.

"Git on top."

"You're a tough guy Gabe, but you can't fly you know. I know I can't fly. In fact, I don't even think I can walk to that wall."

I am starting to quadruple breathe. My heart thuds against the inside of my chest, looking for somewhere to hide. Gabe is walking too fast for me. It seems like he is running. I wonder for a second or two about the urgency, but I am too busy with thoughts of survival to deal with logistical problems.

"Got me a rope yonder," he says, looking back over his shoulder at me, flipping a gawky hand toward the rock world ahead of us.

It's my worst fear. He's got a rope strung on a craggy mountaintop at over 11000 feet and plans to climb it. My gun slips off my shoulder and crashes into the rocks. I sling it up again. The angle of ascent changes. The slope is now almost vertical like old-time apartment stairs. My left hand acts as an outrigger, counter-balancing the bad angle. I am sweating but my hand is frozen and aching from touching the cold rocks. My feet slip with each step and I am constantly double stepping to catch up with myself. I am panting. My mouth sticks to itself. It feels like I am chewing a piece of chalk. I have forgotten my lip goo and annoying fissures are sprouting everywhere. More rocks, dislodged by Gabe up above, clatter down at me. I stop to rest and to pant. The horses look like saddled jellybeans down below in the trees, tails flicking against the branches. I have a feeling that things are about to get worse.

I can no longer see Gabriel. He has disappeared around a curve up above me – a vertical crevasse in the rock wall.

Elk and Deer can be hunted by far easier means. Despite my complaints, concerns and flat-out terror, this is my method of choice. It's cowboy hunting, and I am a cowboy. It is true; that I have never punched a doggie, roped a steer, mended a fence or busted a Bronc, but I am a cowboy nonetheless, and this is the way we cowboys hunt.

Except for a brief stint when I thought my bike was a motorcycle and I was a motorcycle policeman, I can't remember ever being anything but a cowboy. In the golden years - seven to roughly nine - the first thing I did when I woke, was to strap on a silver-stared, shiny, black, plastic holster and put on my cowboy hat. Then, I would reach under my pillow - where all cowboys kept them - and extract my two white, plastic-handled silver-barreled guns. They were real guns. You could put a roll of red-papered caps on a pin under the hammer, pop off a few rounds, and the coolest whiff of blue smoke would stream out of the barrel. No kid alive could resist sniffing that smoke. I'd blow off a half a roll as soon as I got them in the gun, then save the rest to smash with a tack hammer on the floor in the basement.

My grandmother had a blanket-knitting fetish. We had dozens of them flopped around – gifts for every occasion. They made good saddles. Fold one into quarters, toss it over the arm of my mother's sofa and poof, instant horse.

I rode for hours. Covered miles and miles - most of it through hostile Indian country. I led wagon trains. I was a Major in the Calvary - scouted for them, in fact. I was the town Marshall for most of my career. I roped cats and our small dog Tippy.

Cowboy is in my soul. It would not be an exaggeration to say I have seen every cowboy movie ever made. Gene Autry, Hoppalog Cassidy, Glen Ford, Auddie Murphy, Henry Fonda, Jimmy Stuart, Robert Mitchum, John Wayne – I have been all those guys at one time or another. In the 80's when John Travolta and the rest of the Urban Cowboys danced onto the scene, with over-sized collars, snake-skin boots and hats without a lick of sweat stain on the brim, real cowboys like me felt kind of, well, pukey, I guess. We had to put our cowboy hats away, that's for sure. Better to be doomed to the functionally inferior and esthetically inadequate baseball cap, than to be thought a poseur.

So, yeah, we could be hunting out of trucks or on ATV's but we would not be here and we would not be cowboy.

This is my twentieth - or something like that - cowboy hunt. The difference between this one and all the others is that today, I am, of course, the oldest I have ever been, and I have never before drawn Gabe as a personal guide. I am not sure which of those maladies hurts more.

I can't see or hear him anymore. I know he is up ahead of me only because I am still dodging a shower of rocks. I am essentially alone, almost on the top of a mountain. Fear and excitement are easily mistaken for one another. I am not sure which one I am feeling. My legs are shaking.

The cut in the rock wall bends back on itself, so that anyone looking directly at it could never see it. I stand at the base of it, fighting to catch my breath. The talus slope appears to be losing the battle against gravity. It looks to me that at any minute, the entire thing could cut loose and head south with me tangled up in it, tumbling like laundry in the dryer. But there is another problem. There's fur everywhere - fur and pieces of bone. And, the unmistakable scent of cat pee permeates the air.

"Gabe."

Nothing.

"Gabriel."

I'm shouting, but I can barely hear myself in the thin air. I try to bend my neck around into the crevasse, without taking my back off the wall. My feet slip a notch on the moving slope. "Gabriel."

I've been hearing about problems with mountain lions lately. Their numbers are on the rise in the west, and their habitat is shrinking. People are getting mauled and killed. Last year, when we were out here, a small child had been stolen while on a walk with his parents. We came upon part of the search party while hunting. Their conclusion was that a big cat snuck up on the hikers and stole the kid from the back of the line – in broad daylight. Gulp!

I am not afraid of much in the mountains. Snakes and bugs are startling sometimes, because you can't see them, but they are very rare and usually harmless. Moose and Buffalo are mean and dangerous, but easily avoidable. Bears will eat you if they have the opportunity, but usually are shooed off without incident. Cats are a different story. They tend to stalk you, and by the time you have seen them, they have already marked you for lunch. "Gabriel."

I can neither hear nor see my wilderness guide out here in the wilderness. The avalanche of rock he has been sending down at my head has stopped. My legs continue to shake. It's a combination of excitement and fatigue, I figure - denying fear. I'm having real difficulties catching my breath. I'm having dizzy spells from oxygen deprivation. There is some blood on my pant leg. I can't find the source, but it is fresh and most likely, mine. The horses have shrunk to periods below. We are crowding the twelve thousand foot mark, far above the tree line. My feet are in the shade and freezing, yet, rivulets of sweat stream down from under my hat. I start rationalizing: There's probably not going to be anything up there anyway. I could get killed doing this. Have a heart attack. Fall into these rocks and break my head open. Get eaten by a lion.

"Maybe I should go back down and make sure the horses are okay," I say to nobody.

I wait a few more minutes, chasing demons through the valleys of my mind then, hitch the rifle sling up farther on my shoulder, take a step around the rock into the crevasse and start climbing again. No question that some cat has been hanging out in this crack. The fur and bones are just too obvious. I take one step at a time – one rock at a time - up and up. The crevasse spirals until there is only a cone of sunlight streaming in at the top. And then, I see a strand of yellow, waving in the wind.

I took a mountain climbing class back somewhere in my Cowboy-wannabe youth. When Gabe said he had a fixed rope, I pictured a braided nylon climbing rope fixed properly to the rock with climbing chocks. This is a piece of hardware store, yellow polypropylene fixed to the rock with nothing.

"Gabe, I can't climb this thing I yell."

He doesn't answer. He's cat food. I am here alone, trembling. The rocks continue to shift under my feet. I can scarcely breathe. I can no longer see the horses from here in the crack. I close my eyes. I can still see blue sky. I can see the rocks. I can see the sun glistening off tiny pieces of mica in the granite. And, I can see that rope.

It is decision time. Do I follow this fool, whom I barely know, on this mission of insanity - a mission just to see what is on top of a pile of rocks? Do I risk the rest of my life? A fall up here could be a death sentence - or worse. Do I slink back down to the horses like a what? Whimp? Chicken? Pussy?

Wait a minute. This is my trip. I spent a lot of money for this. It is a hunting trip, not a sight seeing trip. This guy is in my employ. He does what I say. This is a foolish and dangerous thing he's got me into. I make the decisions around here. It wouldn't be slinking back to the horses. It would be making a rational and educated move to protect my own well-being. It would be my right as a prudent consumer.

The plastic rope is frayed at the end. It's come unraveled. It hangs down only about chest high.

"You could have sprung for a little more rope Mr. Short," I yell. I've taken him off the friend list, and use the formal form.

Adrenaline is a strange drug – as addictive as any. It stampedes through my veins like so many Buffalo. I reach as high as I can and grip the damn rope like it is my only connection to the world, which, in a second, is exactly what it will become. It hangs in a trough in the rock where thousands of years of running water have removed even the suggestion of a good toe-hold. My boots clatter against the polished rock. The picture of a bad ice-skater windmilling his way around a rink pops into my head. I hand over hand my way up, wondering what piece of flotsam Gabriel has lashed this thing to. Not much I suspect. The picture of a guy in a full-body cast pops into my head.

I have been trying for years to lose a circle of excess hide from my belly. I am glad I haven't. I hook it over the edge of rock above the trough and use it for grip. A smooth, trim six-pack of muscle would have just slid off. With a grunt, I scramble the last couple of feet and collapse in the rocks on top of the ridge.

My rope fears are justified. The business end of the thing is wrapped just a few times around a big boulder. The wrappings could have undone themselves in a heartbeat and sent the rest of the skimpy rope and me to Hell.

I can't think about that now. I have pressing issues - breathing. I am face down in the rocks. Each breath liberates a micro-cloud of fine dust. It's pulverized mountain – the stuff that works its way to the sea with each rain. I can taste it. It feels gritty between my teeth. Each heartbeat bangs ruthlessly around in my head. I lift my eyes. The ridge slants uphill for another thirty yards ending in a polished knob of rock. Everything in sight is downhill from there. I can see Gabriel, or parts of him at least among the rocks - the brown from his jacket, a booted foot cast skyward at an unnatural angle, flecks of hunter orange, the brim of his hat.

"Gabriel," I gasp.

Nothing. The damn cats got him - ripped him apart and scattered the bits among the rocks.

I spin on my belly in a 360-degree circle, lizard-like, looking for anything cat-like. The rifle was a pain in the ass on the way up, but I am glad I have it now. I manage to sit and lift it to my shoulder, ready.

I can see Gabe now, but he doesn't seem torn to pieces like I had originally thought. In fact, he looks like he's lying on a beach staring out at the ocean. His hands are folded behind his head, and one leg rests crossed over the other. His back is against a sizable boulder and he looks quite comfortable. He cracks a huge smile of approval as I struggle to my feet and begin staggering his way.

"See," he says. "Ya'lls tougher 'n you thunk."

"Yeah, and you're crazier than I thunk too. That rope's not safe Gabe." I don't mention my cat paranoia.

"Reckon it got ya'll up here shonuff."

I find a suitable rock next to Gabe and sit hard. I prop the rifle on another rock and exercise my stiff shoulder. Carrying a gun on a hike like that is not easy. I look at my watch. It has taken over an hour to climb up here. Then, I let my eyes pan the landscape.

"Holy jamokes. We couldn't climb much higher."

"Reckon not."

The Grand Teton, forty miles northwest, is a little higher, but doesn't look like it from here. I can see its snow covered top clearly in the distance. Its sharp peak has ripped the bottom out of a passing cloud. Almost seventy-five miles to the east Gannet Peak, Wyoming's highest point, sits among the Wind Rivers, but at this distance the relative heights are difficult to see. Everything looks like down to me.

"Hey, there's Elk down there Gabe. I tap him lightly on the shoulder and point down into the valley in front of us.

"Yuhuh."

We are on the highest knob of a giant circular ridge, which makes a bowl of sorts at the top of a valley – a typical geographical arrangement for mountainous terrain. The ridge spins away from us almost a mile. The valley below is steep and grassy. On our side, below us, is a giant black forest of timber. We look down on the tops of ancient trees. On the broad side-hill, near the top on the opposite side, dozens of Elk and Deer feed – visible with the naked eye. More dot the bottom of the valley, in a meadow, which ends where a tiny creek drains the bowl. I pull out my binoculars from their hiding place in my shirt.

"Gabe, there's a monster down there. That one bull is huge."

Gabriel has not changed his position. He is sunning himself, hands behind his head, face turned up. He's not even looking into the valley. Must be advanced guide stuff I've not heard of yet.

"Shonuffs a toad, I reckon. Seen him last week."

Toad is Cowboy talk for a big one.

"Yeah, big toad. Let's put a move on him."

"Cain't"

"Why not?"

"Too steep yonder. Couldn't never git to him. Couldn't never git him back up here if'n we done it."

"There's plenty of light, Gabe. We could drop back down to our horses, ride down the valley we came up a mile or two, cross over, and come into this valley from the bottom. Put a good sneak on him and take him back out the bottom. He's a real wall hanger. It'd be worth it. Hell, he probably couldn't even get away. These slopes are so steep."

"Cain't"

"Why not."

This is always a touchy negotiation. We hunters foot the bills. Guided western hunting trips, cowboy or otherwise, are not cheap. We want to get our money's worth. Those of us who do it on a regular basis know a thing or two about hunting. We'd like to be involved in the hunting decisions.

Guides on the other hand are professionals. They know the land. They know the horses. They know the habits of the game. They want you to be successful and are usually in some sort of unofficial competition with the other guides to see who can do the best. We are their responsibility. They insist on being in charge. Most of the time, we don't even know where they are taking us.

I'm looking at one of the biggest bull Elk trophies I have ever seen and I can't hunt it?

"They's a avlunch in the bottom. Cain't get past it. A man cain't climb it. No mule cain't either. Reckon it's a dead end."

"You've not been down in this valley then, Mr. Go anywhere?"

"Cain't. Tried it a bunch."

We sit silently for a minute. I glass every inch of the valley and the rim around it. The grass ends thirty feet from the top and, above that, nothing but shear rock wall. Gabe's right. There is no way we could ever get an animal out over the top, given what we had to climb to get here. The prospect of climbing back down that rope pops into my mind. I know we are going to have to do it, but it is not a task I am looking forward to.

"How do the animals get in here," I ask, after several minutes of examining the situation.

"Cain't figure it yet. They's got secrets."

"You've never been down there in that valley," I ask again

"Reckon ain't nobody's been there," he says, shaking his head.

I glass some more. The trees in this valley are giant - much bigger than any I've seen anywhere in Wyoming. Likely they have been undisturbed for, who knew? All of time I guess.

I don't know how to feel about all of this. I am whipped. I'm bleeding. Rocks are burrowing into my ass. We've expended a lot of effort to get here both physical and financial and yet, he knew we never even had a chance of getting anything.

"You mean we wasted a day, almost killed two horses, and then almost killed ourselves getting here, and you knew all the time we couldn't hunt here? Why would you do that?"

"It's purdy," he says grinning.

"Why'd you let me bring the gun?"

"Reckoned ya'll needed the exterxice."

It's probably exhaustion, but all I can do is chuckle. Exterxice?

It turns out, that the best guide in Wyoming, Mr. Mountain man, Mr. Tough, Mr. Hunter Obsessive Maniac Rope Hanger, has a soft spot for good views.

"It's a virgin," he says. "Ain't none left. Couldn't not never kill nothin' here no how. It'd be agin nature."

He has a point. Time has stopped in this valley. There are no traces of anything human here. The rest of the planet has been pounded into submission by countless generations of people. Human footprints cover just about every square inch of it – except here and maybe just a very few other places. It's likely that very few men have sat where we are sitting to even view this valley. It would have been way too much effort for any pioneers to expend. Native Americans might have made it here during their wanderings, so we might find a moccasin print down there if we looked, but not many. If it weren't for Gabriel's unremitting wanderlust, I probably would never get to see anything like this anywhere else in the world. It is a private sanctuary for animals only. I am not certain we should even be looking at it. Firing a gun here, let alone taking any of these animals would leave a dent in our Karma that would take a million after-lives to smooth over.

A Golden Eagle soars overhead. I settle into the rocks a little and even start feeling comfortable. The Eagle, without reason, does a 360-degree roll.

"Reckon why he done that," Gabe says.

"Why?"

"Cuz he can."

I chuckle again.

"That's why we's here. Cuz we can. I reckon it ain't 'bout the huntin'."

He has another point. I have often felt it is not about the hunting. Nobody in my family will miss a meal if I don't get a deer. It is about the adventure. The head-mounts I have on my walls are not animals. They are stories. They are memories. Hunting is the excuse to come here and do this. We are prisoners of our choices, in life. This is how we cowboys escape our mistakes - if only for a short time.

The sun slips low. Horizontal rays fan out through a bright cherry sky. We are not merely witnesses. We are engulfed - part of the spectacle. The rocks glow red. Our skin turns red. The intense color settles around us like a hot chocolate bath. We are glued to our rocks, unable to move or speak. The wind relaxes its relentless assault. I feel gentle vibrations and hear the soft hum the mountains make on the lee side of the breeze. Given our unique perspective, I am certain Gabe and I are the only ones to experience this particular sunset in this particular way. These minutes will be etched in our memories for eternity.

Gabriel is fascinated. "Reckon I ain't seen one this red never," he says.

We've been smelling smoke all day. I try to explain that there have been forest fires in Idaho, fifty miles to the west, and so the sun's rays are being shifted to the left end of the spectrum as they pass through, but I don't think he understands. I don't think he cares. This is a man who lives only in the moment. He does a 360-degree Eagle flip whenever he can. Like the desert sucking spring rain, he absorbs the sunset, oblivious to the dance light waves make to create it.

We head back in the dark. I am dreading the rope. We walk easily down the ridge for a mile and come off only a few hundred yards below the horses.

"We could have come up this way, Gabe."

"Reckon it's longer."

"Not that much."

"The rope's more funner."

Dinner back at camp ends in the usual way. Each of us, beat to hell, makes his parting comment. Then, we all rush to our drafty tents for some much needed rest. My buddy Tom and I lie on our log cots. He tells me about all the game he saw and about his near miss on a nice Bull. He wants to know about my day. I tell him.

"We didn't hunt much," I say

"Man," he says. "That was a pretty expensive sight-seeing trip. You wasted a good hunting day and worked your ass off too."

"Yep."

Everybody seems to want to point out the obvious today.

It's true, there's one less day for me on this trip, and each of these days can be looked at from a financial perspective. They are pricey. But, looking back, it occurs to me; if I had a hundred million dollars and could do whatever I wanted on any day that I wanted, I would have done today, exactly what I did. I'd have ridden the horse. I'd have trudged up through the talus. I'd have climbed the yellow rope. I'd have sat during prime hunting time and become part of a sunset. Gabe knew all along what I really wanted from this trip.

If old Gabe and I had brung a millionaire up yonder with us, I reckon, we'd a all been fairly right equal, danglin' on the end of that rope, skitterin' up that hee-el. Wouldn't a made a speck a difference if'n we'd a had a dollar or a hundred million of 'em.

The hot white light, from the lantern hanging from a modified coat hanger between us, fades to brown and then hisses out. The tent, with no Big

Dippers or Crab Nebulas, is far darker than space. Tom is probably sleeping, but I lean his way in the darkness and whisper. "It isn't the money and it isn't the hunting. It's the adventure. It's the memories. It's what separates living from merely existing. Want to know who the Million Dollar Cowboys are, Tom? They're you and me and Gabe and Florida Dave and Dead Eye George and Michigan Slim. We've always been the Million Dollar Cowboys, and didn't even know it."

TIP - COWBOY HUNTING: Cowboy hunting is waking in the God-awful dark to the sound of bells clanging on the necks of horses as they are chased in from their night pasture to begin the day. It is cold, cold mountain air that smells like bacon and sneaks up under the back of your shirt - shivery like a lover's hand. It's hot coffee and lots of it.

TIP - CLOTHING: If you plan on taking a long horse ride, where you might have to get in and out of the saddle many times, wear pants that are just a little too big. Tight ones will bind, and you will have an even more difficult time.

TIP - CLOTHING: A day in the saddle can rip the hide off your legs. Consider wearing a pair of polypro long johns under your jeans. Even though they can be hot, if the insides of your thighs, as well as other even more private areas, have not been pre-callused (an unlikely condition in the normal person), the double layer of material will greatly reduce chaffing.

TIP - GUNS: If you have a rifle, or worse, are thinking about borrowing a rifle from someone, which has a beautiful finish, you might want to think twice about taking it on a trip like this one. Scabbards are brutal on bluing. One ride and the blue will be rubbed to silver in several spots. Stainless steel barrels aren't safe either. A small rock or a grain or two of sand will etch trenches in a gun in just a few miles on horseback. Custom finish stocks are doomed. If the scabbard doesn't wreck them, rocks along the trail will. Composite stocks are far more resistant, but then, they lack the character of a nice wood finished stock.

There is the other school of thought, though. Twenty years ago, my gun had a nice finished stock. The barrel was blued and the gun looked sharp. Now, the stock is a collage of dings and scrapes, and the blue is flat out gone on large portions of the barrel. More than once someone has mentioned that my gun is not in very good shape, and I should maybe think about having it refinished.

"After all," they say. "Have some pride."

It's true the stock is starting to look like two beavers have had a tug-of-war with it, but refinishing? I don't think so. Just as each mount hanging on my wall is not an animal, but rather a story, each ding on that gunstock is a reminiscence. I know where all of them came from. I got one when I leaned the gun against a rock on the top of Pow Wow peak, and it slid off into a crack. Beautiful day, killed a huge buck about an hour later. There is a scrape on the side I got falling off a cliff on a trip up the Greyback – got some rock chips permanently stuck in my elbow to match it. Another big divot was dug into the gun by a rock when a horse decided to take a roll in the dirt one hot afternoon. If I had known he was thinking about a dirt bath, I would have taken the saddle off or at least pulled the gun out of the scabbard - saw two bull Elk fighting about two hours later. The missing blue? It's from days and days in the saddle. There's a smooth part on my ass to match that rub on the barrel. Yet, I figure at its current rate of deterioration, my gun will hold up until long after I die. If it looks too ugly at that time, just bury it with me.

TIP - GLASSING: Other than your underwear, the piece of equipment you will use more than anything else on a cowboy hunting trip is your binoculars. Have them with you at all times. Game can be hard to see, and even though you'll be scanning huge tracts of land, generally higher magnification is more useful than size of field.

Start as close to you as possible and work away. Many times, animals will be standing right in front of you, staring at you, while you are looking far off on some distant slope. Go slow. Sometimes you can look at the same spot for an hour before you see an animal standing there. When the sun changes, the scene changes, and what was a shadow can become a deer. What looked like a bunch of sticks a few minutes ago can become a huge rack.

Many times, a spotting scope comes in handy. They are a bit of a problem to carry on a horse, but if you can manage it, by all means take one – the smaller the better.

TIP – HUNTING TRIPS IN GENERAL: Try not to focus too much on getting an animal. Chances are you will get one, but that's not really what it is all about. Actually pulling the trigger on a Deer or an Elk, is only about 10% of the experience. Focus instead on the adventure. If you live in Ohio, for example, and work in a cubicle, or at some counter, or behind some desk, or even building houses, chances are at some point or another, your job and your life will become ordinary. That's really what Cowboy hunting is all about. It's adventure! It's a life, for a week, which is so removed from your normal life, that you can almost forget who you are. That's the point. A head shrinker would tell you to relax, take a vacation. But let's face it, relaxation is not what we really need. We need excitement. If we get too relaxed, we start thinking about how we'll change everything. That's just more stress and, it never works. Things are the same when you get back from one of those relaxers. If you're hell-bent down some cliff on horse, or even on foot, then, for that instant you'll really be away from it all. You won't even remember your ordinary life and that is truly "getting away for a while."

The trophies are nice, but they are just stuffed heads. It is the memories that come with them that are really important. When you're cowboy hunting, getting there is way more than half the fun. It IS the fun!

GETTING THERE

TO GO OR NOT TO GO
BAR TALK

Gustafers was a typical sports bar. The room, already too loud, flashed, video only, on its six TVs. Some form of game, or some discussion of some form of game ran noiselessly across each screen. Young waitresses with low hung slacks and low-slung necklines, darted about, oblivious to everything except their current missions. Tables were scattered around a central brass-railed bar. The barky stench of Nachos, Buffalo Wings, perfume and cigarettes floated thick in the purple air. Budwieser, Miller, Molson and all of their rivals had scattered themselves everywhere throughout the joint, depending on the relative strength and effectiveness of their advertising campaigns.

The Lions were losing again, no surprise to the hundred or so patrons clustered unevenly around the various tables, and lined along the edge of the bar on fixed, swivel stools. Few actually watched the misery. They'd seen it all before and each, man and woman alike, had an opinion as to why the carnage continued and what best to do to stop it.

A whirlwind of sound twisted above the tables until its roar stomped out the sound of a single voice. At the bar, men cocked their heads toward one another, sipping their beer, bitching about their jobs. Three of them had clustered around a single woman each leaning in, scattering scent, hoping to get lucky. At a cluttered table in the middle of the confusion five women sat, long cigarettes held high by long decorated fingers. They had come to escape their men, husbands and boyfriends alike, but so far had not stopped talking about them. One man sat at a table across from a middle-aged couple. Papers were strewn out before him, and a matching set sat untouched in front of the couple. He was selling something. They were not buying – sports trumps business sometimes, even bad sports. And, squeezed into a corner booth, six men ignored the game, ignored the women, passed on the food, and barely sipped their beer. They were preoccupied with important goings-on. They were there to finally get serious about hunting. This was it; no more putting it off, no more indecision, no more dreaming. They were going west this year, and that was all there was to it.

    TJ had grown up in the shadow of an Elk – literally. His father owned an auto repair shop. He'd bought it from another man who had been a hunter. A giant Elk mount came with the place, and TJ had been staring at that head since he was old enough to stare at anything.

    "I don't care where we go, but I finally got the money, and I am gonna get me an Elk," he said to the group.

    "My brother-in-law knows a guy who has a ranch in Colorado," Rollie said. "He says we can just come out any time we want and he'll provide everything we need. Save us some cash."

    "I've heard the best place to go for Elk, is Montana," Shorty said. "We might as well go for trophies. Besides Montana is cool. I've always wanted to go there."

    "The real big ones are in New Mexico," Walmart Will said.

    "No, Montana," Shorty insisted.

"I think we should seriously consider hunting mule deer, while we are at it," Digger said.

"Those Licenses are expensive," Rollie said. "I don't know if I can go for two things."

"It's easier to get a big mulie than it is to get a big Elk."

"No," TJ chimed in. "Elk are easier."

"Why don't we let an outfitter decide," Max said.

"Outfitter. Boy that'll be really expensive," Rollie said. "I bet we can do it ourselves. We don't need an outfitter. "

"What about antelope?"

"Why not a bear?"

"I want to go to Wyoming."

"We could drive and haul the stuff back ourselves."

"No let's fly and ship it all back."

"There's a lot of Movie stars in Montana."

"Ooh I'd like to meet one of those."

"I like that Sharon Stone. She is too much."

"Did you see her in that movie with Michael Douglas?"

"You know who else lives in Montana?

"Cher?"

"No she lives in New York, or something like that."

"Harrison Ford."

"No he lives in Wyoming."

"That's Kevin Costner."

"He was great in Butch Cassidy and the Sundance Kid"

"That was Clint Eastwood, you idgit."

Three hours, six cheese burgers, three pounds of fries, eighteen beers, four bowls of popcorn and almost thirty chicken wings went by. The lions, half naked in the locker room, were explaining to the press about how they needed to pull it together and focus on the next game. The five women went home to the husbands, and boyfriends, from whom they had wanted so desperately to escape. The slinky waitresses tapped their fingers waiting for closing time. The bartender wiped a very experienced rag, soaked in something that smelled flammable across the bar.

In the end, the would-be fall hunters made no decision.

TIP – Cowboy hunting: Cowboy Hunting is blue jeans, maybe stiff Carharts and a flannel shirt – a worn knee here, a torn pocket there. Cowboy hunting holds little tolerance for fancy hunting britches with little designer insignias and leather patches where there are no holes. It's a hat with sweat stains crawling up the front, which look like the mountains themselves, etched against the sky at the end of a flat plain. It's making a final tie of well-worn laces on well-worn boots – boots that have lost chunks of hide as big as quarters, but fit like feathers on a duck.

TIP - Decisions: Make the commitment. Either you are going or you are not. If all you do is to sit around a talk about going hunting, that IS all you will do.

TIP - Talkers: The day you start verbalizing your intentions to go out west Cowboy hunting to your friends, you will get any number of guys offering to go along with you. Talking about it is one thing, actually committing to do it is another. Invariably, someone will back out. And if you have made plans hinged on that person being present, you could find yourself losing out on your own opportunity. I can not tell you how many times I have had to call an outfitter on the phone to tell them that one or more of my buddies will not be coming. Not only is this embarrassing, it is frustrating - particularly for the outfitter, who is making economic plans to accommodate you and your friends. Do it too much, and you might find your outfitter unwilling to take your reservation in the future.

TIP - Buddies: It's hard, but you are going to have to weed out some others - those who you know will not actually do it or will not be able to do it.

Obviously, if you know a guy is a yacker but never an actual doer, you know the type, don't even tell him you're going. He will just give you headaches. Tell him all about it when you get back, and be prepared to have him tell you that next year he wants to go with you.

Cowboy hunting is not cheap – no matter how you do it. Thirty five hundred dollars is not an unreasonable amount to expect to spend on a guided combo Elk and Deer hunt. Licenses will be another thousand. Throw in airfare, car rentals, motels, outside meals, tips for guides and taxidermy, and you can easily spend five to seven thousand dollars on a deluxe trip. If you know that those numbers would stretch one of your friends too thin, make him aware in advance of the potential costs. If you are set on him going, you will have to slash your trip down to an economy version, which can have its own set of drawbacks.

If you are planning a horse trip, and one of your friends weighs 350 pounds, you could get out to Cowboy land and find your outfitter unwilling to equip him. Horses can only carry so much. No good outfitter will want to ruin one of his good horses for a one-time hunt. Weed this guy out as soon as possible.

Take other health problems one of your friends may have into consideration. Cowboy hunting is physically exerting no matter how you do it. It is not just taking a casual stroll out to some fancy hunting shack/outhouse in the woods. Whether you take a truck, an ATV, or a horse out into the boonies where the animals live, at some point, you are going to have to do some walking and possibly even some climbing. This can be the stuff heart attacks are made of. There is nothing worse than being sick, or having someone in your party be sick on your trip. Make anyone with health concerns aware of the difficulties before making too many plans. I have seen more than one father-son combinations on Cowboy hunts where the father is stuck in camp, and the son is feeling guilty out in the woods. The concept is great, but the reality can be a very damp blanket.

Overall, experience has taught that it is best to make your plans yourself. Decide exactly what it is that you intend to do, and then tell only those who you think might actually be able to handle it and follow through with it. If they can adapt to your plan, let them come along. It will definitely be better if you can go with one or two friends, but in the end, there really isn't anything wrong with simply going yourself.

TIMING

THE FASTEST ELK IN THE WEST

January in Michigan can be a gloomy time. Frequently, the entire region succumbs to a blanket of hard gray. We smother under its oppression for weeks. It's cold. It's wet. It's depressing. One such monster brought with it the news that none of my hunting comrades could foresee a cowboy trip in the fall. Weddings, divorces, business considerations and what-have-yous looked as though they would gang up and prevent my friends from applying for tags and making plans that far in advance.

That situation has arisen before. I have overcome it by simply going alone. On that particular year, however, I too felt as though my business would need a little special attention in the fall, and I put off applying for far too long. Most reputable outfitters fill up in January or, certainly by February, and time, of course, slips by relentlessly. I let it all go figuring I would make up for it in the fall of the following year by taking an exceptionally long trip or something like that.

I thought I could handle missing a season, but as the summer crawled by, and the shadows began to lengthen, and the cool hint of fall began to sneak in to each day, I flat-out started to panic.

Colorado, still sold tags over the counter for Elk and Deer hunts in certain areas. (They no longer sell Deer tags over the counter.) My old friend Cowboy Truck Roger still had his pickup. And, one day when I could no longer stand it, I called him. I Just wanted to inquire if he had booked his entire season, or if maybe he had a spot, or if he'd seen any worthy critters or, I am not sure what else. I guess I just wanted to talk to somebody who was where I wanted to be.

"I got a cancellation," he said.

"No kidding," I said, not wanting to seem too eager. After all, I could never put an elk hunt together with such short notice.

"Yep. One guy dropped out of a six-man party and I got every other slot filled except that one. "

"When?"

He gave me the date and even though all laws of practicality said no, I immediately pulled out my calendar and started plotting.

"Gees, Roger, That's just two weeks from today."

"Yeah," he said. You comin?"

"Well, I've got all these problems my business, and there really isn't any time, and I doubt if . . . . "

"Does that mean you're coming," he said, cutting me off in mid-sentence.

"I don't know," I said. "I'll call you back."

This is nuts, I thought to myself as I hung up the phone. But damn! I sure would like to go hunting. I stared hard at the calendar. "Four days," I said aloud to nobody. "I could go for four days. I'll make it dependent on the airlines.

Delta, American, Northwest all said no. They had no seats available on any of their flights. Finally, United came through. One seat left from Detroit to Denver. That left a car. If I couldn't rent a car in Denver I would not go. Dollar had one – not much of a car, not four-wheel-drive, but a car nonetheless.

I looked back at the calendar. Four days - one travel day out there, one travel day back – that left two days of hunting. It would be cutting it too close. I called Roger.

"Well," I said. "I can get a flight and a car, but with driving time and all, I guess I'd only have about two hunt days , and . . . . "

"So, you comin'," he said cutting me off again.

Two weeks to the day later, I was sitting in Roger's pickup almost at dark, glassing a balding ridge, watching a big clump of Elk move out of a pine pocket to feed. Opportunity comes and goes fast. You have to take advantage of it when it knocks.

The next morning, Roger dropped me off, on the ridge parallel to the one holding the Elk. It was a warm sunny day. Dust sprung up in tiny tornadoes and slithered across the dry ridge. Grasshoppers flitted around like tiny helicopters. Birds dipped now and then looking for breakfast, and the pines sprayed an intoxicating elixir into the mountain air. I held my rifle in my right hand and my jacket in my left, as I stepped away from the truck. A minute later Roger was gone, off starting another hunter on another adventure, and I was alone again in the Rockies. Ah yes!

I had no plan, but it really was a nice day, so I thought that maybe I would find a little spot to make a stand for a while, do some glassing and just sit in the morning sun. I never had the chance.

The hum of Roger's engine had just died when I looked up at the ridge opposite mine, a half-mile away across a steep valley. It was alive with Elk, and they were on the run – straight at me.

We had spotted several good bulls on that ridge the night before and it looked like they'd be trampling me in a minute or two if I didn't get ready quick. Strings of Elk were peeling off that ridge and the valley below me was clouding over with dust. Something had the entire herd on the stampede. I looked around. The closest cover was a hundred or more yards away. The first Elk, a cow and two calves were staring me in the face, twenty yards away. I could never make it to cover if I ran, and, no doubt, that would scare everything away from me. I froze. The three Elk took me for a funny looking stump and passed on by. Six more appeared in their place. Ten more appeared on my left and ten more on the right. I was standing in the center of two continuous streams of Elk, sprinting by on both sides – cows, calves, spikes, four by fours, five by fives, and then, suddenly a big six by six. I'd been hunting less than five minutes and the Elk I was after was standing, staring at me about fifty yards away.

I slowly dropped my jacket, and lifted my rifle to my shoulder. He did not move. At first the only thing visible through the scope was fur. I sight my gun in at two hundred yards. I don't know how to shoot anything at fifty yards with anything other than a shot gun or a pistol. I had to move the thing around top to bottom side to side, but after a second or two, I found the magic spot and my hunt was over.

"Dang it!" Roger said as he jumped out of his truck. "We thought you dropped your gun and shot yourself. That's why we hightailed it back here."

"No. I was going to take a little rest, but I had to shoot this elk on the way," I said.

"Man you are about the fastest gun in the west."

"It was pretty much self defense, officer."

"That's the quickest I ever seen a hunt get finished."

Roger patted me on the back and I flew back to Michigan that day. As far as anyone knows, that is the fastest Elk hunt, from planning to finish ever in history. That trophy hangs in the corner of our lobby where I can get a wink at it every now and then.

TIP – Cowboy hunting: Cowboy hunting is a breakfast that sticks to your ribs. Quiche is okay, as long as it comes with plenty of eggs, bacon, pancakes and ham on the side. Not much room for gooey granola cereals and cholesterol free, cardboard tasting, processed health food in Cowboy hunting.

TIP - Timing: Getting an Elk after waiting until the last two weeks before the hunt to even make plans was nothing but pure luck. If you think you can wait like I did and even get into a hunt, never mind score a nice Elk, forget it. It was probably a once-in-a-lifetime thing. A cowboy hunt takes a lot of time to plan and you need to do it EARLY!

Good outfitters fill up their schedules fast. In Colorado, where Elk tags can be purchased over-the-counter most outfits are fully booked by mid February – sometimes earlier than that. In states where a lottery is in effect for a license, you might have more time, but you can bet that as soon as the draw results are posted, the better outfitters will start filling their available time slots in a hurry.

Hunting is a business for outfitters. They get one shot each year to make it. They need to do a bunch of planning themselves to insure that you have a good and, hopefully, a successful hunt. And, they need to do it so that at the end of the season, they will have paid all their expenses and made a little money to justify doing it again the next year.

It sounds pretty simple, but it is far from that.

They need to make sure they have enough horses to get all their hunters and all their guides and support staff into the back-country and back again safely. They might need to have trucks and ATVs tuned up and ready to go. They need to hire guides, cooks, wranglers and camp people. They need to plan meals and buy food. They need to lug all their gear into a camp and get it set up. They simply cannot do all of the behind-the-scene stuff that goes into a good hunt at the last minute. In fact, some states like Wyoming who don't publish draw results until July have driven many good outfitters out of business. It's hard to make the decision in January to do Something in September, October, or November, but that is exactly what you need to do. Make the decision to do it, decide where to go and GET IT BOOKED!

SPECIES

CORNUCOPIA

You have to start somewhere. If you want to go out west cowboy hunting, start by deciding what it is you want to hunt

It would be nice to be able to go to one location and hunt all the different Cowboy species at one time, but that can't happen. At best, on a single trip, you might be able (and you should try) to get in three, Antelope, Mulies, and Elk maybe, for example. Two species per trip is more realistic – at least from a logistical point of view.

Big game come in a variety of flavors. Sea Lions, are big game to Eskimos. So are Caribou. Elk, Deer, Antelope, Moose, Mountain Sheep, Mountain lions, Bear, and even Mountain Goats are Big game to Cowboys. If you want to hunt Caribou, call any one of a thousand Guides in Canada or Alaska, take a quick trip up there and shoot one. They come at you in herds of thousands. The guides know where they are from aerial recon reports. You do not have to go far from your camp. You don't really have to aim – just fire. You might get two at a time. That ain't Cowboy hunting.

If you want a Sea Lion, I can't help you.

TIP - Elk: Generally speaking Elk are among the easier of the Cowboy species to hunt. They can usually be found in the lower elevations, and those, which do live high, usually migrate to lower altitudes sooner than other species. Elk tend to pack together into groups. Usually a group of cows will live together with their calves in small herds of up to twenty to thirty animals. In the fall, each group of cows will attract the attention of a bull, who will move in and keep them fairly well huddled together. Other bulls will live on the fringe of the herd and try to move in whenever the urge hits them or they think the herd captain isn't paying attention. As the season progresses, the smaller groups frequently coalesce into giant herds numbering in the hundreds, and in a few places in Cowboy land, thousands.

Elk are easy to spot. They stick out against the background foliage quite well. The big bulls are lighter in color than the cows and younger bulls, making them even easier to spot. They tend to feed out in open meadows where they can be seen from great distances. And, if not pressured, a herd of Elk may spend several days feeding and bedding in the same area. If you spot them at night, you can frequently return to the same area the next morning and find them again.

Elk do not gallop. They trot. But, they can do it pretty quickly and, if necessary, straight up a cliff. Overall though, you can generally get a good shot at one, because they tend to string out. That is, they move in long strings one animal after another. If you have a big bull in mind, you can generally wait for a string of cows to come out of hiding first and then pick the bull off when he finally moves to follow the string. They stop and stare at you a lot too. That makes them an even easier target.

Elk are noisy. You can hear a herd of Elk coming a long way off. They are heavy animals. When they move through timber, they snap a lot of branches. When they run they kick a lot of rocks loose. The cows and calves "chirp" when they move. The young bulls are always trying out their bellowing, which usually turns into a long squeak of sorts.

Elk go into rut early in the season, usually mid September. When they do, they are particularly vulnerable because of that bellowing thing. You can hear a big bull for a mile – maybe more. You can hear them all night and all day sometimes. Worse, they come when you call them. Any animal that comes when you call it, can get shot pretty easily.

Because of the relative ease with which they can be hunted, Elk are the staple of many outfitters. You can almost always find somebody willing to take you Elk hunting.

Trophy Mule deer are a totally different story.

TIP - Mule deer: We have Whitetail deer everywhere in Michigan. So many, you have to drive very defensively on a back road at night to avoid hitting them. I've been tracking them all of my adult life. They live in wooded areas dotted with open fields and marshes. I've hunted them for the majority of my adult life. I have a very good idea where deer tend to hang out – or so I thought.

While driving to the Wyoming ranch where we went on our first deer hunt, many years ago, we saw dozens of Mule deer – maybe hundreds. On the four-hour horse ride to the high country, we saw many more. Every timbered area, and every draw had an Autobahn of tracks leading to and from it. Naturally, when we stopped to do some glassing, I focused my energy on a large timbered area on a ridge opposite our ridge. It didn't take long to notice that all the local Cowboys, guides included were spending their time glassing the highest, rocky craggy peaks in the area. Rock out-croppings without even the slightest hint of anything green were their favorite targets.

"What are you boys looking at," I asked naively

"Rock."

"What for?"

"Mulies."

"Yeah well, if you gentlemen would care to take a look at this nice little green meadow next to this stand of tall timber in the valley below us, you'll see three nice bucks," I said.

"Waar?"

"Thar," I answered, pointing to the three four by four bucks I had found.

"Well, if that's what you want, we can go git em," my guide said. "But, we're gonna watch them rocks for a bit more, while we got day light."

"Do you honestly think that deer would be up there in those rocks where there is no feed or shelter when they can have all the feed they want in that valley and lots of cover in those pines?"

"Yep."

"But there are deer right there."

"Them's babies. We're lookin' for toads."

"Excuse me? Toads?"

"Yeah, that's what we call big ones. One's what got their horns outside their ears. Trophies. They hang out in the rocks."

If you stretch an adult male Mule Deer's ears out and measure tip to tip, you'll get about 24 inches. If you get a deer whose antlers are that wide you will have a nice one. If you get one outside that, you will have a trophy. 30 inchers are getting rare, but they are still out there – some even bigger. But, it's true, the really big brutes "Toads" as they are known, do like to hang out in the rocks. It didn't take me too long to figure that out. They like a big rock, maybe a cliff, as close to the top of a mountain peak as possible. They bed down with their back to it while their sharp eyes and sensitive nose scan the valley below. It is as secure a fortress as possible and a good place to grow big antlers.

That fact alone makes Mule Deer harder to hunt than Elk. It's hard to get to those mountain tops. You can't take a truck up there or even a four-wheeler. You have to use a horse, or walk – sometimes both. Getting them out once you get them, can be terribly difficult. That is not to say that you will never find a big Mulie at lower elevations. You just might, but you'll find far more in the high country – the rockier the better.

Deer are much harder to see than Elk. They are smaller, and colored so that they do not contrast to the ground around them. In fact they look a lot like rocks or logs. Frequently you have to glass for hours at terrain you've already glassed a thousand times before.

Deer don't group as much as Elk. You might find a couple standing around together, occasionally a dozen or so, but toads? No. They're loaners. True cowboys. They stay hidden longer than Elk and generally are much more wary. Their rut comes later than Elk, and they do not migrate until later in the year – many times late November.

Mule Deer populations at the time of this writing are in decline. They are a species, which is much more difficult for Game and Fish departments to manage. Loss of habitat, increasing predator populations, and the virus which causes the deadly Chronic Wasting Disease has seriously decimated their numbers. Tags are getting harder to get.

Few outfitters specialize in hunting deer. Most will accommodate you if you are hunting Elk with them, but because of the difficulties and logistical problems involved, they are not keen on the concept. Don't let that dissuade you. Be persistent. Mule deer are a rewarding and fun species to hunt.

TIP - Antelope: Speaking of fun. Antelope are an absolute hoot to hunt. The rule for hunting Antelope is; bring a lot of bullets. Drive down just about any road in eastern Wyoming, parts of Montana, and eastern Colorado and you will see them by the hundreds - in many places outnumbering cattle. Most Cowboy states have Antelope. Utah has large herds in certain areas. Even coastal Oregon has Antelope, and, in fact, boasts some record breakers. Despite their numbers though, they can be challenging.

Antelope have three formidable anti-hunter weapons; telescopic, laser vision, rocket speed and the ability to appear and disappear at will.

Eastern Wyoming looks flat. Even the hills and outcroppings are flat and bare except for the Sagebrush. But, looks are definitely deceiving when it comes to those wide-open areas. Those flats are laced with small depressions and gullies. With their close-to-perfect coloration Antelope can squash down and hide in anyone of them. Little Sage trees grow to heights of almost three feet in some areas. Two of them next to one another is a fortress - even to a large antelope. Disappearing is no trick to an antelope.

No matter how good your eyesight is, and no matter how good your binoculars are, and no matter how hard you try, an antelope will always see you before you see him. It is not unusual to see a herd of antelope grazing, heads down, two miles away on those flats. Stick one toe out of your truck door, and somebody in the herd will lift a head. Seconds later all eyes will be on you. Seconds after that, they will be moving away. Scare them just a little when they are running flat out, and they will suddenly catch another gear and take off at speeds you just won't believe. A twenty-foot ravine means nothing to an antelope. They'll clear that in a single stride.

Hitting something as small as an antelope at two or three hundred yards with a rifle is difficult. Hitting one sailing along over uneven terrain at forty miles per hour or more is very challenging. Take a spotter to watch for the little dirt clouds your misses make, and give you suggestions for corrections. To repeat; Antelope hunting is a lot of fun.

TIP - Moose: The amazing thing about Moose is their incredible range. The information board at the visitor center in Teton National Park claims they can dive to depths of eighteen feet in ponds and lakes – a scary sight for a scuba diver. I personally have seen many of them above the eleven thousand foot mark in Elk meadows. They are noted for eating pond vegetation but will graze on just about anything a horse will.

Moose are fearless of anything on four feet. You can literally ride right up to them on a horse. Sometimes at night they will ride right up to you. Get down and walk toward them, and they will spook a little more, but not much. They are also fairly territorial. Once they migrate into a particular area, they tend to stay. Therein lies the problem. Their lack of fear and their predictability makes them easy to hunt, once you find them – almost too easy.

Alaska has the biggest moose, Canada the next largest. Cowboy Moose – Shira Moose – are the smallest, but still bigger than your horse.

The hardest part about Moose hunting, other than drawing a tag, is getting them back to the world, once you get them on the ground. The picture of one lanky Cowboy I know, pushing his wife's moose head out of the mountains in a giant construction wheelbarrow, because it was too big for a horse, will remain on the bark of my mind, like Elk bites on an Aspen.

TIP - Mountain Sheep: Mountain Sheep come in four varieties; Dall Sheep in Alaska, Stone Sheep in the Canadian Northern Rockies, Rocky

Mountain Sheep found in Cowboy country, and Desert Bighorns found in well, deserts, like Arizona.

Sheep hunts are for the most part a once-in-a-lifetime opportunity, because unless you want to spend a very large sum of money, that is about how long it takes to draw a tag – a lifetime. Most Cowboys will agree that they are also one of the hardest species to hunt when you do finally get a tag.

Mountain Sheep live in the most remote of neighborhoods. – usually on the very tops of the highest, rockiest, nastiest peaks. They can see and hear a couple of clumsy Cowboys and their horses coming for an hour. They have extremely fine-tuned noses, and can smell a Gnat fart in a fancy candle factory. Cowboys are usually a little more aromatic than that.

If you are lucky enough to pull a Sheep tag, plan on quitting your job and spending whatever time is necessary to get one. A one-week or even a two-week hunt may not be enough time. I have known local, professional Sheep guides who have spent a month trying to fill their own tags. If the tough climbs and the long hours don't get you, the weather will. Granted Sheep hunting in some areas is easier, but in Cowboy country it can be very difficult.

TIP - Mountain Lions: Mountain Lions, a.k.a Cougar are usually hunted in the winter. Although in some places, Idaho for example, you can buy a Lion tag over the counter and hunt them during the regular Elk season. The typical Lion hunt, these days, is done with dogs and snowmobiles. The reason is simple; cats are hard to find. In winter, you can cut a set of tracks and know there is a Lion at the end of them. A snowmobile helps you get to the business end of the tracks in a reasonable time. Cats cover huge territories and just because you have found a set of tracks, does not mean you are anywhere near the animal. When you get close, the dogs will take over. Then it is a question of listening to the barking and howling.

Cat populations are on the rise. Hunting them is a fun thing to do in the winter. Ranchers will love you for it. However, the regulations for getting one are stringent. In many areas, it is necessary to call the state Department of wildlife on a daily basis to make sure the tag you have obtained is still valid. Most states have established quotas for lion harvesting. The quotas are for very specific areas and for very specific periods of time. If the quota for your area is say, three lions, and three other hunters get theirs first, your tag could become invalid overnight. Obviously, when you get a lion, you must report your kill to the Department of wildlife within a certain time or you will be in violation.

If you are a stranger to the area and out in the wilderness on your own, without access to a telephone, trying to hunt Mountain Lions, you will find complying with the rules difficult. Realistically, cat hunting for a non-resident is best accomplished with the help of an experienced guide.

TIP - Bear: In the olden days, actually as recently as the early eighties, Outfitters in Wyoming would wait until one of their horses was about to go paws up in one of the corrals. Instead of dealing with a labor-intense disposal operation, they would march the dying horse up into the back-country and dispose of it via lead poisoning in a likely spot to attract Bear. Modern rules, being what they are, have made this simplified hunting method obsolete.

It is still possible to hunt bear, but there are, once again, large variations in how and when you can do it and how you can obtain permission to do it. In Idaho and Montana, you can buy a bear tag over the counter like you can for Lions, and hunt them during Elk and Deer season. In other areas you have to beg for a permit.

When we talk about Bear hunting, we are talking about Black Bear hunting for the most part. Until just recently Grizzly bear hunting was impossible for Cowboy hunters, because there weren't any around - except in Alaska and in a few of the National Parks, where they are protected. However, the Grizzly Bear is making a comeback, and has actually started roaming outside of the National Parks, irritating ranchers and the National Cattlemen's Association. This has prompted a new interest in Grizzly Bear hunting and renewed issuance of permits. They are hard to get, as you might imagine.

TIP -   Mountain Goats: If you think getting a Sheep permit in one of the Cowboy states is hard, try getting a Mountain Goat tag. I don't think the Pope himself could get one. And, if you think finding a Mountain Sheep is hard, try finding a Goat. If the Pope does draw a tag, he'll need a winged Angel for a guide. It is hard to believe that an animal as large as a Goat, could survive in the rocky altitudes it inhabits, and on the lichens and rock tripe upon which it feeds.

Idaho, especially in wilderness areas like Salmon Selway or Frank-Church have good Goat populations. Colorado has large numbers of Goats in its College Peaks area. But, if you really want to hunt Goat, go to Alaska. They live in extreme conditions there too, but the altitudes are much more conducive to human survival.

WHERE TO GO

THE LAND OF THE COWBOYS

By definition, cowboy hunting can only be done in the land of cowboys. Yeah, yeah, every state has its share of cowboys. But, we're not talking about some guy in Michigan sitting on a bench at the mall wearing a wide brimmed hat, a pair of Bolero boots, a fringed jacket and a big belt buckle, while he waits for his wife to come out of the vitamin store. We're not talking about sitting on a horse, on some farm in Ohio, either.

If you really want to be cowboy and especially hunt cowboy, you need to get west of the Missouri river – that's pretty much it! You need to go where the history is, to where they made the movies. To really appreciate cowboy hunting, you need to get into the Rocky Mountains and the land west of them.

Get a map . Find the place where Utah, Wyoming and Colorado all meet. Start there with concentric circles of cowboy hunting opportunities. Expand each circle to cover Wyoming, Utah, Colorado, New Mexico, Arizona, Idaho, Nevada and Montana. While good cowboy game can be found in eastern Washington State, western North and South Dakota, eastern California, eastern Oregon, western Nebraska, western Kansas, as well as parts of Oklahoma, and Texas, the vast majority will be found in the states in the circles – the Mountain States, the big eight, The Cowboy states.

TIP – Cowboy Hunting: Cowboy Hunting is having to crack ice to fill your water bottle. It's cussin' because there ain't no horse in the world that'll stand still while you tighten a cinch. It's a gun that doesn't care if gets scratched up a little going into a scabbard – heck, it's been dropped off a few cliffs in its time. It's leather - on saddles, on corral hinges, on just about anything that needs tying.

LICENSING

DRAW PARTNER!

"Hey," Mike said to me one day with a palpable note of excitement in his voice. "I'm going out to Wyoming for Mulies this fall, finally after all these years."

This was May. Wyoming doesn't release its deer draw results until July, so I was a little skeptical.

"Elk too," he said again, flipping his hat defiantly toward a hook on our wall.

"Congratulations on the elk draw," I said. "But you could be counting your chickens a little early on that Wyoming mule deer tag."

"No man, we didn't get no tags yet. My buddie's cousin is taking care of all that stuff. He's got a friend that lets him hunt on his ranch and so he's taking care of everything. We just have to show up."

"You still need the tags, Mike."

"No. See this guy who owns the ranch has a friend who is an outfitter or guide or something like that and he can get us the tags. Besides it is all private property and so you don't really need one."

"Is it a game ranch?"

"No man. It's just a big chunk of, I don't know, cattle ranch or something."

"Well, I think you might want to check that out a bit before you leave. Wyoming is just like Michigan. You have to have a license to hunt deer. "

We saw Mike again in January. He had not gone out to Wyoming hunting. Something about needing the tags and stuff like that.

If I had a monkey for every time I have seen that movie, I'd have . . . well, you get the idea.

TIP – Cowboy Hunting: Cowboy hunting is a squeaky knee stepping up into a squeaky saddle. It's a horse, groaning under the weight – they can't figure why we want to do this so early in the morning. It's wind whistling through pine needles. It's the last joke before setting out. It's the jays squawking and the squirrels chattering – they think the forest belongs to them.

TIP - Tags: Once you decide to actually go out to Cowboy land to hunt, and have chosen a species (or two) that you would like to hunt, and a location where you think you might like to do it, you **WILL NEED A LICENSE!**

You can purchase tags for some species in some states or in specific areas of some states over-the-counter. Some outfitters in some states or specific regions of some states can and do have the ability to get you a license – a very expensive license but a license nonetheless. In every other situation you will need to DRAW A TAG in a lottery. For some species this means residents and nonresidents alike. Don't assume a non-registered outfitter or "one of your buddies" is going to be able to come up with a tag for you. Hunting on someone else's tag is illegal, everywhere. You might find yourself in big trouble if you try it.

TIP - States If you plan to hunt in a specific cowboy state, you must obtain a hunting rule book for that state, and BECOME FAMILIAR WITH IT! You may be surprised to find that what you think you are going to do and what you may actually be able to do are very different.

All Cowboy Hunting states have game and fish departments or something similar, which regulate hunting in their jurisdiction. They all will gladly provide you with a copy of their rules. Today, most have web-sites on which you can find most of the information you are interested in. All have phone numbers manned by actual humans to whom you can ask questions.

THE KINGDOM

In days of old when Knights were bold, the King owned all the land - period. He might let a favored Knight manage a certain parcel and even make a profit on it, but he retained ownership. The Knight might let a commoner farm a particular chunk on a profit-sharing basis, and he in turn would likely have peasants working under him for a whatever food they could scrounge out of the leftovers. In the end, the riches garnered from the land kicked back up to the King.

The Federal Bureau of Land Management (BLM) owns huge tracks of empty land, upon which any U.S. citizen can do just about whatever he wants (unless posted otherwise). The BLM is the largest landowner in the country. Unless posted, you can camp on BLM land. You can ride horses, motorcycles, jeeps, ATVs or whatever. You can shoot guns, and hunt pretty much at will (unless a private citizen has an easement through or around some BLM land, and then you must have written permission from the landowner to access the BLM land over their property. Unfortunately, much of the BLM land that I have seen is open, arid, sage brush land. The majority of BLM land has been described as the land nobody else wanted. In all but a few cases - Colorado's San Juan Mountains , for example - it is that land which runs up to the mountains, but stops short. If you are an antelope hunter this land is exactly what you want. Depending on the time of the year, it can be good for deer and elk too. But, if you are looking for trophy deer, most guides will tell you, you need to go a little higher.

The Federal Government, The U.S. Forest Service, The U.S. Fish and Wildlife Service, as well as individual State Government divisions, like Forest Services, and Game and Fish Departments usually own the next division of land (higher up in the mountains), frequently as either State or National forests. Here the air gets crispy, and the pines flourish. Good stands of timber naturally hold a large variety of game. Like BLM land, any U.S. citizen can use this land at will, but there are more rules and more postings, and more closings of areas for a variety of reasons– especially during hunting season. For example, many national forest areas which are open to ATV traffic during the rest of the year, are closed during hunting season (In Colorado and Wyoming, they come with chains and lock the gates). Some are closed to automobile traffic during hunting season. Other State and National Forest areas are open and unrestricted. Hunting is usually good in the Forests, but because of the terrain, many are still unusable by anyone who is not properly equipped. More about this later.

Beyond the National and State Forest, boundaries lie the Wilderness Areas. These areas are the most remote of all the lands. Trophies hide out in Wilderness areas, but in almost all cases hunters are required to have a certified guide present, and drawing a permit is sometimes a problem. Most tags for wilderness areas are now on a lottery basis, and most states are going to the preference point system for hunts in wilderness areas.

National Parks and National Monuments are specific subdivisions of National Forests which play by a rule book all their own. Everything within a National Park or a national monument is restricted. Hunting is strictly prohibited, unless you are one of the very few who draw one of the rare tags issued for those areas. If you are, you can bet, you will have to have a guide, and probably even a ranger to accompany you on your hunt.

And then, of course, there is private land. Access is up to the landowner, but hunting rules are still established by the game and fish departments of the individual states. Don't think that just because you are hunting on private land, you will not need to apply for a license. This is a myth. Somebody will have to have a tag for any game you kill, and in most states those tags are not transferable. They can be purchased for you in some instances - if they are available over-the-counter - and granted to you by a landowner in some cases, but where ever there is a drawing you or he will still need to enter the lottery - private land or not.

TIP – Cowboy Hunting: It's the smell of fresh horse manure and the fresh, turpentine tingle of pine. It's the sweet alluring scent of sage. It's the chemical smell of gun oil. It's clean mountain air, barely spoiled by the stench of civilization.

TIP - Rules: Be sure you know the hunting rules for the area you intend to hunt before you go. There can be huge variations from one place to another, and hunting tags are usually specific to a particular person and to a particular area, the borders of which may not always be easily recognized. All State game departments are more than willing to provide information about any area in which you intend to hunt.

TIP - Wyoming:

Headquarters: Wyoming Game and Fish Department
5400 Bishop Blvd.
Cheyenne, WY. 82006 – 0001
Phone: 1-307-777-4600
Web Site: www.http://gf.state.wy.us/
General Rules:

1.) If born on or after Jan I, 1966, you must have a valid hunter-safety training certificate.

2.) Each licensed hunter must purchase a State of Wyoming Conservation stamp. The cost is $10 and must be signed and in possession while hunting.

3.) It is not possible for anyone other than the hunter himself to obtain a license. Simply put, there is no such thing as an "outfitter's tag," in the state of Wyoming. An outfitter may assist you in filling out your application and he can even deliver it to the game and fish department in Cheyenne, but he will have no influence as to whether or not you draw a tag. All non-resident hunting permits in the state of Wyoming are issued strictly according to a lottery draw. Even some resident licenses are granted in this manner.

There is one minor exception. Each year the Game and Fish department issues a certain number of what they call "Commissioner's licenses." These licenses are granted to certain non-profit organizations These organizations auction them off for very large sums ($7000-$9000 in some cases). Sometimes, they will give them away as lottery gifts in which one's chances of winning are very remote.

4.) The first draw a non-resident can participate in is the regular elk license draw. The application period is from Jan 1st to January 31st. If you are interested in getting a bull elk, this is the drawing you must be in.

5.) The next non- resident drawing is for deer and antelope. The application period is from January 1st to March 15th. If you want to obtain a buck deer or antelope tag, this is the drawing you should enter.

6.) Wyoming also has what they call a reduced-price cow, elk, doe deer, doe antelope. You may enter this drawing for up to two tags, both issued to the same person. The application dates are the same as the regular draw dates. These tags will allow lucky recipients to harvest two extra cow elk, doe deer, or doe or fawn antelope in certain areas only. It is possible and legal for an individual hunter to possess three tags for the species mentioned, by drawing one tag in the regular draw and two in the reduced-priced draw.

7.) After these two drawings and after similar drawings for residents, if the game and fish department have leftover tags, they hold another drawing which nonresidents can enter called surprisingly; the leftover drawing. This is your last chance to draw some kind of tag. There are usually no male species tags left by this time, but you may find one in a given year for a specific area. The application times for leftover is July 10 – July 20.

8.) Frequently, after all these drawings, there are still leftover licenses for specific species, of specific genders, in specific locations. They are usually for cow elk, doe deer and doe antelope. The game and fish department issues these licenses to hunters at their Cheyenne headquarters office as well as at their regional offices. The applications for this drawing can be obtained from the headquarters office or on their website.

9.) Then, if the game and fish department still has left over licenses from their reduced price drawing, they will distribute them to designated sales agents (sporting goods stores etc.), and hunters may purchase them over-the-counter after August 15th.

10.) Mountain goats have a special drawing all of their own. The application deadline is January 1st - February 28th.

11.) The game and fish department holds drawings for Moose and Bighorn sheep but while they claim it is mathematically possible to draw a tag during the regular drawing it is highly unlikely. Instead, if you are unsuccessful, you will be given a preference point. Or, if you wish, you may buy a preference point and not even bother applying during a special period usually in July (check the website for the announcement as to when these preference point only applications will be available). Generally speaking, successful Moose or Bighorn sheep licensees, will be those who have the highest number of preference points.

12.) It is possible in the state of Wyoming to hunt multiple species at the same time – to combo hunt. The seasons for individual species overlap in Wyoming. As long as you have tags, and the season for the particular species you are after is open you can hunt it along with whatever other species meets the same criterion.

Wyoming maintains a link on it's website, which will give you the odds of drawing a tag for a specific species in a specific region throughout the state. It also will give the actual drawing results and harvest reports for given species in particular areas for the previous years. This information can be very helpful when planning a hunting Trip.

TIP - Colorado:

Headquarters:	Colorado Department of Wildlife
	6060 Broadway
	Denver, Colorado 80216
Phone:	303-297-1192
Website:	www.Wildlife.state.co.us

General rules:

1.) All hunters born after a January 1st 1949 must have a valid hunter safety card on their person while hunting.

2.) Types of licenses available.

Limited Licenses - available by application and drawing only - specific for species and unit.

Unlimited licenses - No application or drawing - can be purchased over-the-counter at DOW offices, certain agents, online, or by phone.

Over-the-counter with caps - can be purchased same as above, but are specific for a hunting unit and are granted on a first come first served basis until the designated limit for that unit is reached.

Private land only licenses - available by application and drawing. Remember, you must have permission to hunt private land before hunting. Having the license does not grant permission.

Ranching for wildlife licenses - residents only

Left-over licenses - available at DOW offices and certain agents in August

3.) Hunters will also have to purchase a habitat stamp prior to hunting. Cost: $5.

4.) All Deer tags are by application and drawing only!

5.) Preference points will be given to any unsuccessful license applicant.

6.) Colorado has a number of different hunting seasons based on species and type of hunt. For example: Archery deer begins in certain areas as early as august 16th. And there are three seasons for combined rifle deer and elk. Check the species, hunt unit and hunting method limitations mandated before you apply for a license to make sure that your plans can be accommodated.

7.) Colorado does allow combination hunts.

8.) The application deadline is April 3rd

TIP - Arizona:

Headquarters :   Arizona Game and Fish
2221 W. Greenway Rd.
Phoenix, AZ. 85023-4399
Phone: 602-942-3000
Website: http://www.gf.state.az.us/index.shtml

General rules:

Hunters in Arizona must purchase a hunting license as well as a permit for the specific species and area they intend to hunt. They are two separate things.

The licenses can be purchased at any time without an application for a permit. However, if you are applying for your area/species permit online, you will be prompted to provide you license number during the application process. You can get both the application for the permit and the license at the same time online.

Only hunters under the age of fourteen must have a hunter safety card.

The deadline for applications to hunt Elk and Antelope is February 13th.

The deadline for applying for Deer and Sheep is announced after the Elk Drawing. It is usually in May or June.

Current non-resident licenses are $151. Current Elk, Deer and Sheep permit fees are $595, $232, and $1407 respectively.

Arizona does have a bonus system and unsuccessful hunters will be awarded a bonus point for the species for which they applied.

Arizona has a complicated system of permits for different species and different areas. Study their rules on the website or by requesting a hunting brochure from their Phoenix office.

You may purchase bonus points only in Arizona, but you must also purchase a license.

Some non-permit tags (over-the-counter) are available for deer. Check the Game and fish department for specifics regarding these licenses.

Arizona also conducts population management hunts in specific areas for specific species. Check with the game and fish department to determine if one of these hunts might fulfill your plans.

The Arizona Hunting regulation and application booklet is 85 pages long. Near the end is the application success odds for the given units and for the specific species. Be sure to look there during your application process.

TIP - Montana:

Headquarters: Montana Fish Wildlife and Parks
                1420 E. Sixth Avenue
                Box 200701
                Helena, Montana   59620-0701

Phone: 406-444-2535

Web Page: http://fwp.mt.gov/hunting/default.html

General Rules:

Montana is divided into seven hunting regions. Within each region are many districts. The districts are species specific

Montana's website is very helpful with regards to individual species and the districts where they may be hunted. Click on their Plan a Hunt button for information

Montana has a special super tag lottery where an unlimited number of chances to win a license for any species in any district for $5.

In addition to a license, Nonresidents will need to purchase a Conservation stamp and a hunter's access stamp totaling $18

Montana sells combination hunting tags for Elk and Deer or single tags for Deer, sheep, moose, bear. These licenses are also in combination with upland birds and fish.

The Elk and Deer licenses can be general licenses, landowner licenses, or outfitter sponsored licenses.

All hunters applying for an outfitter sponsored license will be successful. Make arrangements with an outfitter prior to applying

The deadline for applying for Elk and Deer licenses is March 15th. Application dates for other species run from may through June. Check website for specifics.

Hunters born after January 1st 1985 will need a hunter's safety card.

In addition to a hunting licenses you will need a permit for the individual species you are hunting. These permits are inexpensive, but necessary.

Montana does have a bonus point system. Bonus points cost $20 for non-residents and come with the license application.

TIP - Utah

Headquarters:	Utah Division of Wildlife Resources
	1594 W. North Temple
	Box 146301
	Salt Lake City, Utah
	84114-6301
Phone:	801-538-4700
Website:	http://www.wildlife.utah.gov/hunting/

General Rules:

Hunters born after 12/31/1965 must have a hunter's safety card.

The deadline for applying for Big Game is February 16th

Utah has a preference point system and it is possible to buy just a point without applying for a license.

60% of Utah's big game range is on private property. Therefore the Division of Wildlife Resources has established private hunting units called CWMUs. These units are managed by an administrator who can provide licenses for individual hunters in his unit. These administrators usually act as outfitters as well. Contact one before applying and you will likely get a tag.

You may also enter general drawings for tags in specific game units around the state, but the best bet for trophy animals is by hunting within one of the CWMUs.

Utah also has a once-in-a-lifetime hunting program for certain species – Desert Bighorn, Rocky Mountain Sheep, Bison, Moose etc. You may apply for tags for this hunt or buy preference points online.

TIP - Idaho

Headquarters: Idaho Fish and Game
                600 S. Walnut
                Box 25
                Boise, Idaho   83712
Phone: 208-334-3700
Website: http://fishandgame.idaho.gov/cms/hunt/
General Rules:

Hunters in Idaho must purchase a general hunting license as well as a tag for an individual species in an individual area.

The hunting license is $141.50 and the tag for an Elk is $373.50 and for deer $258.50

The deadline for applying for controlled Deer and Elk hunting is June 5th.

Hunters born after 1/1/1975 need a hunter's safety card.

All bow hunters must complete a bowhunter education class either in Idaho or another state.

Idaho allows successful controlled license holders to exchange their tag for another area – one time.

Reduced price bear and Mountain Lion tags are available to nonresidents over-the-counter.

It is possible to combination hunt in Idaho.

TIP - New Mexico:

Headquarters: New Mexico Game and Fish
                1 Wildlife Way
                Box 25112
                Santa Fe, New Mexico
                87507

Phone: 505-476-8000

Website:

http://www.wildlife.state.nm.us/recreation/hunting/index.htm

General Rules:

The application deadline for Deer, Elk, Antelope and Sheep is April 7th.

New Mexico grants 78% of their available licenses to residents, 12% to nonresident hunters who have contracts with outfitters and 10% to the general nonresident applicants.

Only hunters under the age of 18 must have a hunter safety card.

If you are unsuccessful in the draw for a specific species in a specific area, you may be able to purchase an Over-the-Counter license to hunt on private property if you have made prior arrangements with a landowner. If you have made those arrangements you may be able to purchase an OTC license for that land without going through the draw. Check with the landowner first and then with the Game and Fish Department.

Over the Counter tags may not be available for all species in a given year. In 2007 for example, deer are available but elk are not.

If you plan to use an ATV in New Mexico, they must be equipped with a New Mexico approved spark arrestor.

You do not need to wear hunter's orange in many parts of New Mexico while hunting.

If you are hunting, you must have a habitat stamp. They cost $5.

TIP - Nevada:

Headquarters: Nevada Department of Wildlife
1100 Valley Road
Reno, Nevada 89512

Phone: 775-688-7500

Website: http://www.ndow.org/hunt/

General Rules:

Hunters born after 1/1/1960 will need to have a hunter's safety card, and will need to register that card on a separate paper application at least seven days prior to applying for a license.

Hunters will need to have a hunting license as well as a tag for the specific species and unit in which they wish to hunt.

Hunting licenses are $142 and tags for Elk, Deer, Antelope and Sheep are $1200, $240 $300 and $1200 respectively.

You may buy preference points only but you must also purchase a license to do so. Preference points are $10.

Nevada has two draws for big game. The main draw, followed by a second draw for any tags still available. Remaining tags after the draws will be available on a first-come basis.

If you are hunting Sheep in Nevada you will need to attend an indoctrination course sponsored by the wildlife department.

Hunting applications are generally available in mid-March and the deadline for applying is generally mid-April. Check with the department of Wildlife for more specific dates as they become available.

TIP – Cowboy Hunting: It's the dull, flickering glow of lantern light. There's no electricity in Cowboy hunting. There's no fly-in, snowmobile, shoot-a-caribou-out-of-a-giant-herd kind of stuff in real Cowboy hunting. That's for Eskimos. There's no cozy little plywood blinds either and certainly no propane heaters to keep them warm.

TIP - Application Services: If you are not a do-it-yourselfer, there are a number of service companies these days who will do it all for you. In addition some of them offer a wide range of hunting information about each state and each species you may want to go after. Of course, they charge for these services, but for some people, their fees are easily justifiable. They do take some of the headache out of it for a busy hunter.

Search the internet for "hunt booking agencies" and you should be able to find a number of such companies.

TIP - Hunter's Safety Cards: Most states require a hunters safety card to hunt if you were born after a certain date. They are serious about this. In some cases you will be denied a license altogether. Frequently outfitters will require you to show them your card before they will take you out. Game and fish cops will reward you with a fine and probable suspension of your hunting privileges. Do not wait until the last minute to get your card. You can't just buy one. Usually, you have to take a class and pass a test before one will be issued. This stuff takes time. Check with the regulations of the state in which you intend to hunt and if your birthday falls outside their regulations GET THE CARD NOW!

TIP - Bonus Points: Bonus points expire if hunters do not continue to apply in the years following the year in which the year they were awarded. Check with the individual state in which you applied to check their policies on this. You might be surprised to find that bonus points you have acquired in the past are no longer valid.

COMBOS

ONE'S GOOD – TWO IS BETTER

Not a bad morning - only a quarter inch of ice on the water bucket when we got up. An hour later, Gabriel and I had almost thawed out as we rode up the picturesque Cabin Creek canyon. Soon, the sun managed to climb up over the ridge tops and systematically scorch the white crystals of frost, which had accumulated on every exposed leaf and twig, vaporizing them - tiny steam jets rising through the steely, crisp air. The horses were muttering to themselves about the rocks in the trail and the cold, and something about "fat asses" that I couldn't quite catch.

I had a mule deer tag. Gabriel didn't care as long as "we was fixin' to go up in them thar heels to hunt sumpthin." He said, he reckoned a deer might be found on the top of Full Moon Mountain and he had made us a good short-cut trail to the top.

"Gabriel," I said, as he turned suddenly off the well-worn trail we had been on and headed straight up the side of the mountain. "You are such a joker. Come down off that hillside and let's get going on up to the top."

"I ain't jokin'" he said. "This is my short-cut trail."

"We can't take the horses up there Gabe. It'll kill them."

"Naw"

"It'll kill us."

"Yuhuh mayhap."

Fact: you can't argue with Gabriel Short when he's got a vision. I turned my horse toward the solid wall of mountain next to me. My horse took one look at Gabe's horse hopping – galloping sort of – struggling straight up the mountain at almost a vertical angle and turned back toward camp. I managed to stop him twenty yards down the trail and coax him back toward Gabriel's newest not-a-trail trail.

Coax? Wrong word. I heeled that bad boy, and he took off like Elvis heading for a hot dog stand. I turned him at Gabe's horse's hoof marks and goaded him all the way up to where they stood panting, in one long hard push.

"We can't make these horses do this.

"Sho nuff can. Me and this critter has already done it plenty of times."

We were on a small flat spot on the otherwise impossibly steep mountainside. The horses stood gasping for breath, their massive chests heaving in and out. Suddenly, a mile or so to our left, we heard a monster bull elk bugle out at the morning sun.

"Whoa," I said. "That sounds like a real stud."

"Reckon so,," Gabe said. "I done heared him up here the other day, but I ain't seen him yet."

Gabriel's path wound its way up the side of the mountain at an unreal angle. To stay in the saddle, we had to lean far out over the horse's neck and give them all the rein we had. Because they were working so hard to climb this beast of a hill, their heads bobbed up and down a full two feet with every step. We had to be very careful not to get butted on the chin and likely knocked to the ground. To say it was a rough ride would be like saying John Wayne was a tough guy. He was a hell of a tough guy, and this was one hell of a rough horse ride!

To make things worse, Gabriel had not picked a path that ran out in the open. His path snaked between the outstretched branches of a pine forest that grew delicately close to the knife-sharp ridge we were climbing. We were in whisper mode because we were hunting, but there was no way to hide the sound of two horses scrambling up a mountain like that. And, because we were working our way around and through a spider-web of dead tree branches it was impossible to avoid breaking them off from time to time, sending a loud crack sailing off through the clean quiet mountain air.

And, as we worked our way up, our buddy Mr. Big Elk, kept bellowing – closer and closer and closer. We'd move a few yards up, send a hail-storm of rocks skittering down the slope, snap off a few branches and then stop to rest. Each time, the elk would bellow - each time a little closer. Finally, when the Elk seemed to be only couple dozen yards away, Gabe stopped.

"Reckon he's gonna try and gore us," he whispered. "Let's git down and git ready to start sword fightin'."

We dismounted and dropped our reins. Our horses weren't going anywhere. They were too tired to take off, and stood under the pines catching their breath. Gabe and I stepped softly away, turning back after thirty or so yards. The wind was coming up the canyon to our left, and sent a strong bouquet of elk our way.

"He's very close," I said."

Gabe nodded. "You didn't bring your gun, " he whispered, looking me over.

"I don't have an elk tag," I said.

"The hell you say," Gabe said.

"I told you that. We only got deer tags this year. Well, we were having trouble deciding if . . . "

Gabe slapped me in the chest interrupting my rapidly escalating, albeit thin, tirade of excuses why I stood there on that mountain tagless and gunless. He'd heard something.

"Shhh," he whispered.

The horses had turned toward the canyon in the direction of the elk. Their ears were high and cocked. They too had heard something.

My eyes froze on the treed valley where I had last heard the elk, hoping to catch a glimpse of brown, maybe a set of antlers sliding between the branches. One of the horses snorted and stomped the ground with a heavy hoof. And suddenly there he was.

The big elk stepped out from behind a tangle of pine and stood stiff-legged face-on to the horses. Streams of hot breath shot from his enlarged nasal openings. His eyes were wild. He lowered his head and made a mock charge of a couple of steps. He was up wind from us, and up wind from the horses. He strained to try to catch scent, but apparently found none. He seemed unaware that Gabriel and I were there. He held his gaze, steadfast on the horses not sure if they were enemies or just reluctant cow elk who wore funny, misshapen humps on their sweating backs. He moved toward them measuring each step. At about twenty yards he stopped.

The horses were not moving they were not afraid either. This seemed to be a definite puzzle to this old boy. He was used to cows doing what he commanded, and to younger bulls either stepping up to fight or trotting off at his magnificent presence. These two, just standing there ignoring him, confused him. He pawed the ground. He lifted his massive 6x7 white-tipped rack as high as he could flopping it back until its tines scratched his shaggy back. Then, inhaling a gigantic gulp of mountain air, he expanded his huge sides and let out an operatic bugle that would have made Pavarotti himself take notice.

Gabe and I were dumbstruck. We stood there, jaws dragging on the soft pine carpet below. There are still a few 7 bys out there, but I have never seen a rack on an elk that big in the wild. It is still my all-time record, and I am sure would have easily graced many a sanctioned record book – that is if I'd have had a tag dammit!

Talk about helpless. Gabe and I stood there looking at that elk and then looking back at each other like two village idiots watching Lady Godiva strolling by, naked as a pool ball.

"You ain't got your gun," Gabe observed.

"I don't have a tag," I reminded him.

"Naw"

"I told you that."

"Did not."

"Whatever."

The elk stood there in a face-off with the horses, giving us a good five minute, broad-side shot at twenty yards, before noticing that we were there. Even then, he merely walked off, stopping every now and then to look back at the horses. It was as though he knew we not going to be a threat, even though he had given us a hundred opportunities to get him. Gabe picked up a large stick, lodged it against his shoulder and mock shot the big boy as he strolled off.

"Reckon we'd a got him," he said.

All I could do was snarl.

BIG TIP - Licensing: Always try to maximize your hunt by having more than one species tag. Murphy was apparently a hunter as well. It never fails that if you are elk hunting you will see nothing but trophy deer. And if deer are what you want, the hills will be littered with full curl rams. Unfortunately this may not always be possible. Wyoming, Montana, Colorado and Idaho, for example have dual or overlapping seasons for elk, deer, antelope, moose and sheep. New Mexico and Arizona do not. However, in some states it is possible to hunt different species consecutively. That is, deer can be hunted one week and elk the next. You can make arrangements with your outfitter to accommodate you by maybe hunting a few days on the end of one season and a few on the front of another.

Hunting more than one species on a single hunt may be difficult from a logistical standpoint, and you should not necessarily plan your trip to do it, but it certainly doesn't hurt to have the tag just in case.

TIP - Draw odds:

In the past, there was no way to pre-guess the chances of actually drawing a tag for the area and the species you wish to hunt. Thanks to computerization, you can get a pretty good idea if you will be going hunting in any particular year or not. Most states offer a link on their website to the draw odds and drawing results of the previous year's hunt. The results are organized by area and species and in most cases also give the number of hunters applying. This information is invaluable when it comes to planning a trip to Cowboy land.

TIP - T.V. Hunts: Hunting, like everything else has become big business. Big business means marketing and that means television. The reality T.V. craze has put hunting on everyone's screen. And, by God, they've done a super nice job of it. Those early Saturday morning hunt shows have gotten dad up early and forced children across America to switch from cartoons to Elk hunts. Five minutes of watching a show like that will have you picking up the phone to book a hunt with that outfitter in that spot in the coming fall.

Be warned: Unless you are hunting on a private game preserve of some kind, you still have to have a license. Most T.V. outfitters do have licenses available but their price is astronomical and their waiting list to get one is very long. In fact, to hunt a T.V. hunt, you might just have to enter into a bidding war just to get the chance. Ever wonder why there are so many movie stars or sports personalities on those shows?

TIP - Horses: When faced with the choice of doing something – anything – difficult, and returning to the barn, a horse will always choose the latter. They Are not as dumb as they pretend to be. DO NOT give in to them. Make them do what you want - no matter. They are testing you. They will take a mile if given an inch.

TIP - Elk: Elk can be classified more or less by their calls. Generally speaking, the deeper, longer, more drum-like calls are those of the larger bulls. The younger bulls - four-by- fours - can't seem to keep a call going as long, and at the end it sort of it peeters out to a high shrill. Spikes just squeak.

TIP - Horses: If you plan to ride in high vertical country, be sure your saddle has a breast plate or collar of some kind to keep the saddle from sliding back off the horse's rump. A britchen is helpful too for going downhill.

TIP - Elk: Elk have an amazingly strong and distinctive scent. Once you smell it, you will not forget it. Trust it. If it is on the wind, elk are near.

TIP – Cowboy Hunting: Cowboy hunting is grit-your-teeth horseback riding - on forever flats and straight up break-your-neck walls and straight down pucker-your-butt cliffs. Horses are the ultimate four-wheel-drive vehicles. They will go boldly where no ATV, Jeep or Chevy could even think of going. It's riding and riding and riding, until the trail eyes of the horse become your eyes and you flow along in perfect rhythm with him. It's riding until you don't realize you are riding anymore. Cowboy hunting is eating your lunch in the saddle more often than not.

OPTIONS A PLENTY

OPTIONS

EMPTY MEN

Tom Terrific, Deadeye and I were on a plane heading out to our favorite hunting hole a little south of the Tetons in Wyoming. The plan was the usual one: rent a car at the airport, head into Jackson, have some lunch, pay homage to the Million Dollar Cowboys (a.k.a. tip a few at the Cowboy bar), then spend a couple of days acclimatizing by hiking in the foothills around the Tetons before heading out to our outfitter's ranch to saddle up for our hunt. The plane was crowded with men heading out to do the same. The cabin buzzed with certain excitement known only to those about to embark on an adventure – for some, the adventure of a lifetime.

We shared three seats on one side of the plane. Across the aisle six other men took up two rows. They shared loud stories and jokes across the seatbacks. They were already dressed in camo and seemed ready to jump out of the plane and kill something on the tarmac.

"You boys must be going hunting," I said, leaning into the aisle.

"Yep, it's our first trip," the guy next to me said.

"All six of you? You're filling some outfitter's whole hunt. I'll bet he's happy."

"No, No," the guy on the aisle next to me said. "We don't have an outfitter. We're just doing it ourselves. Johnny's friend told us about this place called the Sawback. It's all public land. We don't need an outfitter. There's a road you just drive up along the Granite river, then get out and start hunting. "

"Whoa, the Sawback isn't quite that easy."

"You know where that is? You going hunting too?"

"Yeah," I said, " I know the Granite River and the Sawback. In fact, we are actually going to be hunting on the opposite side of it. Probably a par six or seven from where you guys are going to be."

Four of the six seemed to be in their late thirties. The other two were likely older, maybe mid to late forties. They seemed like ordinary guys, good athletes in their younger days, getting a little soft now that they were dealing with life and families, but still quite healthy and vigorous looking. They were clearly having a good time, and they were not more than an hour or so into their trip.

"Yeah, we got two SUVs rented at the airport and we're going to drive right up this little road right here," he said, pointing to a red slash on a map he had suddenly produced. "Is there any good camping spots around there, do you know?"

"Well, not specifically, but it is all National Forest or BLM land, so I doubt you'll have a problem finding a place. What, do you have someone setting up a camp for you. "

"No, we've got some pup tents and some camping gear with us. Stove, lantern, that kind of stuff. We're going kind of light."

"So, how are you going to hunt? Have you got someone bringing you horses?"

"Naw, were in pretty good shape so we are going to just walk it. Is it pretty good hunting right around there?"

"It can be, but you have to get up the Sawback to do it right and if you are walking your range is going to be a little short. "

"Yeah, what's that Sawback like?"

"Vertical. How are you going to get it out if you shoot something?"

"We'll just drag it out to the road and load it up."

"Drag it?"

The flight attendant dragging the cart through the isle momentarily interrupted our conversation. I continued. "You know those SUVs you rent at the airport aren't big SUVs like Suburbans. They call them SUVs but they are the small ones. Kind of tough to fit your gear and an animal inside of one of them at the same time. You need a pretty good truck. You must be hunting deer right?"

"Elk."

"You know Elk are a little heavy. Tough to drag them unless you cut them into pieces and bring out a quarter at a time. How long you plan on staying?"

"A week, but we can handle it."

I spent the rest of the trip fielding questions from these rookies. They were seriously under-prepared, but full of energy, glowing, and ready to take on the challenge. I was eager to see how enthusiastic they would look on the return trip.

The weather did not cooperate much on that trip. We had some rainy days, which at the higher altitudes meant snow - nothing serious, but enough to make sitting in the saddle a little miserable. As usual, we had a great time hunting, with our favorite outfitter and his gang. We even managed to fill a few of our tags.

My guess was right. We met up with the gang of foot hunters in the airport before our return flight. What a mess. They were no longer smiling and joking among one another. In fact, they were barely speaking. Their gear was strewn around in piles in the check-in line and they used their suitcases as chairs. Their wind and sun-burned cheeks puffed above scraggy week-old beards. Their eyes were blood red and too moist to look natural. Their arms hung flaccidly at their sides and tiny groans escaped their lips with every movement. Their clothes hung wrinkled and dirty on their slumped frames. They needed showers.

"Hey, How'd you boys do," I said as we approached them.

The man I had been speaking with across the isle on the plane spoke. "Not too good." The excitement his voice held a week earlier was gone. His comrades barely looked up.

"Didn't get anything," I continued.

"Naw. Not this time. Maybe next year."

"Did you see any?"

"A few, but we couldn't get close enough for a shot."

"Did you find a good spot to camp over there on the Granite?"

"It was alright. No really good flat spot to pitch a tent. Tough sleeping."

"Did you get up to the top of the Sawback?"

"Yeah, the first day, but that's a tough climb. Took all day going up. So, we just kind of hung out on the side of it after that."

"Nice area though hey?"

"Yeah, but tough to hunt."

I was going to add "tough to hunt on foot," but didn't. These guys were obviously demoralized enough. In fact, one of them looked like he could stand a few days in an intensive care unit.

"Well, better luck next year. Have a good flight back."

OPTIONS AGAIN

Once you make the decision to go, you will have some options you will need to think about long and hard.

You can:

1.) Drive a car out, camp near your hunting area and hunt on foot.

2.) Drive out, pulling a trailer and an ATV.

3.) Fly out, rent a car, camp and hunt on foot.

4.) Fly out, rent a car, rent an ATV, Camp and use the ATV for access and game removal.

5.) Fly out, rent a car, rent a horse, camp, and use the horse to hunt.

6.) Drive or fly out, hire an outfitter to take you to and from a drop camp and get your game out of the wilderness for you.

7.) Drive or fly out, hire an outfitter to do everything for you.

Lets examine each of these options in detail.

Option 1. Drive out and hunt on foot.

If you are on a very limited budget, you can draw a tag through the lottery system of the state in which you intend to hunt. This is the cheapest (although, not the most certain) way to get a tag.

You can drive a car filled with camping gear out to your area, set up camp and walk around the foothills with a rifle or a bow, hoping to stumble upon a deer or an elk. There is nothing illegal about this and some people actually do fill their tags this way. But, get ready for some very serious work, and a very limited hunt.

Remember, even if you are in shape, you are out of shape in the mountain altitude. Game tends to move as far from campers as possible. Unless you bag some poor diddle-brained creature who happens to stumble into your camp, you are going to have to walk a quite a ways just to find something to shoot. And, if you are hunting in the mountains likely that hike will be mostly uphill. Uphill hikes in the thin-air mountains are killers.

So, typically, you hike out a couple or three miles in the morning. You skulk around most of the day and end up shooting something that evening. You get it gutted and maybe drag the head back that night. Then, you hike back the next morning and get it quartered. You put a section on your back and walk it back to your camp – maybe in time for lunch. In the afternoon, you make the hike again and bring out another quarter. The next day, you repeat the process. If you have a five-day hunt, you could spend half your trip lugging meat out. If the weather turns south, your task could be impossible. If you shoot your trophy in a difficult spot, you could be totally euchred. If you shoot it on the last day of your hunt . . . well, you might really be out of luck then. Remember, in all states it is illegal to leave dead animals in the wild.

This scenario doesn't consider the time it takes to drive to the hunting area, finding a good spot to camp (somewhere reasonably near where you intend to hunt), setting up a camp and breaking a camp down and packing it away. If you plan to hunt by option one, consider extending your hunt for an additional week (which, in the long run, may end up costing you much more money). And, you can all but forget about getting a trophy

Option 2.) Drive out with a trailer and an ATV.

This is a much better plan. Having an ATV - quad, four-wheeler, whatever you want to call them - around can save you a lot of work and tons of time. They are also a lot of fun to buzz around on. Unfortunately, they can't go everywhere a horse can. They need a trail wide enough to carry them, and that is about three times more space than a horse needs. If you need to pass through a stand of timber, where there may or may not be a trail, you'll have a tough time getting over deadfall. If you have to cross a deep stream or river, the ATV might not make it. If you plan on hunting, high wilderness areas where the big ones live, you might have to walk a long way past where your ATV can get you. If walking is okay, the ATV is okay. If you are hunting wide-open BLM land, I can't think of a better vehicle – way faster than a horse.

But, there is another problem. Most states have set limits as to where they will allow ATV traffic, in general, and more specifically and more dramatically for hunting.

Colorado, for example, has recently passed legislation which dramatically limits where a rider can take his ATV (or Jeep for that matter). Other western states are considering similar legislation. This is a big problem. Most wilderness areas are closed to ATV traffic, period. Others will allow ATV traffic but only in corridors, which border the wilderness area, but ban it in the area itself. If you take an ATV near an area then shoot an animal, which runs a long way off (a trait they are known for) you could have a serious problem trying to get it out. You will still have to drag or carry sections of your kill back to the ATV and then ride back to your camp. Be sure to check the regulations for the area you intend to hunt first, or you might be disappointed. Generally speaking an ATV can be taken up roads or marked trails but cannot be taken off that trail for any reason.

It is amazing how creative hunters can be when it comes to trailers and ATVs. I have seen what looks like entire cities being hauled out behind a truck - ATVs, freezers, tents, Port-o-johns, generators, and yes, more than one kitchen sink.

Option 3.) Fly out, rent a car, hunt on foot.

This option is not much better than option one. In fact, it might be worse. Having to deal with airline schedules and rental car return policies adds another layer of complication and considerably more expense to your adventure. If you have a time limitation for your hunt, the added headaches planes and cars create can seriously limit the fun you have.

Further, it is very difficult to take enough camping gear for a week's stay in the mountains on a plane. Today, with airline financial losses reaching new levels, and with the increased security at airports, most carriers are enforcing their limits on excess baggage. You may find that baggage charges will be greater than the fair you pay as a passenger.

Rental cars aren't what they used to be either. Auto companies have down-sized what we used to call an SUV. Rental car companies have taken the principle to a new low. What they call an SUV barely qualifies as a car. You just can't pack enough stuff in one of them to keep two guys comfortable on a one-week camping foray into the mountains. Their inventory manifest might offer a larger car or truck but, when you get to the airport the likelihood of them actually having the bigger vehicle available is slim. Even confirming a week or a day in advance that you will be getting the car you want won't work. These companies do not care. Their counter staff are chosen for their ability to turn to absolute stone while you are bitching about not being able to get what you reserved. You'll end up with what they have or with nothing at all.

And if you should be lucky enough to actually bag something, an elk for example, you'll find stuffing it into one of these mini SUVs very difficult .

Option 4.) Fly out, rent a car, rent an ATV, Camp and use the ATV for access and game removal.

Years ago, it was virtually impossible to find someone who would rent an ATV. Today, it has become a cottage industry and you can rent one just about anywhere. However if you are thinking about renting one for your hunting trip, make arrangements far in advance or you may not be able to find one. Most guys who rent ATVs in the summer are also hunters or guides in the fall. They may be using their machines themselves or have pre-contracted with another outfitter to provide equipment for him.

You will, need to make sure too, that the car you rent is capable of towing a trailer and you will need to make sure the ATV rental guy has a trailer for you. If not, then he will have to deliver your ATV to you and pick it up when you are ready to leave.

While it is possible to rent all this stuff, remember, renting cars, trailers, and ATVs can get very expensive - way more than what an outfitter would charge.

Option 5.) Fly out, rent a car, rent a horse, camp, and use the horse to hunt.

It's funny. A guy will rent you his car, or his ATV or even his wife - all far more expensive and infinitely more dangerous than a horse - without much more than a casual question or two.

"You ever rid one before? Well, don't get yourself kilt."

But try renting his horse, and you'll have to pass more tests than a NASA astronaut. You will have to demonstrate that you know more about horses than just having ridden a few on the Merry-go-Round at the Bloomington county fair. You'll have to prove yourself worthy. You'll have to prove that you can care for a horse and keep it healthy. Drive a guy's ATV off a cliff and you'll be writing a check for a new one. Kill a guy's horse or even hurt its feelings, and you will be in a whole heap of trouble. You know horse thiefin' used to be a hanging offense in Cowboy land. The "used to be" part of that statement has been forgotten by a lot of locals.

Even if you do have sufficient animal husbandry skills to keep a horse healthy, you will have to practice them during your hunt and that in itself will take up more time than you will typically have. Horses need water. They need food. They need to be trailered around. They need to be properly corralled or hobbled. They need to be caught in the morning and bridled - on and on. Taking care of someone else's horse on a hunting trip is a hassle no one needs.

Option 6.) Drive or fly out, hire an outfitter to take you to and from a drop camp and get your game out of the wilderness for you.

We hunters are an independent breed - self-sufficient too. We don't really need anybody telling us how to do something we have been doing all our lives. Just get us out there amongst 'em and we will take care of everything else ourselves.

Well, it is the taking care of everything else part where the problems come.

Drop camp hunting is an excellent method of getting your adventure fix and you won't find it difficult to get an outfitter to accommodate you. What you will find difficult; is everything else.

Drop camp hunting means cooking for yourself, which means more planning. Not only do you have to procure all the food, you have to get it into the camp. Then, you have to cook it. There is nothing better than coming back to a camp after a hard days hunting - frequently in cold wet weather - to a nice hot meal and a ready bed. If for a million reasons, you were miserable out on the trail, come back to a drop camp, and you will be just as miserable, but you'll have a ton of chores to do as well. More than one drop camp hunter has crawled into a cold sleeping bag after a only a hot dog and a cup of half-warm tea as his evening meal. And if that is not quite appealing enough for you, remember, the morning will be worse. Dragging your tired, wet, hungry ass into a sleeping bag at night is one thing. Pulling it out of a warm sleeping bag into the dark cold morning is another. Want a cup of hot coffee to start the day? Well, get down to the stream for some water or chip the ice off a bucket to get some. Then fire up something to cook on, propane or wood, while your fingers freeze and you body shivers. Getting the picture? It's okay if you've got the time, or a designated cook and camp tender. But if you and your buddies are trying to do it yourselves, get ready to make a few enemies. Few drop campers manage to keep their friendships alive let alone their plans for a return trip the next year.

And, what about the hunting itself? Drop camp hunting means no guide. Yes, you will be saving a few dollars, but think about what you will be giving up.

When a guest comes to your hunting world, don't you pass on the benefit of your experience? Don't you say things like: "See that little marsh. The deer use that to get from that woods over there to this one over here. And if you wait right here, you'll probably get a good shot . . .?" Of course you do. No one knows your area better than you. That small service you provide to new guys in your area is invaluable. It carries then that a guide can provide valuable services to you.

7.) Drive or fly out and hire an outfitter to do everything for you.

If you have only a short window of opportunity in which to cowboy hunt, hire an outfitter. If you would like to increase your odds of being successful, hire an outfitter. If you are unfamiliar with he area in which you intend to hunt, hire an outfitter. If you want to have an all-around better Cowboy hunting experience, hire an outfitter. If you are in the habit of listening to and taking the advice of many old-time Cowboy hunters who have come before you and have at one time or another been in your shoes, hire an outfitter.

Getting the picture? We will assume through the remainder of this book, that you are listening and intend to **HIRE AN OUTFITTER!** Their services begin long before you even put in for a tag, and continue until your trophy is hanging on your wall.

TIP - Rental Cars Never try to take a small two-wheel-drive sedan - the only car left for rent at the airport - antelope hunting. You just might drive a rock through the transmission case and end up walking fifteen miles back to the world. The tow bill to get the damn thing back will be astronomical. Been there.

TIP - Rental Cars Don't drive around for a couple of days with a carcass in the rear of a rental car - especially an antelope - even if the temperature is in the twenties. The bill for getting the stink out of the damn thing will be astronomical. Been there too!

TIP - Travel: If you fly, **BOOK EARLY!** Oh yeah, you would be surprised at how fast flights dry up during hunting season. We have waited almost too long a couple of times. Airlines aren't dumb. They know what is going on in September and October. If you book your flight early, and something comes up which prevents you from going, you can usually cancel, and use the tickets another time. Airlines understand this, and are willing to change arrangements. It might cost a couple of bucks, but the security of knowing you have the flight is worth it.

TIP - Hunt Insurance Who'da thunk that you could buy insurance to protect you while hunting, but you can. You can even buy insurance that will pay to get you airlifted out in case of an emergency or an injury. Just search the internet for Hunters insurance and you will find plenty of companies willing to provide coverage.

TIP - Guns and Airports: Walk through an airport with a rifle and the air will freeze so solid that you can almost reach out with a hammer and shatter it. A million eyes will fall on you like butterflies to bagels. All guns must be in **hard** cases! You do not have to remove the bolt or the clip, but you will probably have to demonstrate to someone that the gun is unloaded, and sign a declaration to that effect. Bullets actually make the airlines more nervous. If you take them with you, be sure not to put them in the case with the gun. Stash them in your regular duffel, and check them through. Still, they might get x-rayed in the baggage area these days, and you might have to answer some questions. Try to keep your ammo in its original box. For some reason they have a thing about original boxes. If you reload your own, get an empty factory shell box and put your reloads in it, to avoid hassles. Expect to be searched if you reload. The airports have amazingly sensitive methods of detecting gunpowder. The smallest trace amount left on a shell box will start bells ringing. Take every precaution to eliminate as much trace as possible to ensure an easy passage through a turnstile.

Handguns really get airline people jittery. You will not need one on any western hunt. If you insist on bringing one, for some reason, it too must be in a case. Get ready to answer a lot of questions. It's a good idea to call the airline security office ahead of your trip and ask them their policies. Even at that, you may have to answer questions from some check-in people. Plan to spend a little extra time in security these days if you are on a hunting trip.

TIP – Cowboy Hunting: Cowboy hunting is dirt, but not the kind you feel like washing off. It's clean dirt, the kind you sit in without thinking about it. It's the kind that feels good to the touch and smells even better. It's mostly ground rock, mixed with pine needles and ancient fibers from ancient plants. It's not really dirt, it's planet, as pure as Mother Nature can cook it.

OUTFITTERS

FINDING A REPUTABLE OUTFITTER

If the government acts like the King with regards to the divisions of the land, then the outfitters are the Knights who watch over the bounty.

If you provide assistance - provide equipment, horses, assist in bringing game out of the back country, or even give directions, to any hunter in the State of Wyoming, for example, for a fee, you must have an Outfitter's license. Period. If not, you can be fined. Each cowboy state has similar rules.

Outfitters purchase permits to take hunters into a specific area – usually the drainage of a particular river or creek, sometimes a tract of private land , maybe a large ranch in Colorado. The permit areas in a particular drainage are somewhat hazily defined using the meets and bounds system – something like this: all of those lands drained by Elm creek, from the midpoint of highway 31, south along skyline of Mitchell Ridge, then west to Dog Ear Point, then north along Black Mesa to highway 31.

These permits are not cheap – upwards of $10,000 pre year in some areas. They do however give the outfitter some exclusivity for a specific area, and of course this is something cherished by most hunters. If the permit is for an area on State or Federal land (excluding Wilderness Areas), ordinary citizens are still allowed to hunt for themselves, but technically no other outfitters or guides are allowed to bring clients into the area.

Outfitters are required to be licensed by the states in which they hunt. You can call the state licensing office to be sure that they are. Or you could settle for having the outfitter supply his number to you. In addition, most reputable outfitters are members of their individual State guides and outfitters association. You can call these associations for information about them, as well. If they are not a member, maybe you should be a little more cautious before signing any contracts.

The outfitter's associations of the Cowboy states are listed below.

Wyoming Outfitter's Association: (307)-265-2376

http://www.wyoga.org

Colorado Outfitter's Association: (970)-824-2468

http://www.colorado-outfitters.com

Montana Outfitter's Association: (406)-449-3578

http://www.montanaoutfitters.org

Idaho Outfitter's Association: (208)-342-1919

http://www.ioga.org

Nevada Outfitter's Association: (775)-964-2145

http://www.huntandshoot.org

Utah Outfitters Association: No Phone

http://www.utah-adventures.net

New Mexico Outfitter's Association: (505)-743-2504

No Website

Arizona Outfitter's Association: No specific phone – Multiple organizations – search internet

http://www.arizonaguides.net

Today, many outfitters also maintain web pages, which can be extremely helpful in assessing an outfitter's qualifications.

THE NO GOOD, THE JUST BAD AND THE REALLY UGLY

Reputable outfitters? Does that imply that there are something other than reputable outfitters? Oh Yeah! Our very first outfitter back in the 1970s was a very poor outfitter, and we were too inexperienced to know better.

He told us he would pick us up at the Jackson Hole airport, when he didn't show, we should have suspected that we were in for trouble. We had spoken with Clark the night before and thought everything was A-okay. It was a beautiful day though, so we were content to sit in the airport and stare out at the Tetons —for awhile. Finally, after we were unable to reach him by phone (for a couple of hours) we decided to hire a Taxi cab to take us to the address, where we had mailed our deposits. There were three of us, and we had a bit of gear, so squeezing it all into a cab was a little rough. It didn't get any better when we pulled up to a run down house in a fairly shoddy part of town (yes, there were shoddy parts of Jackson Hole back then). Finally after banging on the door for several minutes, we were able to waken Clark Jr., the outfitter's son, and the guy who was supposed to have picked us up.

He came to the door in a dirty t-shirt, and pants that appeared to have been slept in -- for the last week. "Sorry. Forgot," was all he had to say.

We had been dreaming about this trip for months. Our spirits, which had been soaring were starting to loose their lift. A friend of a friend of a friend had given us Clark's name, and suddenly we knew that we might be just one friend to far removed from the truth. After what seemed like forever, Clark Jr. was finally ready, and we loaded all of our gear into the back of a rusty pickup, and squeezed four guys into the front seat - to head first to the post office, then to the bank, then to Clark Jr."s girlfriend's house, and finally out to the farm where Clark Sr. worked as a hand.

His wife met us at the door. Except for the fact that she seemed a whole lot meaner, she looked more like Darth Vader's wife than an outfitter's.

"He ain't here," she said, spitting something black out of her mouth, which we all hoped was not tobacco. "When he gits back, he's got some chores to do, and then he'll have his lunch. After that, he can go huntin' with you boys." She didn't offer any lunch to us, and after looking at what was smeared on her apron, I for one, was not too interested in having any.

It took the two Clarks about three more hours, before we were ready to go. They'd rustled up another old (dirty) guy to help out with the horses. We watched while they tossed our gear into the truck like they worked in the baggage department of Benny's Bargain Airlines. A pack of unhappy dogs kept us standing where we were told to stand.

Soon, we were back in the truck, bouncing in the upholstery-free back seat. I lost two fillings on the ride up to the trailhead. There was a divot in the top of my head, where a rivet sticking out of the roof of the cab had impaled itself, on a particularly brutal bump, and I think one of my ribs was broken or at least seriously bruised by one of my buddy Tommy's elbows. I wished he was a Chiropractor.

Clark Jr, never said a word. Nor did he change his T-shirt. He just sat there, right arm over the steering wheel, and his left arm working a cigarette in and out of his mouth. He had a .38 caliber pistol strapped to his hip.

Eventually, we made it out of the truck and were up on the back of some animals, which in many ways, resembled horses.

I'd always heard that if you could see more than 6 or 7 ribs on a horse, it was undernourished or sick or something. I could see all of the ribs on mine as well as its pelvic girdle, and it was coughing. They told me to approach it on its right side so it could see me. Only his left eye didn't work. Tommy's had open sores on its hip and chest. Our other friend Jim, was on a multi colored beast that had kicked him, kicked two of the other horses, kicked a dog, and seemed to actually have foam dripping out of its mouth. I'd never seen that in a horse before – a real pleasant mount.

We rode, or sort-of staggered, along a treed ridge next to a softly gurgling stream, for about an hour until we came across four tents, a rudimentary coral and a broken, rotted outhouse, up ahead on the trail. All three of our companions were chain smokers. As we road along, they literally lit one cigarette off the glowing butt of the last one. Worse, they were pitching the still-glowing stubs left and right, along the trail.

If you listen to my wife, she will be happy to describe the status of my car. Pigpen will come up several times. My desk is strewn with the remnants of projects in progress, completed or forgotten – papers, magazines, trinkets, toys, computer parts, what-have-you. But those are my personal man-made worlds. I really don't care about them that much. I certainly don't care if anyone ever rides in my car. However, I am a fanatic when it comes to the natural world. If I am hiking and come across even a scrap of old Snickers wrapper, I pick it up. I bury my campfires. I really do think that no one should be able to see any evidence of my presence when I leave the woods. With each arching white flick, I was getting madder and madder. By the time we road into camp, I'd seen a hundred or so cigarettes arching into the brush on the side of the trail, and I was furious.

At the tents, the two Clarks and the old wrangler dismounted with out a word, and began tossing our gear onto the ground. "That's your tent," Clark Sr. said, through a blue smoke haze and a cough.

We dragged our stuff into the shabby tent. Tom asked if I had noticed them tossing all those cigarettes. All I could do was to glare. He and Jim knew that I was steaming. They were none too happy either.

Tents are tents, and I have been in both good and bad. This one had no floor, and one of my major concerns was that it had been pitched in a rock pile. I had brought along a neoprene sleeping mat, but on rocks I knew it would be insufficient. Neither Tom nor Jim had one. When they went out to inquire about whether there was anything around which might act as a cushion, they were met with; " You should have thought of that before we lugged you all the way up here."

Unlike me, Tom and Jim are two very mild-mannered people. But now, they were fuming too.

It was only about four o'clock – still plenty of time to hunt, we thought, at least do a little scouting. We asked about maybe taking a little ride up one of the ridges to look around.

"You just got done ridin' an hour. What do you want," little Clark said.

They could have lit their next smoke off my forehead.

"We gotta wait for the cook, and help get her set up. "

We were becoming very uneasy about our decision to hire these guys for our hunt. We were inexperienced and didn't really know what to expect. We decided to just be polite and see what happened. After all, we had a full week and we didn't necessarily have to end up friends with these guys as long as they were able to get us each an Elk. We decided to take a walk up in the hills to calm down. When we returned, the cook was in the camp. It was Mrs. Darth Vader. We should have known. There didn't seem to be any additional horses in the herd, so we assumed that she'd come on broomstick.

"You boys almost missed dinner ," she said.

It was true. They hadn't waited. The cook tent was a blue cloud of choking smoke. Presumably they had stopped smoking long enough to eat, and then lit up again immediately after. Remnants of dinner were strewn around the table cold as ice.

"We only serve it one time," she said. "Be here or you miss it."

I was about to let go a blast of pent up resentment and see if I couldn't scorch a little of that nasty off that ugly woman, when Tom tapped me on the shoulder. He could sense what was coming and as usual wanted to try to calm things down. "Hey," he said. "You wouldn't happen to have a beer would you?"

"Water and coffee. That's it," Clark Sr. said.

I grabbed a plate of whatever and stomped out to sit among the poor Auschwitz-looking horses, who were infinitely friendlier.

There was no camp fire or any such camaraderie at this camp. Tom and Jim and I stood outside in the starlight for a couple of hours and then slid onto the rock pile to try to sleep. We were stunned awake by a series of shouts culminating in a single, deafening pistol shot. Finally, I thought. Somebody shot her.

We scrambled into our pants and boots and stumbled out into the black morning. Laughter rang from the cook tent, and when we opened the door and peered in through the smoke Clark Jr. stood gloating over a dead porcupine, which lie on the dirt floor bleeding. Apparently he had made a visit to the outhouse and found the harmless creature wandering around nibbling on grass. You would have thought it had been stealing babies like some crazed Dingo. You would have thought no one in that group had ever seen a porcupine before. You would have thought that if they were truly hunters they would also be conservationists as well. Most hunters are.

Our hunt continued to go down hill from there. The area these guys hunted extended no more than a mile or so from their camp, and at that, it seemed like they were forever looking over their shoulders, waiting for someone to come and kick them off. We rode over the same trails time and time again. We rode over them, and then walked back over them being sure to step only in the tracks made by either Clark Sr. or Jr.. They were very adamant about that for some reason. I never saw any Elk, except for some, which had obviously been butchered there in the field. I saw at least one carcass fully intact - except the antlers had been removed. It made me sick.

I had been hunting with Jr. who constantly admonished me about making too much noise, while he sent clouds of smoke down every canyon and across every ridge. Any Elk with a nose had left the area long ago. Tom on the other hand had been out with Sr. and had a similarly bad time. Sr. had wanted him to begin firing into a batch of cow Elk they had come across. We only had bull tags. Sr. said there was a bull in the bunch and that Tom should kill it immediately. Tom never saw any antlers. He was livid.

When we awoke the next morning, the trail below, where we had just come was smoking. Clearly there was a forest fire below us, and my heart sank. I am certain to this day, that our outfitter and his son started that fire with their careless handling of cigarettes. We made them take us back to town immediately. We rode back down through over 200 firefighters flown in from everywhere. Later we filed a complaint with the State of Wyoming. We never heard anything more from them about the fire.

THE GOOD THE BETTER…AND DICK

We still had three days left on our Wyoming Hunt, after Darth Vader and family dropped us off in the middle of the town square in Jackson. We stood under the Elk archway for a while trying to figure out what to do. Finally, we dragged our gear over to the Antler and got a room. The effort made the Million Dollar Cowboy Bar look mighty inviting. The bartender had a sympathetic ear, or maybe he had seen poor desolate cowboys before, and knew when they were about to self-destruct on trail whiskey. In any event, he suggested that in the morning, we should get a car and head out to see an outfitter he knew named Dick.

Dick's ranch sits on 65 acres of sage and pines, nestled in rolling hills, on the remains of an ancient flood plain deposited by the Hoback river. The river was named after a guide who had been commissioned by John Jacob Astor - the prominent New York business man, whose great grandson later perished on the Titanic - to bring fur trappers into the Jackson Hole area in hopes of capturing a share of the lucrative Beaver pelt market.

The ranch consists of a several guest cabins – roomy, heated, private bathrooms, comfy beds, etc. – a couple of barns a few staff cabins, some corrals and a luxurious main lodge with cable T.V. Pool table, bar and a large eating area. If you stand on the front porch of the main lodge and look out, you will see Highway 191 as well as a host of man-made objects. If you stand on the back porch, you will be looking into a painting – looking into another world, devoid of anything touched by man, devoid of time itself. If you walk a few hundred yards around a bend in the Hoback, you will be unable to hear anything man-made, unless a jet sails by overhead. Take a few more steps up the trail, and you might as well step a few hundred or a few thousand years back in time. This was paradise, and Dick and his crew would redeem the worth of all western outfitters and guides - in our minds at least.

The Hoback trail runs literally through Dick's back yard. That afternoon, Dick's staff got us saddled up on three beautiful horses and headed up the Hoback trail a half a mile to where it meets the Poplar Creek Trail. From there we followed the Poplar for four or five hours or about 16 miles to where Dick maintained his high camp.

16 miles on a flat road is one thing. 16 miles in the mountains is another. The trail wound through open sage and wild flower meadows, along bubbling creeks, and up through cool stands of very old timber. Sometimes it was all uphill, and at other times it dropped down at a grade that threw us back in our saddles just barely holding onto the reins. The land on both sides was open at times, like riding across a giant football field. At others it was so narrow, we wondered if we could squeeze through. More times than I care to remember, the trail narrowed down to just a foot, bound on one side by a sheer mountain wall, and on the other by a drop-off of 50 to 100 feet to the river below. From the back of a horse, those drops always look far more treacherous. But given that, there is nothing like a ride through the mountains on a nice day to lift the spirits of even the most dejected cowboys.

High camp here was not much different from high camps anywhere - tents. Everything that is taken to or from a high mountain camp must be packed on horseback. Therefore, camps are by necessity austere. What differs is the effort the people put into making them homey. Dick' tents had cots – rough sawn from the local timber, and covered with a six-inch piece of foam rubber. They had propane lanterns. They had individual potbellied stoves, which when fired up could drive even a desert nomad out into the night for a breath of cold air. A mirror hung on a large Pine in the middle of the compound served as a common shaving-face-washing-tooth-brushing stand. Water was provided in tin buckets, fresh from the creek. They froze a little each morning and the first man to use them had to break through the crust.

      When we arrived at Dick's high camp, somebody immediately met us and took our horse. The cook, an attractive blond woman, greeted us with a big smile, and a can of cold beer. She ushered us into a spacious cook tent, where a plate of chips and dip, waited. Introductions were made and the jokes and stories began. A few beers and a lot of laughs later, we were shown our tents. To our surprise, all of our gear had been carried the hundred yards up from the horse corral, and stacked inside next to our cots. Fires crackled in our stoves making the tents warm and comfortable. We felt appreciated. I felt like I was home - finally home.

FINDING OUTFITTERS II

To be honest, short of actually finding a trophy on a Cowboy hunt, the hardest part of the whole thing is finding a good Outfitter. And, despite what you may think or what somebody tells you, finding a good outfitter is the key to having a successful Cowboy hunt. It may take a few trips for you to realize the truth in that, but that is really the key to everything. Remember, a successful trip is not always defined by how many or how big the animals you harvest are. A number of my favorite memories and best times came on trips where no one shot anything.

You don't really want to think of it that way, but any veteran cowboy hunter will tell you that is the way it is. A good outfitter can make a bad hunt into a great trip! And, in the end, a good outfitter is your best hope for finding a good trophy.

Spend some time on this. Don't just take the first one you find who can accommodate you. Be careful to check out a referral from a friend. Just because one of your buddies had a good trip does not mean you will. His expectations may be way different than yours. Be mindful of how far away the referral is. Was it your friend who actually went with the outfitter in question or was it a friend of a friend of a friend? Referrals tend to get muddied along the way just as stories tend to get changed every time they are passed around. Our first nightmare with the smoking Clark family was the result of a friend of a friend referral.

Admittedly, this filtering of outfitters gets easier every time you do it. Your first-hand experience of being an outfitter's client helps you to choose the next outfitter you go with. It will at least give you some idea of what questions to ask, and what answers to expect.

TIP - Reference: Don't feel bad about asking for references. Most outfitters will be more than willing to provide them for you. In fact, most will provide them for you before you ask. The good news is that most of the really bad outfitters and guides are gone. Natural selection, when it works, is a marvelous thing.

TIP - How to read references: The first thing to realize is that no one will give you the name of someone, whom he thinks will give him a bad reference. So, if you talk to one, don't ask him whether he liked the outfitter or not, he did. Ask him instead, what the camp was like. Ask him about the staff. How many guides were available? Was there a wrangler? A camp helper? How was the food? Did he see much game? How large an area was he able to access? Was he successful? How much did he tip? Ask lots of general questions about the hunt, not so many about the outfitter.

TIP - Hunting Trade Shows: RV and Camper shows. Boat shows. Builder's shows. Lawn and garden shows. Craft shows. And yes, today, even hunting shows. Putting on and going to shows, seems to be an American passion. Hunting is big business. Millions and millions of dollars are spent on hunting gear and hunting books and hunting trips and hunting this and hunting that each year. So, hunting shows and hunting banquets are a natural.

What's interesting is the number of bad hunt stories that come from those who have purchased hunts at hunting shows. That doesn't mean that every hunt purchased at a hunting show will be bad. It just means that a number of them are.

It's the big business thing. Because hunting is such a big business, some aggressive outfitters have focused more on bookings than they have quality. It is those outfitters who end up at hunting shows, where huge concentrations of wannabe hunters concentrate. BE VERY CAREFUL! You could find yourself in a camp with twenty other hunters. You could find yourself riding out with ten of them in the morning all heading for the same place. You could find yourself heading out with the same ten the next morning heading to the spot the other ten went to the day before. Been There!

The best outfitters don't really have to advertise and they certainly don't have to attend trade shows.

TIP - The Internet It is easy to get fooled here too. The same principals apply. Hunting is big business and the internet has become synonymous with big business. Ruthless outfitters, who are more interested in good booking numbers than good hunts herd up in cyberspace by the hundreds.

That is not to say that good outfitters don't have websites. They do. Just about everybody has a website today. Just be careful!!

TIP - TV Show Outfitters: Talk about big business. You know there is big money in a business when you see entire TV shows devoted to it. And, these days, there are several. They are fun to watch and certainly generate a lot of money for the lucky producers of the show, but here is the thing. Actually booking on a TV show hunt is very difficult. Those guys are booked so far out, it's guaranteed that you will wait until you can't even find your gun before you can get in. And expensive? You have no idea. Take a look who's on those shows – Rock Stars, Movie stars, Pro Athletes, Politicians, Big businessmen. If you can get booked. You better start pawning stuff right now, so that you'll have the cash when your hunt time comes up.

TIP - Success Ratios: Outfitters like to keep track of and usually brag about their success numbers. Take this stuff with a grain of salt. It's easy to lie with statistics. Good outfitters measure their success by the numbers of animals on the ground – better yet, trophies on the ground. Other outfitters measure theirs by counting opportunities. They figure that if you get to see some game, their job is done. Others, throw in another qualifier - shots taken. Some figure that if you get to shoot at an animal, you are done. You are certainly done hunting if you wound an animal.

Well, these things happen in hunting. There isn't an honest hunter out there who has not missed a shot. And, unfortunately, just about all of us have hit one and then lost it. It happens. Good outfitters know this and accept it.

Good outfitters consider their job done when you are driving away with a cooler full of dry ice and some nicely packaged steaks.

Listen carefully to an outfitter's pitch. If he mentions his opportunity rate too much, listen a little harder to the rest of what he is saying.

I had a discussion with an outfitter a few years back about possibly coming to his place in British Columbia to hunt moose. After he told me how nice it was to sit in one of his nice cabins and play cards for the fourth time, I started getting nerved up about how good the actual hunting was.

TIP - Outfitters: When you are talking to an outfitter on the phone, ask him to describe a typical day on one of his hunts. If he gives you a very specific answer be leery. Hunting is a hit and miss thing with no particular structure. If he says something like: "Well, we usually ride up in the hills and start glassing until we figure out a plan," he is a man who has done it a few times before. You need to be flexible to be successful. A good outfitter is one who is willing to do whatever it takes for you to get your mount.

In the end hunting is being in the right place at the right time. If an outfitter tells you something that sounds too far from that reality, your hackles ought to start getting stiffened up.

TIP – Cowboy Hunting: Cowboy hunting is post-card perfect panoramas. It's cresting high ground and stepping into drop-your-jaw beauty. It's pausing for a minute or an hour to just sit there and stare off into the distance. It's feeling humbled by nature. It is knowing that if you were to leave a boot print in any of the canyons or timber patches before you, it might be one of only a few others since the dawn of time – a native' American's, a sheep herder's, maybe a lonely cow puncher's. It could be the only one, ever.

GUIDES

JOE MENJI

Bobby earned his high school varsity letter in Bronc Bustin'. I didn't even know they had such a thing. To say he knew a lot about horses, would be like saying Joe Montana played football. I always imagined him standing on some mountaintop, yelling a secret melody, and all of the horses in Wyoming, Colorado, Utah, and Idaho picking up their ears running to him like elephants to Tarzan. I learned most of what I know about horses from Bobby and his father.

Bobby was born in southern California, but at the age of two, his mother and father bought a guest ranch a few miles outside of Jackson Wyoming. A guest ranch in Wyoming means horses and his parents had plenty of them.

Face on, Bobby had those rugged, Marlboro-man good looks, but if you watched him walking away from you, you'd notice two things. You'd know a horse was supposed to fit between his permanently bowed legs and you'd gawk at the width of his shoulders and the muscles in his neck and back. He didn't even look natural. In fact, he reminded me of Joe Menji.

When I was a young child, my parents took my brother and me to the Detroit Zoo. They had a Gorilla exhibit there, housed in a separate, meticulously tiled building. Joe Menji was the star and on the day we were there, he stood alone, behind the bars, staring out at the crowd. At his side was a giant, tractor tire, which stood five feet high and weighed well over a hundred pounds. Joe stood there motionless with one hand on the top of the tire, his eyes fixed on me. I could barely see over the safety bars that stood between the viewers and the Gorillas, but I am certain that Joe, for whatever reason, had singled me out among the onlookers and was directing all of his attention toward only me.

Joe's lack of motion and the fact that there were no other Gorillas present on that day, soon bored the crowd, and they - including my parents - drifted on. Big Joe had mesmerized me however, and I lingered behind. Soon it was just Joe and me, alone in the Gorilla house, staring into each other's eyes. When he was certain that we were alone, Joe did a remarkable thing, a thing I will never forget. Suddenly, with astounding agility and fluid grace, Joe Menji, grabbed the big tire, like it was nothing more than a doughnut, held it straight out in front of him, toward me, then crushed it like it was so much tissue paper. He then set the tire down, put his hand back on top to steady it, grinned a giant monkey grin and stood there, motionless again, just as he had been when we had come in.

I had had my own private Joe Menji performance and what a magnificent performance it was. I have often wondered if Joe stood like that often, silent, motionless, waiting for an opportunity to perform for a single child, without the critical eye of any adults. How many of us are out there who have had that unique privilege? I remember when he died many years ago. The Detroit News did a story on him. I remember wondering if he had taken our secret with him to his grave.

If you told me Bobby could do a Joe Menji on a tractor tire, I would believe it. Bobby was exactly the person you wanted in a tough situation. Not only were his horse and wilderness skills excellent, his physical presence in tough situations was comforting. Besides, if you ever did get an animal on the ground, Bobby was invaluable getting it schlepped back to camp.

Bobby grew up with paradise as his playground. From the front porch of the family ranch, you can look north to the Gros Ventre mountain range, which stretches a hundred miles and forms the eastern and north eastern border of the historic Jackson Hole. From the back porch of the ranch you can look south up the Oak Creek drainage to a land unscarred by a road or anything man-made for over twenty five miles. In the United States, a wilderness like that, is getting to be as rare as lips on a chicken. It was Bobby's back yard. There were no trails, only a few trees and even less rocks, which Bobby had not, at one time or another, ridden on, picked a needle off, or kicked with a boot. And, he remembered every one of them.

When you're in the back country with Bobby, you feel safe – well, safe in terms of not getting lost - sort of safe – well, a little safe anyway.

TIP - Cowboy hunting: I guess we've just seen too many movies. They've filled our heads with images that are hard to remove. When I think about the lone mountain man sitting on his horse in the wilderness taking on whatever Mother Nature sends his way, I can almost hear the testosterone gurgling out of my glands.

Don't give in to the urge to go solo in the mountains. Don't pester your guides and outfitters to let you go it alone. The mountains are just too dangerous. Horses are just too unpredictable. To many things can go wrong. Your well-being is the responsibility of the guides and outfitters. Don't put them in a difficult situation. Don't place the extra burden of worrying about your safety on them.

Don't "Cowboy up" and do it on your own without even telling anyone where you are going.

Always take Joe Menji with you when you go into the wilderness. Not only can he save your life, he can make your time there a lot more pleasant.

TIP – Cowboy Hunting: Cowboy hunting is not worrying about wet boots. It's fording a river on horseback with ice-water up to your crotch, for crying out loud. It's suddenly taking off on a John Wayne gallop after a herd of sprinting Elk. It's sliding down a rocky slope on your butt. It's engaging in an accelerated dismount, when some horse decides he's had enough of your boloney for the time being. It's blisters, cuts, bruises, aches, pains and even blood – yours. Cowboy hunting is not for the feint of heart or the smooth of skin.

MORE GUIDE STUFF

To guide anyone hunting, on BLM land, National or State Forest land, and even on private land, you must have a guide's license, and be sponsored by a licensed outfitter or be a licensed outfitter yourself. That is not to say, that two friends can't go hunting together. They can, but technically, if one provides all of the equipment, the horses and the expertise to the other, he is guiding, and, if you run across an unsympathetic conservation officer, he might fine you both. If you hunt in a designated Wilderness Area, you must have a guide. That is the law.

Good guides, although they would hate this analogy, become almost like personal wilderness valets. Their day begins long before yours and is devoted to enhancing your hunting experience and watching out for your safety. Even if you have a wrangler in camp to help with the horses, it will probably be your guide who saddles yours and holds it for you while you mount-up. He'll make sure you remembered to bring your lunch, your water, your gun, and your camera. He'll make sure throughout your day that you and your horse don't get into too many arguments. He'll make sure that horse will take you where no other four-wheeled vehicle can and, he'll make sure you don't get lost getting there. A good guide will make an effort to educate you about the area in which you are hunting as well as provide tips about surviving and hunting in that land. A good one will fill the blank spots in a day with yarns and tales that will last years after your hunt is over. Most good guides will see game long before you do. (I have often wondered why this happens, but have given up looking for a good reason. It just happens.) He will then help you form a strategy for getting a shot and spot for you after you take it, making it easier to find your game. I have even seen guides carry rifles and packs up mountains for struggling hunters so that they can get in position to even see game.

But, once you get your trophy on the ground, you will realize the true value of a good guide.

Field dressing a Deer or an Elk, is something most hunters know how to do. But realistically, even the best hunters do it only thirty or forty times in their lives. A good guide might do it thirty times in a single season and there is no way you will do it as well or as fast - especially if you are exhausted from riding and climbing and hiking telling stories (and lies) all day. Fast doesn't count you say? You are right - unless, of course, it is getting dark, or it's raining, or it's ten below zero or you are perched on an almost vertical hillside . Then, fast becomes more important than well.

The record for field dressing <u>without caping</u>, as far as we know, is held by a young rodeo Cowboy named Shirley. (Don't say anything about his name. He stands about 6'5" and weighs in with around 225 pounds of lean hard muscle. He is never without a well-formed Stetson and a six-inch silver belt buckle announcing his Champion Bronc Bustin' status. When he turns to the side you'll swear you've seen his face on a billboard, advertising Marlboros.) We timed him one day. Just under six minutes on a big Elk. And he did it without getting a single drop of blood on his shirt on his boots or on his jeans.

Field dressing game is one thing. Getting your trophy back to camp is another. It is not unusual for hunters without guides to spend more time getting a single animal back to camp than they do hunting. Having a guide makes this most important task infinitely easier.

MILE MARKER NUMBER EIGHT

Gabe and I had been at it since before the Crack-a-Dia. We had gotten up early to ambush a nice buck we had seen the day before, but he had failed to show up. We had been wandering ever since and now, with the sun beginning to eyeball its landing spot below the western horizon, we were almost eight miles from our camp. I was beat. We'd ridden much more than the eight miles to get where we were, way out on Sawback ridge. In addition, we'd climbed several steep hillsides looking for Mr. Big Horns and at this altitude, every little climb drains your battery to almost nothing. Gabe wanted to go a half mile farther and peek into one of his secret hiding holes. When he suggested that I tie up and find a place to do some glassing, until he got back, I gladly took him up on it. Sitting on a mountaintop, staring off at the rest of the world is one of my favorite things to do.

I hadn't been there forty-five minutes when a very nice Mulie walked calmly out into the fading sun about two hundred yards back on the trail we had come up on. He stood for a minute gazing out into the same valley I had been watching. The sun glittered off his impressively tall rack. He wasn't the big boy we had been looking for, but he was a nice trophy just the same. And, he was just standing there, in front of a very tired hunter, who had only two days left to score. Bang.

It took Gabe a few minutes to react to the shot. He came riding up slowly as I stood over the carcass. The deer looked much bigger on the ground than he did standing - something that always makes me happy. "Reckon you's luckier when I ain't around. That's a mighty fine lookin' critter you got yonder."

"Thanks, but I was just thinking about how we're going to get him back to camp. I don't think we can get back and bring a pack horse up here before dark. We'll have to come all this way all over again tomorrow."

Gabe looked at the sun. "Reckon not. But we can walk him out."

Oh man, I thought. Unlike an elk, you can get a deer quartered up and stuffed into the panniers of a single packhorse. I had heard of guides and their hunters quartering one and tying the parts to two saddle horses (if the horses are willing) and then walking back to camp, so I knew it could be done, but I was not looking forward to an eight mile, up and down, mostly in the dark hike. No way. My vote was for coming back tomorrow, even though I still had an elk tag and losing a full day of hunt time might mean that I would not be able to fill it. Fortunately, Gabe had other plans. I could see them brewing behind his squinting eyes.

"Reckon if we done it right, we can git it on one horse."

I had seen Indians and Mountain Men hunters ride back into camp with a deer slung over the saddle in front of them in the movies, but those were stuffed deer skins not real deer with actual meat on them. I really wasn't sure what Gabe had in mind.

"You want him caped," Gabe asked.

"Well, I thought I might. He's a pretty good one and would look good hanging in an empty spot I've got on one wall."

Gabe had begun unleashing the small axe he always carried on his saddle. A few minutes later, he had field-dressed the deer and caped out the neck. Then, with a few deft swings of his axe, he separated the head from the neck and removed it and the cape, leaving the majority of the carcass and the quarters in tack. While I held the legs apart, Gabe then took a series of small delicate swings of his axe, and like a surgeon split the back-bone length-wise, leaving the hide of the back untouched and intact. We now had the two halves of the deer swinging free, held together by the tough hide. Gabe then put a small hole - about two inches long - in the hide between the two halves about a foot or so from the neck.

The package was ready for loading, but Gabe and I could not lift it up high enough to drop it onto the back of his horse, without totally freaking him out and we did not need a mountain-top rodeo at this point. So, we led the horse down into a little gully where we could stand on both sides and have his back at about arm length. We tied his head to two trees on either side of the gully just to make sure. With the horse relatively stabilized, we stood on opposite sides, and hefted the deer carcass up over the his rump and dropped the little hole Gabe had made in the hide over the saddle horn. We then set the head horns and cape on top and snatched the whole mess together with pieces of rope we always carried and, even the belts of our pants.

As I rode along in the fading light, behind Gabe who walked the entire eight miles with a smile on his face, I realized once again how valuable a guide can be on a Cowboy hunt.

NEED MORE PROOF?

We were riding along the top of Sawbuck ridge one day with our old friend X-ray. We were at one of the highest and steepest points along the ridge when our guide Randall suddenly put his fingers to his lips and jumped off his horse. After a few seconds of glassing down the side of the ridge into a little valley, he motioned for us to dismount. "Hell of a buck down there," he whispered, pointing down toward a little island of trees along the side of the rocky valley.

It took X-ray and me a minute or two to find it with our binoculars. How he had seen it with his naked eye was a puzzle, but he was right, it was a very nice buck. The trouble was, he was sitting in a very well hidden spot, with only a small percentage of the his kill zone exposed. To make matters worse, it was a long downhill shot of about 500 yards.

"I can make that," X-ray said.

"I doubt it," I said.

X-ray was notorious for looking at things a little differently than the rest of us did. He could see things most of us couldn't. He was usually full of horse whoopy.

"I know I can make it," he said, drawing his rifle out of its scabbard.

"It's a long shot," Randall said.

"I can do it."

The deer was so far away, that it hadn't even seen us and just sat there, staring down the valley. Randall stood with his hands on his hips surveying the landscape. "I don't know how the hell we'll get it out of there if you do get it," he said. "I guess we'll have to ride all the way back to the nobs and take the little trail from there down to Ash trail, then come back up it, then sidehill over to it from there. Probably take two hours. Long walk, but there ain't no way we can get it back up this way."

"It's a nice one and I'd like to try," X-ray said. It didn't appear anybody was going to dissuade him.

"Okay," Randall said, reluctantly.

X-ray took a position next to a fallen tree trunk and rested his gun on it. It seemed like it took an eternity for him to get the shot off. Randall and I stood there with our binoculars on the deer. We waited. And waited. None us mortals could see what X-ray could. Finally Kaboom!

I flinched a little when the shot finally rang out. It took a millisecond for me to reacquire the spot where the deer had been. And, of course, no deer. I dropped the glasses and used my eye to see if I could spot something running away. Randall had done the same. The three of us stood there watching. Nothing ran out the bottom. Nothing climbed out over the other side of the valley. Nothing moved. We watched for several minutes.

"I think I got him," X-ray said triumphantly.

"I doubt it," I said.

"Only one way to find out," he said. "We've got to ride down there and check it out. We can't just leave him."

"If we do that," Randall said. "And he ain't down there, we won't have no more time to hunt the rest of the day."

"We can't leave him," X-ray said.

We all stood there for a few beats, pondering the situation in silence. Finally, Randall said, "I'll peel over this cliff and climb down there. If he's there, I'll signal you boys and then you'll have to ride all the way around and bring me my horse. I'll get him dressed out while you do it. If he ain't there, I'll climb back up the cliff and we'll take off from here."

"That's a hell of a climb," I said. "You sure?"

It was a fairly warm day and Randall had already taken his jacket off. "Hey, we gotta do what we gotta do, you know," he said.

Before I could say much else, he was over the edge.

By my watch, it took him about thirty minutes to reach the spot where the deer had lain. He shuffled around in the trees for another thirty minutes before heading back toward the cliff. It took almost another forty for him to climb back to us. When he finally crawled over the edge, his shirt was sweat stained and he was breathing heavily. X-ray and I had been sitting on our fat asses the entire time.

"So?"

"Nothing. Not a drop of blood. No tracks. Nothing. I have no idea what happened to that deer."

X-ray and I had not taken our eyes off the valley. If the deer had been hit but was not dead, we figured that maybe it would bolt as Randall approached. X-ray had his rifle ready. Nothing.

The deer had simply vanished. They can do that.

The bottom line? If we had not had Randall, and if old X-ray had remained stubborn, we could easily have wasted an entire day on this ghost deer. I for one was extremely glad we had chosen to spend the extra money on an outfitter and guide.

WRANGLERS – WORTH THEIR WEIGHT IN WORK

Once you get your game back to camp, your guide's work is not finished. Somebody has to unpack it and get it stored away for the night. You can't leave your meat or your cape and horns lying around for too long. They will begin to deteriorate rapidly, especially if the weather is mild. You need to get it to a processor fairly fast.

Then, you have to deal with the horses. You have to put saddles and tack away. The horses will need to be grained and watered before they can be turned out to pasture for the night. If you don't have a good place to pasture them, then you are going to have to hobble or corral them and give them hay for the night - simply graining them is not enough if you expect them to work again tomorrow.

Most reputable outfitters run a shuttle service on the side, ferrying supplies into camp and hauling meat and horns out.

If you are on a one-week combo hunt, depending on when during the hunt you bag the first one, handling the myriad chores going on to support your trip might cost you your second species or might, in fact, consume more time than you spend actually hunting.

Outfitters frequently, hire what is known as a wrangler or a camp helper to assist your guide with these many and necessary tasks. Some do it themselves. In any case, when you are paying for an outfitter, you are also buying this little service, which in itself is worth the price of admission.

DINNER – YOU DIDN'T THINK OF THIS ONE?

It is not unusual to extend a day of hunting in the mountains well into the night when the only thing on your mind is a bed and a night's sleep. But then, of course, you haven't even had dinner yet.

Our good friend and hunting partner Tom Terrific is an excellent cook. In his home, in his kitchen, I'd put him up against Graham, or Emiril, or Martha , or any of the new breed of T.V. wonder chefs. But, stick him out in the mountains, exhausted, in the dark, with a Coleman Stove and an open fire, in the rain, after a long, hard day in the saddle and after climbing a couple dozen mountains and guess what, I guarantee you'll be eating what most wannabe Cowboy hunters end up with - beans right out of the can and a hot dog stuck on a stick and held over the flame for a few minutes.

You can not imagine how comforting it is to pop your sorry draggin' ass into a warm, dry cook tent and smell a nice hot dinner ready and waiting - even if it is only beans and hot dogs!

Just having a cook along on your trip is worth every penny you spend on an outfitter.

A cook's day starts long before anyone else's. The hot coffee you drink first thing in the morning didn't get air-dropped in by aliens in the night. Your cook busted ice off the water bucket or maybe even went down to the creek in the dark and snow to fetch the water for it. She got a fire going and boiled it long before even the horses were up.

Even a bad cook can fry eggs and make pancakes. Even a bad one can slap meat on bread and come up with lunches. Just the fact that she's doing it and you aren't is well worth the few sheckles you are paying. But, most Cowboy cooks go far beyond cracking eggs. Some of the best and most elaborate meals I have eaten in my life were cooked over a wooden stove in a tent at an elevation of almost ten thousand feet.

Our old friend Betty would never think of offering hot dogs to anyone, unless she had made hors d'oeuvres out of them by cutting them up, wrapping them in cheese, bacon and Bisquick and baking them in a Dutch oven. She wouldn't think of having Chinese food out of a can. Betty spends all day - while you are out hunting - making her own eggrolls and wanton so that Chinese night will be complete, right down to numbers one through ten off "Johnny Chen's" deluxe menu. She can't offer Mexican food in the form of a simple Taco. Mexican food to Betty means both beef and chicken Enchiladas, with Chile Rellenos and Tomales thrown in. And, would you think someone could make Thanksgiving dinner on a wood stove in a tent? Oh yeah, complete with roasted turkey, mashed potatoes, dressing, gravy, cranberry sauce - the works!

Of course not all Cowboy cooks are the same, but most reputable outfitters have one good enough to make the cook tent your favorite place in camp.

TIP – Cowboy Hunting: Cowboy hunting is Elk, Deer, Moose, Antelope, Mountain Sheep, Mountain Goats, Lions, an occasional Bear and possibly Buffalo. No self-respecting cowboy would shoot a Yak or a Seal. And a Zebra? Well that's just a horse with stripes. You might get yourself hanged for shooting one of those in the wrong place.

TIP - Hunting: If your cape gets too warm, the taxidermist will have a problem with hair falling out after it is tanned.

TIP - Hunting: Get an outfitter! Get a guide!!!

COSTS

It would be nice to be able to say; " A Cowboy hunt will cost you X." But, that is impossible. The **ACTUAL** cost of a hunting trip in Cowboy land varies as much as the colors of fish. And today, with the new trend of outfitters selling exclusive tags, it can bounce up to unreal levels.

At the time of this writing, a quality Elk hunt with horses, food and typically, a base camp and a high tent camp will run between $3500 and $5000. It might be a few bucks different depending on whether you go as a two-on-one guide, or as a one-on-one guide. (The latter being about 20% more). Add in the cost of the non-resident license and right out of the chute, your costs will range from $4000 to $6000.

But, the actual hunt is only the beginning of the equation. You have to get there first!

Basically, you can fly out or you can drive out.

If you drive, you will have to swallow today's high cost of gasoline. You'll need some lodging along the way, and probably a night or two on each end of the hunt. If you are doing this on your own, the costs pile up quickly. If you can car-pool out, obviously you'll save.

The problem with driving in general, is the time. If you own your own business, or are an employee for someone else, the time you are away from your job, can cost you more than the entire hunt. Every day is precious. Flying cuts that number down.

But, flying has its own expenses. Just the cost of the flight is one of them. The economic conditions being what they are, flights are not getting cheaper. Then there is the baggage problem. Most airlines are now enforcing number and weight restrictions they ignored in earlier times. Because they count a cased rifle as one bag, you automatically are over the limit with regards to checked baggage. (see the chapter on packing). If you try to cram all your gear into one big bag for flight purposes, you will be over the weight limit. Either way, you pay more.

Some outfitters will come to an airport and pick you up. If however, they are nowhere near an airport – frequently the case – you will have to rent a car. The problem is that you can't just rent it for the day you will need it (once on the front and once again after your hunt), you will have to rent it for the entire time you are gone and just leave it sit. Again, this can be costly.

There are other costs. Once you get an animal on the ground you will need to get it to a slaughter/ packaging house. Good outfitters will handle that problem for you and actually pack it out and drop it off at their favorite packing house. Others will charge a fee for that additional service. If you have to fly into your camp on a small plane (you will in some wilderness areas), the airline company will charge you an additional fee to get your game out of the wilds. This is a very good question to ask you outfitter before you book your hunt. If you don't have an outfitter to take care of this stuff, and are trying to shoestring a hunt together get ready for a big punch in the belly when you get the bill for this little service.

Then, you have to add in the cost of the processing and packaging of your meat. This is definitely not cheap. Figure $400 or $500 for the average Elk. If you want it caped, that will cost even more. Incidentally, most good outfitters include this service in their ordinary bill, just like they do transporting your game out of the field. You might want to toss in a little extra tip for the guy who actually takes care of this for you.

Once it is packaged, you have to get it home. If you drive, that means a ton or two of dry ice and a quick ride east. If you fly you have another problem altogether. Extra baggage and extra weight charges can add up fast - $80-$100 per box. Also, believe it or not, dry ice is considered a hazardous substance and you will have to pay an extra charge for it. You'll have at least three, frequently four, boxes of meat for an Elk plus a head charge if you want to bring the horns back.

The other option of having your meat shipped back home for you used to be viable. Now, with the increased costs of shipping, having a load of processed Elk shipped from Wyoming to Michigan can be more than the flight and end up driving the per pound cost of the meat to caviar levels. Elk is tasty for sure, but you will have to decide if it is that tasty. It will cost $400-$500 just to ship it!

Then, there's the taxidermy. Think positive, you are going to bring something home, which will demand mounting. If you drive, you can bring the horns and cape or the entire head home with you. The taxidermy bill will run between $500 and $750 for an Elk, but can be much higher in some cases.

If you fly, you will have two choices. You can pay another baggage fee (maybe two) and bring the cape and horns home on the plane. Or, you can find a Taxidermist near your hunt. The problem here, if you use a Taxidermist in Cowboy land, is once the head mount is complete, you have to ship it home. Get ready for this bill. You'll probably have to sell your Corvette for this one.

And, then there is the tip. Most guides do not make enough money as pay from their outfitter to make their efforts economically viable. They rely on the tip you give them to make ends meet. Tips run anywhere from 10-20 percent of the cost of the hunt. I've seen guides drop off cliffs and hike miles to fetch some animal a hunter shot. I've seen them caping out heads in the dark and the snow and the sleet and then carrying the meat out on their backs. I've seen guides carrying rifles and backpacks for fagged out hunters. These guys really do work their Turbans off and deserve whatever you decide to give them – usually much more.

The important thing to remember here is that the stated price of a particular hunt is one thing. The bottom line you will actually have to pay is another. Add up the numbers here. Cowboy hunting is not cheap and therefore it is not for everyone. I have seen hunters standing at counters in meat packing houses who have not included the cost of packaging their kill into their budgets, negotiating with the butcher, trying to get him to take a portion of the meat as payment – something butchers will not do. This is not a pretty sight. Plan ahead!

TIP - Airports: If you want to bring a rack back with you on a plane, each tip on the rack must be protected by a piece of rubber hose, taped on with duct tape so that it extends one inch beyond the point. Again, a reputable outfitter will take care of this for you. Or you'll be searching for a hardware store near the airport to buy tape and rubber hose before you leave.

TIP – Baggage: It is often a good idea to explore the costs of shipping your baggage straight to your outfitter using the good-old postal service before your trip. You might find you will save much more and reduce your hassle factor considerably, than schlepping all that stuff around an airport.

TIP - Taxidermists: Elk, Mule Deer, Moose, sheep don't grow just anywhere. It is very possible that your local taxidermist may have never even seen one in its natural habitat. Just because you have some guy in your backyard who has done a good job on a white-tail or two does not mean he can handle a nice Elk. Ask if he has ever done one before. Ask to see it or pictures of it. This is important stuff. You may never get a good Elk again and you really only have one good chance at mounting him correctly. You might be better off choosing a Taxidermist in the area where the animal was harvested - one who has seen lots of them and knows how they should look.

TIP - Special Hunts and Special Tags: A number of very lucky outfitters in Cowboy land have been able to work out a deal whereby they control the tags for a specific hunt area – landowner tags, district management tags etc.. You can buy that tag as well as the hunt all directly from the outfitter. Be prepared to give up a first-born child to do it. Some of these licenses can run as much as $10,000 in addition to the hunt and all the other stuff. Gulp! You can usually get a pretty good trophy this way, but if money is an object – think twice.

HOMEWORK

GETTING READY

Okay, you've decided to actually go. You've chosen a species to hunt and a location. You've applied for your tags or purchased them through an outfitter who has access by one means or another. You've made arrangements with your outfitter for the actual hunt and paid your deposit. You've decided on how you will get there and made transportation arrangements. You are ready to go.

Well… not quite. You still have several months to wait and some very serious work to do.

TRAINING

A SCENT ON THE WIND

Cans are clanking together. I am in a strange building. It is very dark. I can barely see the faded brick walls. It is cold. I have been in this building before, but I don't know where it is. Susan is speaking, but as usual, I can't make out any of the words. Children are everywhere. Their teeth are pointed and menacing. They are a little scary. I have the feeling that we should try to get out of here as fast as possible. The walls are getting darker. The light is almost gone. The children are laughing but not in a sweet childlike way. Cans are clanking somewhere.

Time passes. We are suspended in it, and then Susan is gone. The children are gone. The building fades to black. I am alone in the dark. I am cold. I have to pee. The clanking is getting louder.

They are wrangling the horses already. I press the button on my glow-in-the-dark Timex. A faint blue light fills the void. It is only 4:45 A.M. Jesus. I hope my tent mate Tom will do something he never does; make a fire in our wood stove. I have to pee. I can hear the horse's hooves clacking on the frozen ground as the camp wrangler brings them in from the night. Their bells clank as they run.

I venture a finger up through the opening of my sleeping bag and let in a blast of frigid air. Damn! I wish Tom would just once make a fire - or somebody would. I poke my head out a little. I can just make out a yellow light, probing in through the flaps of our tent. Through the canvas, I can see there is light in the cook tent. I know there are coffee grounds boiling unrestrained, turning clear mountain water into asphalt black soup.

I dive back into the bag into the darkness. Various body parts are calling in their morning reports and the news is not good. We're in for a day of pain – another day of pain. I have to pee.

The horses are in the corral. The clanking of their neck bells has all but died out. Tom still snores. I count, like my kids before they jump into our cold swimming pool: ready, one, two, three, oh no Daddy I can't, okay, ready, one, two, three. I sit up. A dagger of pain bores relentlessly into my lower back. I stand. I am in my underwear. My socks have worked their way down and hang a couple inches out past my toes. I can't bend over to fix them. I have to pee.

I brush back the tent flaps and step into the frozen Wyoming night – well, morning, but it looks like night to me. A billion stars have punched holes in the canopy of space. As usual, I am awestruck by the sky in the mountains. I step a few feet away from the tent, shivering. Light from the corral lantern skitters across tiny sheets of ice grown overnight in every footprint or depression in the ground. Frost clings like cake frosting to every rusty brown stem of grass still vertical after the short summer. I hope I am not peeing on my socks.

I step lightly back into the tent. The iron stove door sings a sour note as I open it. A small contingent of renegade coals from last night's fire glow against the cold, insufficient in number to warm anything. I toss in a few sticks of split wood from our pile, thinking the coals strong enough to ignite them. They are not. I toss in a handful of kerosene-soaked sawdust from a rusted coffee can. Still the fire does not ignite. My teeth are clacking together and my feet are beginning to ache from the cold ground. I search around for a match in the stale light from the cook tent. It takes several swipes on the side of the stove before one ignites. I toss it in and the kero-dust flames up immediately. My right ankle is killing me.

I hear Tom yawn as I jump back on my cot and bury myself in my sleeping bag.

"Good morning there buddy," he says.

I wonder what he means by that. I have known him for most of my adult life. I love him. But, I just can't work up that much cheer in the morning. His blood alcohol level is probably still high enough to ward off pain. He has done everything I have in the last couple of days.

"Man I slept like a rock last night," he says.

Okay, I hate him.

My teeth are still clattering. I know I have to get up. By now, everybody will be getting dressed and heading toward the cook tent for some of the savage black fluid. Tom's up. He lights the lantern. Good boy. The hot white light hisses and I can see it fall through the gaps in my fortress. I have got to get up. My shoulder hurts. I have a headache.

Experience has taught me. In cold camps, I place my clothes strategically for easy access in the morning. Smart boy. Ready, one, two three, I lunge back out of the warm sleeping bag. Fortunately, the stove has kicked in and the world inside the tent is more hospitable. Shirt on. Pants on. Boots, well they are going to have to wait. I can't bend over that long yet to tie the laces. I pull them on and shove the laces into the top. I'll get to them later. I grab my jacket liner and head to the cook tent.

"Good morning. " Betty the cook is another one of those perpetually sunny people. "Coffee's on the stove," she says.

It's about a four-gallon iron pot. I can hardly lift it. On a normal morning I can hardly crack an egg this early, but today, after yesterday's abuse, I can't even lift an egg. Hefting the pot makes me swear and grunt under my breath. I spill a lot of the black fluid just trying to fill my cup. I take a sip. The sensation is not unlike what I imagine bungee jumping to be.

Betty Jean is an amazing wilderness cook. We're having tomato, cheese and mushroom quiche today, with side orders of bacon and dollar pancakes. Last night was Chinese night - three different dishes with made-in-a-tent egg rolls. She cooks only with a long wood stove and Dutch ovens buried in the coals of a dying fire. She is particularly amazing when you consider that everything in this camp, including the stove has to be hauled sixteen miles over wicked mountains, on the backs of mules. She has no electricity, no running water and no help. Betty can ride and shoot better than most men. She is cuter than hell, and if it means anything an excellent dancer.

The cook tent is a roomy 20x20 canvas affair with a wooden plank floor, which has held up quite well to many years of ten-foot high winter snow. It is a little smoky, but the real problem is the table. It is a plank picnic table with fixed side benches. You can't slide in or sit down and then scootch up. You have to lift a leg, drop it in, balance, lift the other leg, drop it in, and then finally sit. I can barely lift my leg high enough to get it over the bench. Balancing causes me to grunt audibly. I almost put my hand in the butter trying to get my other leg in. I crash down almost sitting on the guy next to me. Nobody says anything, but I know everyone noticed. The guides just smile.

I over-eat at breakfast. What's new?

My guide Harry stands, drops his dishes in the big tub, and then sits down next to me. He's got his "let's talk" face on.

"I had a vision last night," he says lifting his eyebrows as if to entice.

"Yeah," I say. "That's never good. What did you see?"

"I seen you and me climbing up Loomnum."

"Oh Jees." I say.

"You up for it," he asks.

"What'd you see up there in your vision?"

"A big one. A big old toad."

He's talking about Aluminum creek. All these guys pronounce it Loomnum. I have been there before a few times. It isn't fun. From camp, you ride about five miles – the last bit almost straight up. It damn near kills the horses. The problem is that when you get to where the horses can no longer make it, you hike, or rather climb for at least two more miles. Harry loves it.

Harry left his Michigan home fifteen years ago, when he was just a teenager. He wound up in Wyoming, where he found a job as a carpenter. He learned the ins and outs of the horse world the hard way - from a bunch of old cowboys. He is tall, skinny and looks like any cowboy out of any magazine or movie ever made. He has one of those Adams apples that sticks out and looks like it would love to bounce up and down to a good Yodel. He loves to walk. Actually, he prefers to walk. And, he has a great sense of humor.

I can't tell you how many miles I have ridden behind Harry's horse, while he has walked ahead of it. One time several years earlier, Harry led a string of us hunters on a long ride to a secret honey hole. He walked just about all of the way up there, and all of the way back. As we neared camp, one of the rookies, who had only known Harry for a day, said; "Hey Harry. You walk so much out here, why do you even bother bringing a horse?"

Without missing a beat, Harry said, "Oh, I could never walk all these miles and carry that saddle. I need that horse."

"So what do you think," he says to me again through a haze of blue cigarette smoke.

I cough and take another bite of my coffee. It seems like everyone at the table has paused to hear my answer. They are all looking at me as though I am about to make a decision that will release nuclear weapons on Russia. "Sure," I say. What else can I say? I am, after all, a Cowboy too.

"Good, " Harry says. "I'll be down at the corral. We ought to leave now, cuz it's a long ride."

"Yeah, even a longer walk," I mumble under my breath.

My horse is as happy to see me coming as I am to see his sorry ass. I have all my gear, and I think someone must have mentioned Loomnum in his ear. "You run one time today, you son-of-a-bitch, and I'll hit you with a monkey wrench," I say as I start stuffing my rifle into a scabbard on his right side and fill the saddle bags.

"It'd be just like you to bring a monkey wrench," he says. "Why don't you leave that junk here today? Bad enough I gotta carry you."

He and I argue like this every morning. After I get him loaded up, I check the cinch , grab the reigns and pull him out to the trail where I can get on a little easier. With considerable effort, I step up into the stirrup, swing my leg over his back and drop into the saddle. Yes, right back where we were last night – same horse, same saddle, same pain.

The saddle is cold and a little wet from the morning frost. Instantly it resumes its mission of rearranging the anatomy of my ass to fit it. The pain swarms. My back is really killing me. The horse and I grunt and groan in perfect harmony. My right knee is on fire already. My ankle on that side is sore too. I'll need to lengthen my right stirrup the next time I get down. Not now. I just want to sit here for a minute and savor the agony.

I lean forward and remind the horse. "No running."

"Everybody ready," Harry asks.

He is leading us out. I fall in behind him. The other guides and their charges fall in behind me. We'll all ride together and then split up when we reach our trails. Tom is with Kelly. The poor sap. They're headed to Half Moon. It's every bit as difficult as Loomnum and, it has a little twist. There's a shortcut off the top of Half Moon, which drops you into the valley only a mile or two above the camp. You can't go up that way, but you can come down. Unfortunately, it is so steep that it'll just about scrape the bottom off your boots. It's a knee breaker, for sure. Tom has never been up there before. It will be interesting to see just how chipper he is tomorrow morning.

We ride in semi-light. The sun is just beginning to climb the eastern wall. Huge clouds of steam rise from the nostrils of the horses. Small puffs of steam rise from nostrils of the riders, as we work our way through the heavy scent of early morning pine.

We ride in relative silence, each man lost in his particular dominant thought of the day. Occasionally a horse hoof clatters in the loose rocks along the trail. A cough echoes out against the canyon walls from time to time. We are not yet in full hunt mode, but we're getting there.

I am personally coming alive. My ass has numbed against the saddle. My back hurts, but no more than usual. My knee and ankle are of particular notice this morning. The cutoff to Loomnum is just ahead. We will be stopping to let some of that nasty black liquid escape. I'll fix my stirrup then.

Harry and I splinter off from the main group and begin the agonizing climb up Loomnum. We pee clear, which means the black of the coffee stays in us. Hmmm?

When you ride uphill, the idea is to lean as far forward as necessary to keep your weight from dropping back on the kidneys of the horse, and to keep your own back vertical relative to space – simple enough in theory, but as the angle of the ascent increases, gravity forces your body down, and, because your feet are still engaged in the stirrups, to maintain stability, you must bend your body jackknife-like. In physical fitness circles this is called a crunch or for us old-timers, a sit up. Worse, while this is going on, a steep climb will cause the horse to buck his way up, rather than simply step up the trail. Bucking on flat ground is difficult to counter. On an almost vertical grade, it is impossible.

We stop frequently to let the horses rest, but still it is not enough. When their giant chests stop heaving and when they start looking around for something to eat, it is time to prod them on, but each time it gets harder to get them going. Mine labors to take each step with his front legs, and then bucks his back legs to follow. I am sliding off his back. I have to hold on to the saddle horn – a move considered poor form in Cowboy circles – just to stay on. Finally, we can drive them no further and have to dismount.

This is where agony ends and something worse begins. We are somewhere above the ten-thousand foot mark. There is no air up here. I hold the reigns in my hand and start one-foot-after-the-othering, leading the horse up through the rocks.

I took a mountaineering class one time. They taught me to take a step and then totally stiffen the knee of that leg. This places your weight on the bones, not the muscles and gives them a rest. It lets the other leg muscles rest for an instant, as well. Nice theory. It doesn't work very well. Both legs are tired. They taught me to forcefully blow all of the air out of my lungs each time I exhale – "power breathing" they call it. The idea here is that by totally expiring all the way, the lungs can fill with a larger volumes of fresh air. I wonder how they tested that? Not dragging a lazy horse up a rocky mountain trail, I'll bet.

We have been at it for fifteen minutes. I power breath and stiffen my knees with each step, yet I am exhausted. Exhausted is not a strong enough word, but three-quarters dead doesn't really cut it either. Harry is getting farther ahead each minute. He is fooling around with something in his shirt pocket. If he lights a cigarette, I think I will shoot him.

It's not like I didn't know this was coming. I've known it for months. If you plan on taking a hunting trip in Wyoming in October, you have to start filling out applications and arranging things in February. If you are smart, you start working out as soon as you send in your first check. I have worked out for seven months. I've walked and climbed stairs and ridden bikes and moved furniture and built stuff and cleaned garages and cleaned basements and walked up barren, snowless ski slopes. I am not sedentary. I've lost weight and I don't smoke. What more can I do?

"This is a young man's sport," the horse says.

"So now you are a mind reader too," I say. "Young men can't afford to do this."

"You talking to me," Harry says, shout-whispering.

"No," I whisper back. We are starting to get into full hunting mode and silence is critical.

He stops and waits for me to catch up. "How you doin'," he asks.

"Doin'," I say.

"We only got maybe a mile or two left."

"I know."

"We ought to be able to do a mile in say twenty minutes if we go slow. So forty minutes or so."

"Unfortunately not all miles are created equal, Harry. Put me down for two hours."

Harry laughs. He thinks I am kidding.

It troubles me to have so many physical complaints. In my youth, when Testosterone flowed like spring snowmelt, I was impervious to all weather and even fairly significant injuries were usually nothing more than a momentary annoyance. Now, Testosterone comes via skin patch, I'm actually looking forward to global warming, and the smallest discomfort fairly well cripples me for days. The scent of my mortality is on the wind.

We've left the main trail, and are slowly making our way up a side hill, which leads to a high ridge where we can watch a big valley below. It is nice not to have to walk in all those rocks. However, the soft dirt of the hillside is not much better. One leg is at least a foot or so above the other making stiff kneeing impossible and even regular walking difficult. I hold my left arm against the dirt – an outrigger of sorts – for balance. Some kind of dirt-digging rodent has made a mess of this slope. It's riddled with ankle-busting holes and caverns. Every other step lands in some kind of trench, and whatever energy I save by stiff kneeing, is used up trying to pull my leg out of the dirt. I am literally gasping for air. Harry is far ahead of me again. He will reach the ridge long before I do.

They have a calculation for determining your maximum heart rate. It's a permutation of your age and some other magic number. The point is; the heart apparently has a maximum rate. What happens after it reaches that rate and you still need more beats? I am worried that I have reached that point. I can feel the horse's head against my back. He's actually trying to shove me along. Traitor.

Harry and his horse are just spots up ahead. I have reached my limit. I can't take another step and drop down on both knees. The horse does not like standing on such uneven ground and jumps around trying to find a good place to rest as well. I have to let my heart rate get back down to normal or the thing is just going to explode. I can see Harry looking at me with his binoculars. I raise a thumb indicating that I am all right even though I am not.

I have been tired before. I have been to my limit in sports before - when I was younger. I have never felt like this. I can go nowhere, and this is an impossible place to stay. The scent of my mortality is much stronger now. My life does not flash before my eyes, but I am consciously thinking about it. I am trying to remember back to times when I thought about my death - to how I tried, back then, to imagine how it would be. Where I would be? What would be wrong with me? Would there be a bunch of people standing around my bed waiting for a gruesome death rattle or something? Would it come quick, like from a gunshot or a car wreck? Would I keel over in a crowded restaurant? I never imagined I would simply surpass my maximum heart rate on a mountainside in Wyoming. I am blacking out and ... .

Well, it's been several minutes and I am not dead yet – a good sign. The goddamn horse is starting to feed again, standing on one leg here in Gopher land. He looks like he has one leg stuffed down a hole for balance. Doesn't he realize the severity of the situation here? I was over my maximum rate, and I still can't breathe. I got off him so he wouldn't have to suffer this and he's having lunch again. There's no gratitude among horses.

Ready, one, two, three, I say in preparation to stand. It doesn't work - oh Daddy I can't. I repeat the mantra. Ready, one, two, three and I'm up, standing on one foot mostly here on the steep slope. The horse gives me a nudge with his nose.

"Knock it off asshole."

One foot in front of the other. Each step harder than the last. I like to count when I walk. I'm one hundred steps farther up from where I sat down. Soon, it is two hundred, then three. And, finally, I am standing next to Harry at the top of the Loomnum.

I love it up here. And, I don't smell anything on the wind.

TIP – Walking: At some point on any Cowboy hunting trip, you will be walking, and believe me, it will not be the proverbial walk in the park. It does not matter how young you are or what kind of physical condition you are in, you need to start preparing for this inevitability months in advance. This point cannot be emphasized enough. I have seen hunting trips virtually ruined because the hunter could not physically get to the game. I have seen men sitting in camp, too tired and too sore to even go out. I've seen the look on their faces when they have to sit while their buddies take off. I have seen men sick from over-exhaustion. I have been there myself. The mountains are relentless. They are like nothing else on earth and treat the human body with little, if any, respect.

TIP – Training: Cardiovascular training is very important. Your heart and lungs will suffer ten times more in the mountains than they will on flat ground. Run if you can. If not, try a bicycle, but remember, be sure to include some uphill walking in your regimen. The muscles used to walk up and down hills are not necessarily the same ones used on flat land (or at least they won't feel like it), and they are not the same ones you use when riding a bike.

TIP – Training: Wear a backpack when you train. It is likely you will be wearing one when you hunt.

TIP – Training: Uphill hikes in the mountains are all about heart and lungs. Downhills are actually more abusive and account for more injuries. Downhills ruin knees, ankles, backs and feet. It is equally important (probably more important) to include downhill workouts in your routine.

TIP - Training: Train in the boots you intend to hunt in. There is nothing harder than trying to survive mountain hikes in shoes you are not used to. Get them just a little loose fitting in the toe area. You won't notice boot trouble much on uphills, but downhills tend to cause the foot to jam into the boot and if there is no room for the toes, they will get pretty mangled in even a short distance. Give them some room to slide.

TIP - Training: Cut your toenails. They **will** get sore if they are too long.

TIP – Training: Don't neglect the rest of your muscles and joints. Lift weights. Cowboy hunting is not just about walking. It's about lifting saddles and game and rocks and gear and more stuff than you can imagine.

TIP - Training: Other than choosing a good outfitter, your personal physical conditioning is the single most important limiting factor with regards to your success as a Cowboy Hunter. Poorly conditioned people simply can't handle this sport.

TIP - Training: Altitude will kick your butt! It does not matter how much you train and what kind of shape you are in, you simply cannot counter-act the effects of altitude. You will be on your knees gasping at some point no matter.

The rule is that it takes one day of acclimatization for every one thousand feet of altitude one advances. Personal experience says that you will feel totally useless for at least four to five days and then you will begin to recover - just in time to go home.

Altitude affects different people in different ways, and can affect the same person differently every time they are in it. Most times, it just makes any task, even packing a duffle bag or walking to a cook tent a major chore. Other times it will make you flat out sick.

Headaches are common. Not just little nuisance headaches, but real headbangers that make everything miserable. Drinking a lot of water usually helps here, but not always.

Triple and quadruple breathing is also common as your body tries to compensate for oxygen debt. Plain old panting is required for most tasks above nine thousand feet.

The only way to train for altitude is to spend time in it - period. We've even tried drugs, all of which have failed. You just have to be there for your hemoglobin to catch up to your activity level.

If at all possible try to add a few days onto the front end of your hunt trip that you could spend in the higher altitudes. Get there early. Take hikes up into the high country. Try to do your panting and wheezing before your hunt so that when you do finally spot a nice trophy, you have the horsepower to get on it.

TIP - Timing: We talked a little about timing in terms of filling out applications for permits and licenses and timing with regards to finding outfitter, but timing should be viewed from another perspective.

We only get one life to live. Don't wait too long to do this stuff. Continually saying: "Someday I'm gonna," will catch up to you. Someday is probably today. Cowboy hunting has not gotten any easier over the years that I have been doing it. In fact, it is harder each year. A point comes, when old ankles and old knees gang up and stop old men.

PACKING

BAD WEATHER

Elk Tooth, The Gunslinger, Bobby and I road along a steep trail near the top of a wide open bowl, under a perfect blue Wyoming sky. We couldn't see the entire sky because of the rim of rock above our heads, but the shaft of open air above us was sweet – or so we thought. We were fairly well above the tree line at that level, and pretty much out in the open. The remains of summer's green grasses blanketed the ground, and what had been, at their prime, large yellow flowers stuck up like brown spear-shafts everywhere in the meadow.

We were about to begin a series of dire switch-backs, which would lift us up out of the bowl and deposit us on top of the ridge, where we figured we would do some glassing.

"Let's hold up here for a minute," Shotgun said. "I gotta' pee."

Of course just the mention of bladder relief primed the horses, and in a heartbeat all four cowboys and all four horses were contributing to a small, yellow, river, which would eventually work its way down the mountain to the sea.

"Nice day," someone said, just as the only cloud of the morning poked its ragged head over the edge of the rim.

Before we could remount, the cloud had plugged the clear sky-tunnel above us, choked off the blue, and turned ugly. Thunder cracked and within seconds, rain fell like nickels in a hot Las Vegas slot machine. Zig-Zags of lightning screeched across the sky. Then came the hail – small pea-sized at first, gradually increasing in size. We started looking around for some cover. The nearest trees were two hundred yards back down the trail. The horses nodded their heads – let's go. The hail grew to walnut size and stung like bees when it hit. We were soaked to the skin. The horses turned themselves around on the trail and fought against their reins. Thunder shook the ground. The wind roared. Hail ball walnuts thudded on hats, shoulders, saddles, heads and rocks. The horses cried – those sissies. And the four cowboys? They ran for it, right? Never. They stood there, too dumbfounded (make that just; too dumb) to even move.

And then, as rapidly as it had appeared, the nasty little cloud packed up and moved to parts unknown. The blue filled our little patch of sky again. The horses began their ceaseless munching as if nothing had happened. The birds chirped. And the four cowboys stood there dripping.

"Ain't life in the mountains grand," the Bobby said.

REALLY BAD WEATHER

Sometimes, the instant you wake, you just know it's going to be a bad day. Maybe it has something to do with the barometric pressure, or maybe it's the nagging from an old football injury. Maybe it's just one of those primitive instinctual things, that has no explanation. Of course when you go to bed in the rain, and you listen as it splashes against the roof of your tent all night, you can usually kind of figure it out. It's going to be a bad day.

At about six in the morning, we flipped the tent flaps open and looked down the valley. The camp was pitched around the nine-thousand-foot mark. The bottom of the giant cloud we had been under for the last three days was at about ninety one hundred feet. It was like lifting the bed sheets and looking down at your feet. We couldn't see the mountain peaks, which presumably stuck up through the cloud cover. We couldn't see very far down the trails. We could see our breath, though, and it was damn cold. Damn cold and damn wet.

"Great day for hunting, hey boys."

Every camp has a guy who tries to make the best of things. I hate those guys. It was a terrible day and bound to get worse. The rest of us were miserable and happy to just wallow in it.

We lingered for a long time around the breakfast table, sipping at extra cups of coffee, making lame jokes and re-telling boring stories. It was obvious that nobody was in too much of a hurry to head out into the suffering. But we did. We saddled up our horses and rode slowly out of the camp in search of some suicidal elk herd who just hated life so much that they were willing to dive out of the cloud cover and run out on the trail in front of us. Each man among us knew that that would be the only way we were going to get anything on a day like that.

The trail turned to my mother's oatmeal - slippery, clumpy, and virtually unpalatable. It clung to the bottom of the horse's hooves like Gummy Bears in a Cub Scout's teeth. With every step, their legs slipped to the side, making them groan. On uphills, they had to scramble to keep making forward progress. The downhills were roller coasters.

The heavy cloud ceiling a few feet above our heads dipped down to trail level from time to time, forming a white wall ahead. Each rider in turn disappeared into the wall leaving the rider behind staring into nothing. The wall slapped each man's face, with an icy cold, wet, glove, then dove down the back of his shirt collar and massaged his spine until he shivered in the saddle.

We rode like that for over an hour, seeing no game, seldom seeing the trail we were on, and never seeing the side walls of the canyon we were ascending through. Conditions were worse at the top. Rain fell in buckets, each drop hovering somewhere between wet and solid, like soggy miniature snowballs. We were wet cold and miserable. My horse kept looking back at me with this "You sure this is how you want to spend your vacation," look on his face.

We needed shelter from this torment, but there was none to be found. Finally, we rode into a small clump of thick trees, tied the horses, and huddled as close as we could get to the trunks hoping the branches would at least deflect the rain a few feet away, rather than straight down our necks. At our feet, we built tiny fires with whatever pieces of dry material we could find hiding in nooks out of the wet. We sat for another three hours like that, half asleep, each man taking turns to scrounge a few small sticks to keep the fire smoldering, then ate our lunches.

We spent the afternoon the same way, and road back to camp when our watches told us it was probably getting too dark to hunt. We followed the same pattern the next day, and the next, and the next. In fact, we spent an entire week, wet cold and virtually blind when it came to finding game. I heard the week after we left was beautiful.

HORRIBLE WEATHER

We met up in Bondurant on the eastern side of the Wyoming range. The day was overcast, but dry. We'd heard rumors of snow in the mountains. We trucked the horses back a few miles into the hills and then saddled up. Three hours later, we were riding in a blizzard. The snow fell sideways, driven by a fierce wind. When we reached the camp a three-inch blanket of snow covered everything. It took an hour or so to stow our gear and get things set. By lunch, the snow was four inches deep and the wind was a witch on a broom, screaming through ratty teeth.

Given the poor conditions, we decided not to hunt that afternoon or even scout, which would have been our normal routine. Instead, we sat in the cook tent swapping lies or sleeping in our tents. Dinner came and went. We were out of tales. We were not tired. We were plenty bored and, the way it had worked out, strangers.

For whatever reason, each of us had booked the hunt late, and were singles because our usual hunting partners had for whatever reason had not booked that year. In my case, I had never hunted with this particular outfitter. The hunt was put together at the last minute and so far, it had not started well. Night clamped tightly around the canyon choking off the dim light. It did not dampen the storm in the least. By the time we retired to our sleeping tent, the snow had reached the eight-inch level.

I do not recall sleeping that night. I was not particularly tired. Being strangers, we had used up just about all the pleasant conversation we had. And, the wind was trying to blow the camp back to Nebraska. It literally tore at the tent walls, and poured in wherever it could find a weakness. We had a camp stove but because of the brutal wind, we were having a difficult time keeping it fired up. We fairly well froze most of the night.

By morning, the wind had let up, but the snow had not. I open the tent flap to almost two feet of snow. It hung heavily on the branches of the trees, weighing them down until they were just white cones sticking up along the valley walls. The horses turned their heads in their corral and looked at me. "We want to go home," they said in perfect ten-part harmony.

"You boys have a good sleep," the outfitter asked as we sloshed our way into the cook tent for coffee.

"Perfect," I said, forcing a smile.

"I don't reckon we'll be doing much hunting, if this keeps up," he said.

"If this keeps up," I said. "I'm worried that we won't even get back down."

"Well, I don't think that'll be a problem," he said.

"You don't think?"

"Naw."

"You've been up here in this much snow before, right?"

"Nope, ain't never had this much snow this early. "

"How long have you been hunting up here?"

"Thirty years."

"Wait," I said a little more than concerned. "You have been hunting up here for thirty years and you've not had this much snow before?"

"Not that I can recall."

"And you are not worried about getting out of here?"

"Well, a little, I guess, now that you mention it. But we only been here one day, and things change quick in the mountains."

"Yeah, they get worse quick."

The outfitter chuckled, as if I had just made a joke. I was not kidding. I was getting about as nervous as a cat pissing razor blades. "Have we got a radio," I asked.

"Yeah, I got that little transistor one, there," he said pointing to a small box on the table. I've had it since 1967. Still works."

"No, I mean an emergency radio that we can use to call for help, get a helicopter or something."

"Nope, ain't got one of them. Never needed it."

"Well, of course. You never need one until you have the emergency, but if you don't already have it, the emergency comes and goes, and you wake up dead. You get an emergency radio before the emergency, so you'll have it . . .."

The cook cut me off just when I was getting going. " We got some good pancakes here, how do you like your eggs?"

"Served at a fancy hotel, back in civilization, sitting in a warm restaurant," I said.

The outfitter chuckled again. "You are a funny guy, but don't worry, I seen horses one time, walking around just fine in snow up to their bellies."

"Were any of them walking down a steep mountain trail carrying a fat hunter?"

"Ha, ha, ha, chuckle, chuckle, chuckle."

I had only known this guy for a day, and already he was getting on my nerves. Maybe it was all the time I was spending with my tent mates – A dentist from California ("Dude, this is bitchin' powder snow, we should have brought our skis."), An engineer, from Cleveland (Continual problems with countless small items, each individually categorized in small plastic bags.), and a Pharmacist from Peoria (slept for at least fifteen straight hours, took some kind of dietary supplement with each meal).

"The snow is almost to their bellies."

"Yeah, won't be long," the outfitter said. "Reckon there's nothing we can do until it quits. Then we will come up with a plan."

It quit about noon the next day. I was just about insane from sitting in that tent. The sun looked marvelous when it finally popped through the clouds and shown brightly on the slopes. The snow was three feet deep in most spots, and drifted much higher in others. The horses had managed to stomp it down around themselves and stood munching hay in the corral. They always tended to whine about nothing.

Tiny streamlets of melting snow began to form almost as soon as the sun came out. We waited until the next morning before we ventured out. By then, the snow had already melted and packed itself down by at least fifty percent. The sky was blue, and cloudless. We went hunting.

TIP - Weather. If you have to get off your horse in the rain, or if it looks like it is going to rain, flip your stirrups into the saddle on both sides. That'll help deflect some of the water and make things just a little less squishy when you climb back in.

TIP - Weather. Mountain weather can be more erratic than a golfer's Tee shot. It can literally change in a minute and the changes can be dramatic. Do not trust it! Never leave your camp with out a jacket, some kind of rain gear and a means of starting a fire – even if the weather looks good.

TIP - Weather. Weather presents a huge packing dilemma. The goal is to pack light, but because of the potential for poor weather, you need to bring just about everything you own. Try to kill as many birds with a single stone as possible.

DOING IT RIGHT

If you want to watch a guide's face change from friendly to nasty in a heartbeat, all you have to do is over pack.

We used to let this guy we called the Gunslinger hunt with us in Wyoming. We don't anymore. One reason he doesn't get the invite anymore is because of the unreasonable amount of stuff he always brought along.

Generally speaking, a packhorse or a mule can carry about 150 pounds of gear. They can carry heavier humans, but because of the weight distribution of a pack saddle, overloading the pack animal will mean lots of problems along the trail and possibly the "soring up" of this valuable resource. Soring your horse is a big no, no in cowboy land.

Guides and outfitters figure about one pack mule for every one and a half hunters or two mules for every three cowboys. Do the math. You can take a maximum of about one hundred pounds of gear on a cowboy hunting trip without raising too many hackles.

The Gunslinger invariably showed up with two mules worth of goods sometimes three. He always brought a sleeping bag (packed separately) that was about the size of a Ritz Carlton king-sized bed - except it was heavier. He would bring two (sometimes three) rifles each packed in a separate case. He brought two or three massive parkas and an extra-heavy pair of bib overalls suitable for a month in Antarctica. And, he would add to that load at least two or three giant duffle bags of miscellaneous inventory. The wheels on the little carts the porters at the airport use to lug stuff around would squeak and moan and almost grind themselves away on the concrete as they tried to lug his load away from the baggage carousel.

In the corral on the first morning of the hunt, The Gunslinger's pile of gear always looked like a small mountain sticking up above all the other tidy piles of stuff that needed to be hauled up to the hunting camp by the packhorses and mules. You could almost see the cloud of curse words streaming up from the guides like campfire smoke as they tried to figure out how to get all that stuff into the pack string. There's nothing worse than pissing your guides off before the trip even gets underway.

  A pack saddle is a cross-bucked affair of wood or aluminum that fits on the back of a horse. It does not resemble a conventional saddle. Two bags or boxes, called Panniers, are hefted up on each side of the horse and their big canvas or leather straps are hooked over the tips of the crosses so that they hang down on each side of the animal without actually touching him if possible. Each Pannier will hold a medium sized duffle bag. The two Panniers need to be balanced in weight as closely as possible so that the load will not shift as you plod up the trail. Figure each duffle bag to be around forty pounds. Most packers actually have a scale they use to balance duffle bags. It is that important.

  Once the panniers are on the horse, you can load additional gear directly on the back of the horse or mule. This is done by wrapping individual duffle bags in a large piece of canvas called a Manny. Once the Manny is balanced on the back of the horse, it is lashed in place with a heavy rope and by using a series of complicated knots, usually referred to as a square. Don't bother trying to learn how to tie a square. Every packer and every horseman seems to have his own brand on just how this knot is to be tied. Sometimes, they actually get into fights about how it is to be done and most of the time, they don't do it the same way twice.

  Packing a string of mules for a long trip into the wilderness is an art. Packers actually have contests in which two-man teams bring a string of mules into an arena where they are charged with packing up a pile of unrelated gear – including kitchen sinks and bicycles – and hauling it to the other end of the arena. The team that gets their pile loaded up, hauled down to the other end and unloaded first wins. Really, these guys do this and they are dead serious about it!

So, figure on three duffle bags of gear – two forty pound medium sized duffle bags and a third one which ought not to be much more than twenty or so pounds. Obviously, you can cheat a little, but keeping the load to around 100 pounds is a very good guideline – especially if you intend to fly.

The rule at the airport is "two checked bags and one carry-on." In the olden days (pre-911 and pre-economic meltdown in the airline industry) this rule was only loosely adhered to. Not so today. If you check your rifle, that is one checked bag. You only have one more. In the semi-olden days (after 911 but before the economic mess) you could trick them. You could take your two forty pound duffle bags and stick them into one large duffle bag – a hockey gear bag say. Then you were still only checking two bags. These days, they weigh everything and charge for extra weight (anything over fifty pounds) and for extra numbers of bags. And, these extra charges can be very high!

Check your rifle and two forty-pound duffles and you'll pay an extra bag charge. Check your gun and one eighty pound hockey bag and you'll pay for the extra weight. They get us one way or another.

TIP – Packing: If you fly, call the airline in advance. Find out what the extra baggage fees are and what the extra weight fees are. Pack accordingly.

TIP – Packing: The hockey bag with the two duffles is still a good idea. Yeah, it is an eighty pound bag, but these things come with really nice handles and little roller wheels on the end. You can snatch it off the carousel and string your carry-on over the handle, carry your rifle in the other hand and roll the whole mess out without a porter or one of those little rent-a-dollies. When you get to your base camp, you can yank out the two duffles for easy Pannier packing and leave the hockey bag stashed at the base camp (or ranch) until you return. When you do return, if you've decided to bring back more than you took (like some Elk meat or a frozen cape or a set of horns or one of the camp girls) you can check the two duffles and use the hockey bag as a carrier for the extra stuff. You still have to pay but you don't have to think. Everything has it's value.

TIP – Packing: Try to stick to the one hundred pound rule. You'll pay less, save on valuable horsepower and impress your guides.

WHAT TO BRING

You are not going to be able to change your clothes every day on a Cowboy hunting trip. If that is an absolute necessity for you then maybe this is not your sport. That said, please consider changing your underwear and your socks everyday. It is considered bad form to out-stink your horse.

The best way to plan is to start from the bottom up and the inside out.

As mentioned, it would be a good idea to change your socks every day or at least every other day. You will be wearing a pair when you fly or drive out. You will need another pair on the day you fly back. So, you will need to add a pair of socks to the total number of days you are hunting. If your hunt is say seven days, you will need eight pairs of socks.

You may not need to take all eight with you to the actual place where you will be hunting. If you are spending your first night at a ranch or a lodge, you can probably leave all the clothes you flew out in, as well as the clothes you intend to fly back in at the lodge while you are hunting. This will reduce the load you will have in your duffle bags. So figure seven pairs of socks and seven pairs of under pants.

Most cowboys do cheat on this number. In fact, most of us cut it in half – despite what was said about out-stinking your horse. You really do need to keep the weight of your duffle down.

You will need at least two pairs of long underwear. Polypropylene is still the best bet, although in recent years a number of alternatives have been developed. Remember. If you are going to be riding all day and into the night, you should be wearing long underwear. Having the polypropylene sliding against your wool or denim outer pants is far better than having your skin sliding against it. Experience has taught that you should wear a pair of long Johns even if the weather does not dictate it.

You will need seven (three-and-a-half) T-shirts.

Weather will dictate the remainder of your wardrobe. This is where planning and packing gets very tricky. Check the weather reports for the area you intend to hunt constantly and remember, if you are going to be in the mountains, the weather can change in a heartbeat.

Having at least one long-sleeved undershirt to put on over your regular undershirt is a very good idea. Even if the weather is mild, if you are in the mountains, it will be very cold in the early morning. There will probably be ice on the water bucket every morning. Most Cowboys dress fairly heavily in the early part of the day and slowly shed layers as the day progresses. The long-sleeved T-shirt is a nice, easily shed layer. If you have drawn an early Elk muzzle loader tag in Colorado, you probably won't need it. You'll be plenty warm enough. If you have a late season tag anywhere, you will be very glad you have it.

You'll need two pairs of outer pants – although unless you get wet, you'll probably only wear one. Most cowboys choose either wool or denim. Both are good. You can also get a pair of heavy cotton ones at most hunting supply outlets. These also work well. Remember to get them just a little big. If they are too tight – especially over long underwear - getting on and off your horse will be more difficult.

You'll need two shirts, but again, only if one gets wet. Wool, cotton or flannel all work well. Make sure the shirts have pockets. It's guaranteed that you will find something to put in them.

One hooded sweatshirt is a very good item to have along. You can use it for an extra layer on a cold day, but more importantly, they are very nice to sleep in. The hood comes in very handy on a cold night – especially if you are getting a little sparse in the hair department.

A vest is a good idea. You don't really need a bulky down-filled one. A simple, thin fleece one will work very well and will make a good extra layer in cold weather.

You'll need a hunting jacket. The best are the combos with a removable down liner. You can just use the outer part on a mild day or you can wear the liner if it is a little colder. You can wear them both on a really cold day and it still won't be enough.

Some Cowboys like fleece some like pressed cotton or Gortex. They all have advantages and disadvantages. Fleece tends to pick up burs and other flotsam from the surrounding flora. This is not a big problem in the mountains. Pressed cotton and Gortex have the reputation of being noisy. They are only noisy to the Cowboy wearing them when hunting at a very close range. The game doesn't hear them all that much especially at the ranges where most Cowboys find themselves hunting.

There are two essential features a hunting coat should have.

1) Pockets. The more the better. Again, you will find something to put in them.

2) It must be waterproof! That said, none of them really are. Even Gortex can spring leaks in very wet weather.

You might find a pair of bib overalls will be helpful. Check the weather report. If it looks like you'll be in for a very wet or snowy time take a pair along. If you wear them over a pair of regular pants and a pair of long Johns getting on and off a horse will be very difficult. The good news: If it is cold enough, snowing, raining or sleeting enough that you need overalls, you will have enough general misery that difficulties mounting and dismounting will just blend into the mess.

Good hats are essential. Notice the plural hats. No cowboy in his right mind would tell you not to wear a Cowboy hat. In years past, they were the only option. Today, we have plenty of others.

Basically you will need two of them – a light-weight one and a heavy one. Again, the prevailing weather will dictate which you use. A good combination plan is to wear a baseball hat and carry a good tight-knit stocking hat in one of the pockets of your hunting jacket. That way you can switch back and forth as the climate conditions dictate. Start out with the stocking hat in the cold morning. Switch to the baseball hat as the day warms. Then, switch back to the stocking hat as the night comes on.

The lined baseball style hats with the flop-down tie-up ears also work well. Get a good one of those and you might find that just the one hat will serve all your needs. Most of the hunting jacket combos come with a hood. You might find that helpful if the weather will be very cold.

Some kind of a Dickie or scarf is essential in cold weather. Sealing off your neck will help keep you warm. You can fold a Dickie into one of your hunting coat pockets and barely know it is there.

Cowboys of old didn't have these, but the ultra thin head socks that snow-mobilers wear under their helmets or some skiers wear under their regular hat can be very nice to have in cold weather. Again, their size and weight allows them to be easily packed into a pocket of your hunting jacket.

Two pairs of gloves are good to have – a light-weight pair and a heavy pair. The light weight pair can be just a pair of ordinary, brown, cotton work gloves. They are more than sufficient to fight off most of the bad weather you'll be riding through and protect your hands from trail abuse even in good weather. The heavy ones will be essential if the weather turns bad. Mittens are okay, but a little less accommodating when it comes to horse stuff – reigns, bits, bridles, cinches and what-have-you.

You'll need rain gear – rain pants at least.

You have a couple of options here. If you trust your outer hunting jacket to be waterproof enough to protect you from what could be many hours (seven, in October of 2007 – just a few strokes from the southern border of Yellowstone National Park) in the saddle during a sleet storm, then you can probably just bring along a good pair of waterproof pants that you can put on over your regular pants. Legs, hanging down over the flanks of a horse, exposed to the elements, brushing against wet foliage along the trail can get soaked through in a heartbeat. Waterproof pants are critically important.

A good addition to the pants is a military-style hooded poncho. A poncho can be rolled up pretty tight and stashed just about anywhere. In the saddle they can be worn and spread out over the saddle and some of the gear you may have tied on.

They can also serve in a number of other functions. If it becomes necessary to dismount and build a fire to get warm, the poncho can become a personalized tent of sorts under which a frozen Cowboy can huddle. It can also become a nice ground cloth for those times when a Cowboy just has to sit down or take a nap and the ground is already saturated.

On the downside, a poncho does not provide much protection from the wind and a Cowboy can all-but freeze to death from the leaks.

If you don't trust your jacket and are not into ponchos, you'll have to bring along a two-piece rain suit. These things come in a variety of different configurations styles and colors – most of which are a little too dandy for most cowboys.

We are down to boots. Did we mention that it would be a good idea to check the weather reports just before you leave?

I mild conditions, you will need just one pair of very good, very tough boots. Spend some bucks here!

One time on a trip we made to way-back-in-the-wilderness Wyoming, old Florida Dave did not follow this rule. He bought a pair of cheap work boots at his local discount store and jumped on the plane. It is a damn good thing that someone had stashed a full roll of duct tape into his gear. Watching Florida fighting with those boots all week – taping them round and round several times a day was disturbing and drove the point home. Cowboy hunting holds little tolerance for poor boots! You will be walking only on uneven ground - never anything flat. You will be kicking rocks and boulders along the trail almost constantly. You will be sliding your boots in and out of stirrups a hundred times a day. You will be walking through streams and snow fields. You'll be stepping in horseshit. Well... you might be if you aren't mindful of the fact that horses are rarely considerate of where they take care of personal hygiene duties.

Nuff said?

Some Cowboys like to bring along a pair of lesser boots or shoes for knocking around in the camp and for wearing while their boots dry next to a fire. Camp shoes, they call them. I personally never felt the need to have them. My experience is that by the time I get back to camp, I am so tired that about all I can do is to stumble into the cook tent, eat and then crash. In the morning I am scrambling to get my act together in time to be ready to mount up and leave when everybody else is ready. I simply have never found the time on a cowboy hunt to be slipping out of one pair of boots and then sipping into another like I was going to cocktail parties and such. I always try to set my boots by the camp stove at night where they might get a chance to dry, but usually they only get sort-of dry anyway. Wet boots are just another misery Cowboys love to love.

What about snow boots?

If it looks like you are going to be in deep snow or very cold weather, snow boots might be a good idea, but there are problems. First of all they are very heavy. If you toss a pair of snow boots into your gear when you don't actually need them, you might as well toss in a kitchen sink too. And, here is something else to consider. Most reputable outfitters use over-sized stirrups. Check to see if yours does. Over sized stirrups will allow you to wear a pair of medium weight snow boots - Sorrels or the equivalent. They will not allow you to wear those giant moon-boot things that are only good for the ice in Antarctica. Not only will you not be able to get those things into any stirrup, you'll never be able to walk along the trails and climb the peaks that will need climbing.

So, snow boots – yes if the weather report is gloomy. Stay-puffed marshmallow boots – no!

You will also need some hunter's orange. Different states have different rules about this, but just about all of them require you to have it on while hunting. Many times they delineate a specific number of square inches of orange, which must be visible on each hunter. An orange hat works okay in Wyoming, but Colorado requires that you wear an entire vest. Check with the game and fish department of the state where you intend to hunt about their specific requirements.

Do not forget to take a good belt. You'd be surprised how many Cowboys do and end up with their pants roped up. This looks bad and can be a real pain-in-the-ass. No one would fault you for taking along a good pair of suspenders either. In fact, suspenders can be quite helpful especially if you end up with a few other items hooked to the belt. The pants-falling-down look does not quite cut it in Cowboy land.

Okay, we got you dressed. Time to accessorize.

Remember, you've only got a hundred pounds or so to work with. All the clothing items above have taken a sizable chunk out of that, so it is time to ask yourself, "Am I really gonna need that?"

The hunting/camping accessory business is worth billions. The number of products available to fight off the angry assaults of Mother nature is huge. The Cowboys of yesteryear had none of them and did just fine.

You'll probably need a sleeping bag. Check with your outfitter. Some have sleeping bags already in their camps for the use of their hunters. Some Cowboys don't like sleeping in community bags. In either case, the trick to staying really warm in a sleeping bag (other than to wear everything else you brought) is have a thin cotton blanket to wrap around yourself, inside the bag. These things are very light-weight and can be stuffed inside the bag itself, taking up little room during transport. A cotton inner blanket like this can reduce the size and bulk of the actual bag considerably. There is no need for the ten-inch thick, fifty pound monster that our old friend The Gunslinger used to make everybody haul around for him.

You might need a pillow too. Make it small. Some Cowboys use the inflatable ones. Your choice.

There is usually no need to bring along a mattress or ground cloth of any kind. Most outfitters equip their hunting tents with cots and mattresses – or at least giant pieces of foam rubber.

TIP - Personal Medication:

You might want to toss in a few of your favorite anti-inflammatory pills to fight off the effects of sore knees, backs and ankles. In fact, bring a whole bottle of those. If you are prone to indigestion, consider your favorite antacid too.

TIP – Personal Hygiene

Don't forget your toothbrush and some toothpaste. Your comrades will appreciate it if you brush daily.

TIP – Personal Hygiene

You might want to bring some soap and a small towel. Hanging around horses and hunting camps can get a Cowboy a little dirty at times. It's nice to wash up occasionally.

Most camps keep a wash-pan of hot water near the cook tent so you can at least wash your hands. Some, actually have a shower tent. The problem with that is you need to have someone heat up a bunch of hot water. This is a lot of extra work and can make your guides and camp people a little cranky.

Most Cowboys just take an ice water wash cloth bath in the creek if they really feel like they need it.

TIP – Personal Hygiene

Cowboy hunting bathrooms are an imperfect breed. In fact, bathroom is far too strong a word for them. Most are simply a small tent stretched imperfectly around a few imperfect boards stacked up over an imperfect hole in the ground. Most are so cold that there is literally ice on the whatever-it-is you are supposed to sit on. If you are lucky, that's a piece of plywood with a seat. If you are not so lucky, it might just be a piece of plywood with a hole. If you are really unlucky, it might just be a few small logs arranged so that one can prop himself awkwardly on them and hopefully position his sphincter roughly above the hole in the ground.

What ever the case, you are virtually guaranteed to be less-than-pleased with the facilities available for daily waste elimination. Performing post-defecation cleanup never results in the same quality of work, which one might accomplish under different circumstances – say your home toilet or one in a Ritz Carlton. Add the rigors of scraping ones posterior anatomy against a saddle for ten or so hours a day and it is not difficult to believe that certain anatomical structures will get SO GODDAMN SORE YOU'LL THINK SOMEONE SHOVED A SOLDERING IRON UP YOUR ASS! Please excuse the shouting.

It is a very good idea to bring along some sort of medicated wiping pads. There are a number of different brand names available in any drug store. Tucks ® is one example.

TIP – Personal Hygiene : The problem of chaffed peri-anal and sub-testicular areas is huge on a Cowboy hunt. Those big tendons that run along the inside of the legs and come together in that region can get so raw that walking can be a problem. One old Cowboy trick is to bring along a tube of baby diaper rash cream. Yeah, I know, it's tough for a Cowboy to even think about it, but that stuff will work wonders. It will shut up a screaming baby and a miserable Cowboy in a New York minute.

TIP – Personal Hygiene:

It is a good idea to have along a stash of your own toilet paper. Yes, you can always steal some from the out house tent, but for some reason toilet paper seems to be a short ration on every Cowboy hunting trip.

A good idea is to start collecting ¼ rolls from your own home a few days or weeks before your trip. A whole roll is too big to carry around easily. A ¼ roll can be put into a Zip-locked baggy and stashed inside a hunting jacket or in a pouch on your survival/hunting belt.

TIP – Personal Hygiene: Enough already!

TIP – Flashlight: Yeah yeah, Cowboys of old didn't have them. But, those guys went to bed when the sun set and got up when it rose. You won't be on that schedule.

You'll need to have a flashlight with you pretty much at all times. You'll probably need it in your tent at night for one thing or another. You'll need it in the morning when you are getting your gear and your horse ready to head out. You might need it along the trail on your way in at night.

Be sure to check the batteries before you leave and you might want to consider bringing along a couple of extras – just in case.

TIP – Flashlight: Head mount flashlights are very useful – the kind with the straps are perfect for getting a horse ready in the morning and for gutting out some game after dark. But, they are hard to pack and carry around - another good reason to have a hunting coat with lots of pockets.

TIP – Flashlight: Don't shine your flashlight on the ground from your horse, so he can see the trail at night. He can see it just fine without your help. In fact, if you do that you will actually be blinding him. If you are in a tough spot along the trail where walking is indicated, it's okay to use the light for yourself, but be careful about shining it the eyes of your horse. They are very sensitive, like any animal's are, and can gather plenty of light from ambient sources to see where they are placing their feet.

TIP – Water: You will need to have water with you. If you don't drink during the day, you can get sick - especially in any kind of altitude.

Chances are you will either have saddle bags for carrying your personal gear on the horse, or you will be slinging your day-pack over the saddle horn. In either case, a simple plastic water bottle will do nicely. A full quart is mandatory and depending on circumstances two quarts might be appropriate. The hotter it is, the more you will need. The higher you go, the more you will need. The more walking you do, the more you will need.

Those round metal canteens with the wool or sheep-skin coverings look cool in the movies, but are hard to strap to a horse. They tend to flop around and bang against stuff or catch on passing foliage.

The fancy bottles you can find these days for runners or bicyclists with the molded plastic sides and the flip up sipper straws are a little over-the-top and frankly don't hold as much as a simple plastic water bottle does.

There is also little need for a wine-skin. It's just one more thing to hang on your saddle and screams; "Look at me. I are a mountain man," just a little too loudly.

TIP – Water: Giardia, a.k.a. Beaver fever, is a huge problem in the west. It's a parasite, which cycles through animals and then ends up in the water from their feces and whatnot. The Giardia produce these little cysts that hatch into some very evil little monsters. If you swallow the cysts, you might not be swallowing anything else for a while, because you will get very sick. A case of Giardia will leave you sicker than you have been since that night with Southern Comfort – or whichever particular poison you still avoid, all these years later.

The cysts are heavier than water, so they tend to sink. If you have to dip water out of a stream, don't go too deep and you'll reduce your chances of picking up any of those little bastards.

The Giardia themselves and the cysts from which they come can be filtered. The hunting/camping industry has developed a ton of machinery to get the Giardia out of the water. The problem is that they are all somewhat bulky and can be quite expensive.

So, do you need a Giardia filter? If you go with an outfitter, probably not. The outfitter and his crew will have been living in the area for most of the summer before your hunt begins. They have a lot of setting up and getting ready work to do and they have to drink too. If Giardia is a problem, you can bet they will have figured out a way to deal with it. In the olden days they had to boil the drinking water. These days, they will probably opt to purchase a larger commercial Giardia filter. Boiling water is a big chore.

Call the outfitter before your trip and ask him about this problem.

If you choose to hunt without an outfitter, you will need to think about this. And do think about it. If you get Giardia, not only will your ruin your trip, but you may ruin the next several weeks as well. Giardia can be persistent.

Here is an irony. The name Beaver Fever is a bit of a misnomer. Cowboys have been drinking water right out of the mountain streams since... well, since there have been Cowboys. During all of that time, there have been Beavers and Elk and Deer and Sheep walking around with the same personal hygiene habits that they have today and guess what? No one ever got sick from Giardia.

Giardia did not become a problem in the mountain streams of the American west until cattle were allowed to graze in the high-country valleys. No one will say that it is the cattle grazing that has caused the epidemic but the inference is obvious.

If you are in an area where there have never been cattle grazing, or high enough up that the cattle have not been there – even though the beavers and Elk have – you can probably drink the water and not worry about Giardia. Cowboys do it all the time. In fact, if you are in a high-altitude camp, your outfitter will just be dipping the water right out the stream and not worrying about it either.

If you see cattle or sign that they have been there, don't drink the water.

TIP – Binoculars:

Binoculars are one of the most important things you can take on a Cowboy Hunting trip. You will spend hours peering through them. "Glassin'" in Cowboy lingo. Take small ones.

You can buy binoculars that look like two thermos bottles linked by an auto bridge. Or, you can buy a pair that look like a cell phone. Cell phone is better. Usually they both have same magnification power and usually there is not much difference in field size either.

Again, get the small ones. You are going to be carrying your binoculars on a staring around your neck. Ten pound binoculars are going to put enough strain on that string to damn near cut your head off. Every time the horse bounces up or down – every few seconds – they are going to smash against the saddle horn and drive you nuts. You are going to have to get off the horse and walk around with them. They are going to have to fit under jackets and compete for room on a Cowboy's chest with his gun sling. Take small binoculars!!

TIP – Binoculars:

When you are riding, it is a good idea to open one button of your shirt or leave your jacket unzipped a couple of inches so you can tuck the binoculars inside the shirt or jacket. When you need them, you can just slide them out. The problem, is that if your horse makes a sudden lurch or if for some reason, you need to do a little running or galloping, if your binoculars are dangling around, they can be quite troublesome.

Our friend The Gunslinger learned this lesson the hard way too. Not only did he like to bring a thirty-pound sleeping bag, but he had the monster binoculars to go with it. They looked like they should be on a podium on top of some building for tourists to use to see the sights of some city. One day, we jumped a herd of Elk, as we came around a bend in the trail. The Elk took off, of course, but our guide figured that if we hurried, we could get to a place on the other side of the ridge where we might be able to ambush them (another good reason to have a good guide).

"You boys feel like ridin'," he said and without an answer took off, like he was in the Preakness.

Did we follow? In a heartbeat. What Cowboy worth his beans and coffee wouldn't?

When we finally stopped galloping – about fifteen minutes later – The Gunslinger was spitting blood. Those massive roof-top binoculars he had, had been sailing everywhere while he held on to the horn and in the course of the action had poked a sizable hole though his upper lip and chiseled the end off one of his front teeth. He tried stuffing them into his shirt after that, but they were just too big. He couldn't have stuffed them into one of Dolly Parton's shirts. He ended up carrying them in his saddle bag, which meant they were hardly ever available for actual use.

TIP – Bullets: Theoretically, you will only need one bullet on a Cowboy hunting trip – two if you are hunting on a combo tag.

All right, all right. I can see you veteran Cowboy hunters laughing at that one. Theory and reality are often as far apart as politicians and honesty.

You'll need some extra rounds. But one box is plenty. The Gunslinger brought at least ten boxes – maybe more, depending on how many extra guns he brought. A single box of bullets is a very heavy item. Doubling up on them is not necessary and adds a lot of extra weight.

Even if you want to sight your gun in one last time, after you get to camp, it should not take more than a couple of shots to do it. One box of bullets is plenty.

But, there is an exception. If you are Antelope hunting bring two extra boxes. You'll most likely have a car or a truck with you then so the extra weight will not be a problem. The problem with Antelope hunting is getting those buggres to stop running long enough to get a decent shot off at them.

TIP – Licenses: Don't forget your license. Don't forget you license. Don't forget your license.

When your license comes in the mail, find your hunting coat, put the license in a plastic baggy and stick it in the inside breast pocket of the jacket. Your outfitter will need to see it as soon as you get to camp. Get the jacket. Take the license out and wait for him to write down all the info. Then, put it right back into the jacket while you are standing there. Your guide will need it immediately after you get something on the ground. You must have it with you <u>at all times</u>.

"There's no game officers out there in the wilderness." Wanna bet? I have been approached by more game and fish representatives while Cowboy hunting than at any other time in my life. I would say chances of running across one are in the seventy percent range. "I forgot it," will not get you by. Don't forget your license!

TIP – Hunter Safety Cards: Most states are requiring hunter safety cards for people of a certain age. Some states require that you present the card in order to get the license. Others require that you have it on your person just like your license.

Call the Game and Fish department of the state where you intend to hunt and check to see what their rules are.

TIP – Knives: Get this. If you go on a Cowboy hunting trip with a good outfitter and a good guide, you don't really need a knife. In fact, you'll probably never even draw it out of its little holster unless you want to clean your finger nails or hack off the duct tape you had around something.

If you get one on the ground, your guide will jump on it like a duck on a June bug, gut it, and cape it out for you while you stand guard. Your best bet is to just let him do it. You might want to help out by holding the legs apart or by helping him flip it over, but your knife work will not be necessary.

That said, nobody - Cowboy, Hunter, walker, jogger or bird watcher should ever venture into the wilderness much farther than to look for a lost ball from an errant drive off the fifth Tee without taking three essential items: a lighter, some toilet paper and a knife.

TIP – Knives: If you are going to be on a horse, or anywhere near horses, it is a good idea to have a straight-shank knife, rather than a collapsible one.

Let's say you need to cut something with a free hand while you hold reigns or lead ropes or saddles or tails or what have you with the other. Let's say you are being dragged down the mountain with one foot stuck in the stirrup like you see in the movies. It can be a real pain-in-the-neck to have to monkey around with opening a collapsible knife under these kinds of circumstances. If you are around horses long enough, it is almost guaranteed that sooner or later you will find yourself in some kind of undesirable situation.

TIP – Knives: The Gunslinger had a Bowie knife. It was more like a sword. It hung down the side of his leg like a crutch. He couldn't even get on a horse without dealing with that damn thing. It weighed a ton or two. He must have watched Rambo just a few too many times.

All you need is a small, sturdy hunting knife. Having it sharp is far more important that having it big.

TIP – Knives: If you are going to be around horses or a lot of hunting gear, a small utility tool, like a Leatherman or a Gerber or a Kobalt can be a handy thing to have. It might be all you actually need. Be careful. Some of them can have a few too many features or can be a little big and can get a bit heavy.

TIP – Belts: Of course, you don't want to forget a belt for your pants, but you might want to consider a second one for your hunting gear.

You need a knife. You need a lighter. You need some toilet paper. You might want a Utility tool. You need a few extra bullets. You need a flashlight... . Trying to get all this stuff hung on the belt that holds up your pants can be a problem. Just fitting it in between the belt-loops is a hassle. Having a second belt, which is just used for hunting stuff really helps.

Sporting goods stores are full of small pouches you can hang on belts. Get one, stick some toilet paper in a plastic baggie and jam it in the pouch. There will probably be enough room in that pouch for a lighter too. But if not, get another one and put the lighter in it along with some fuel sticks for starting a fire. Find a knife case and match a small flashlight to it. Hang that on your belt. Hang your knife, utility tool and a small bullet case on it too. Get another case and stick a compass in it.

What you will be making is a separate hunting belt as well as a pseudo-survival kit. Anytime you go into the woods – maybe just on a short hike, you can grab this belt and know that you will have the minimum equipment necessary to facilitate your walk and maybe even save your life. The first step in survival is being prepared.

And for hunting? It can't be beat. Get a belt just a little large so you can put it on over a few layers of clothing or even around your hunting jacket. In the morning you can get dressed, put on your hunting belt, grab your jacket, water bottles and rifle and head off to wrestle with your horse. No looking around to make sure you have this and that. Those essentials will be on your belt and they won't be weighing your pants down. And at night, when you stagger back into camp after a day of Cowboy hunting, you can just reverse the process. Put your horse away, grab your jacket (if you aren't wearing it) take your water bottles and rifle and head back to your tent. Drop all that stuff off, shed your hunting/survival belt and you are ready for dinner. Over the years, this has proven to be a great way to deal with small but important gear.

TIP – Belts: If you make yourself a hunting belt, equip it with suspenders. You'd think two belts would really help hold your pants up. Wrong. It's the opposite. The hunting belt will ride on the other one and actually make things worse. Suspenders cure the problem. No one would fault you for wearing two sets of suspenders – one for your pants and another for your hunting belt.

TIP – Snacks: If you are with a reputable outfitter it is highly likely that the food will be terrific. That's usually the hallmark of any good hunting trip, Cowboy or otherwise.

That said, it's nice to have a little snack late in the day when you are riding along the trail and, I have never really thought that there has been adequate snacking items on any trip I have ever been on.

Maybe it's me. I can't tolerate a lot of sugar – especially late in the day. I'll be asleep in seconds if I eat too much of the stuff in the afternoon and the staple of Cowboy hunting snacks seems to be candy bars. I love them, but I need something more substantial to keep me going. My choice? Hunter's sausage. Over the years, I've learned that having a stick or two along has made a long afternoon horse ride far more enjoyable.

TIP – Boots: Be sure to break your boots in. If you don't, you might want to bring along blister kit.

TIP – Boots: Don't get boots that are too tight. Make sure they have some room in the toes. You will be walking downhill at least as much as you are walking uphill. If there is not enough toe room, you'll be jamming them into the boots on downhills and it is guaranteed you will have some pretty sore pinkies about mid-week.

TIP – Socks: Ultra heavy socks are probably not necessary. Check the weather report. Too big or too heavy a sock can actually make your feet cold. Good circulation is essential to keeping toes warm. A sock that is too heavy or too tight can interfere with circulation and freeze your feet.

TIP – GPSs: I love hand-held GPS units. If you will be hunting by yourself, definitely take one. The problem is that they are a little heavy. Adding one to your hunting belt just might tip it over the edge of practicality. If you are going with a good outfitter and a good guide you probably won't need it. Weigh the value against the hassle of carrying it and make a decision. It's a toss up.

TIP – Wallet: You won't need your wallet on your horse. Stash it in your gear. Nobody is going to touch it.

TIP – Extra Shells: If the magazine of your gun holds four or five shells keep them in one of your pockets. You will need to constantly load and unload your gun. You load it up in the morning before you get on your horse. **BE SURE TO KEEP BULLETS ONLY IN THE MAGAZINE WHEN YOU ARE RIDING. NEVER HAVE A BULLET IN THE BARREL OF YOUR GUN – SAFETY ON OR NOT – WHEN YOU ARE ON A HORSE!**

Unload the gun before you get back to camp or certainly before you go into your tent.

The four or five shells will probably be all you will need for the entire trip, but it is a good idea to take a few extras in case whatever you are shooting at does not cooperate.

Small belt pouches that hold another five or even ten shells can be found in any sporting goods store. They work well for carrying extras.

TIP – Scabbards: You will need to have a scabbard for carrying your rifle on a horse. The good news is that most reputable outfitters provide them. Check with yours before you go and make sure he does. (If he doesn't, think twice about going with him).

Carrying a rifle slung over your shoulder while riding is necessary from time to time, particularly if you are in a hot area at a hot time, where you might have to jump off quickly and get of a shot. However, it can be a real pain-in-the-ass to do all the time.

TIP – Day Packs: Some outfitters – even good ones – do not have saddle bags on their saddles. You need to have something to carry your water and lunch in on the horse. Your day pack will suffice. The trick is to hang a day pack on the saddle horn to hold that stuff and whatever other gear you might need to have along.

TIP – Horse Packing: The usual saddle configuration is two saddle bags and a scabbard. Obviously there is a limit to the amount of stuff you can bring along on a horseback ride.

You have to have your rifle. It goes into the scabbard with no bullet in the barrel (magazine okay)

You need water. It goes in the saddle bag on the opposite side of the scabbard for balance. Having to constantly shift your saddle back to keep it from spinning around the horse is a pain-in-the-ass.

You'll need your lunch. It can go in the other saddle bag but keep that balance thing in mind. If you have a heavy lunch you may want to put it in with your water.

You'll need to bring your rain gear. Roll it up and tie it to the back of your saddle. There are usually two leather strings on the back of just about every saddle for this purpose.

You'll start out in the morning with just about everything you own on. As the day heats up, you will be shedding layers.

Your hunting jacket will go first. Roll it up and tie it on the back of the saddle with your rain gear.

If you have a smaller jacket - like a liner jacket or maybe your hooded sweatshirt – tie it on the front of the saddle just in front of the horn. You'll find two strings there just for that purpose.

TIP – Horse Packing: You can buy a fanny pack for your horse. It is essentially a long skinny duffel bag that you can tie to the rear of the saddle using the two leather strings. You can roll your rain gear and your hunting jacket up and stick them in the fanny pack. They are nice because they eliminate the worry about sleeves and other stuff coming unrolled and hanging down along the flank of the horse where they can get speared by passing foliage. Horse fanny packs are nice, but they are not necessary.

TIP – Rain Gear: The common pant and jacket rain suit combos sold in every sporting store are good, but usually need to be two to three sizes bigger than you would ordinarily purchase because they make getting on and off a horse difficult when too small.

Further, if it is cold, you will want to put them on over a jacket and sweater.

The cheap ones tend to tear easily and in hunting conditions, tree limbs and branches can shred them pretty fast. Get a good set if you are going to do it at all.

TIP - Rain Gear: The long rain slickers that you see the T.V. cowboys wear are nice, but heavy and kind-of stinky. Cold too. Those things come from another era when they used what they had. Today's technology trumps that old stuff easily.

TIP – Packing: When you are gathering up all your gear – just before you start shoving it in your duffle bags – put those items that you intend to actually wear when you are on the horse to the side. Pack them last.

Chances are that the first night you spend on your trip will either be at a motel somewhere, or at a base camp or ranch. Usually, you will not be actually saddling up until the next morning. You don't really want to spend the morning digging around through your gear looking for the combination of stuff that you intend to wear on the horse. If that stuff is already on top and easy to find, your morning will go easier.

The same thing goes for sleeping at night in a cold tent. Spend a little time just before you turn in arranging the stuff that you will need first thing in the morning. Put it all within easy reach. There is nothing less comfortable than standing in your underwear in the frozen morning looking for something in your bags with a flashlight. You've heard the expression "freezing your ass off." Don't make that come true.

TIP – Booze: All but a few cowboys like to have a beer or two after a long day in the saddle. Some like a jolt of something stronger. Some like to carry a little "trail shortener" in their saddle bags. I even know one guy who drinks wine spritzers. Gag.

Most outfitters provide coffee, soft drinks and water. Some might bring along a few beers to share, but this can become a big expense.

Most outfitters do not mind if you bring along a few beers or a bottle of Old Whatever." Just don't overdo it. Remember everything has to be hauled up to a hunting camp on horseback. Twenty cases of beer is going to put your guides and packers in a very bad mood.

Also, there are "dry" camps. Some outfitters do not allow alcohol in their camps. Check to see what your outfitter's rules are about this before you go.

TIP - Hats: Man, don't you want to wear a Cowboy hat when you are on a horse in the west? I do. But, on a hunting trip, they are extremely impractical. They are a nightmare to pack (which means you have to wear it on the plane and just about everywhere else you go). They blow off in the wind . They don't store well. They catch on just about every branch hanging in the trail and come off. They are not all that warm. But, for managing water drippage, blocking the sun and looking good, you can't beat 'em.

GUNS

GENTLEMEN, CHOOSE YOUR WEAPONS

Mike dropped into the office one day and noticed an Elk mount in our lobby.

"Man, you must have used a canon to get that big old boy," he said, standing with his hands on his hips, staring up at the modest Elk. "That there is what I got my big old 600/40/40 magnum turbo Stratoblaster for. That's what I'd use on one of them. What'd you use on it."

".306," I said.

"You're kiddin,"

"Nope."

"What about that Mule deer? I'd use my 33 over 70 Plainsboy Swiftkick Slapper for one of those. It's the perfect gun for something that size. What'd you use?"

".306."

"Naw. On one of them?"

"Yes sir."

"Ah, I see you got an Antelope. I heard they're pretty quick. "I'd have to get the old 2-22-27 Super Light Cosmo Slingfragelator for that. Shoots far and flat. You know what I mean? What'd you use?"

".306."

"You gotta' be kidding me, man. You gotta size your weapon to you're what you're huntin' don't you think?"

"You ever been out Cowboy hunting, Mike," I asked.

"Nope. Can't afford it. But, someday I'm gonna, and I'm taking all eight of my guns when I go, cuz I want to be prepared."

"Maybe if you sold a six or seven of them you could go." I hated to point out the obvious, but, he started it.

TIP – Guns:
The debate about which gun is the right gun to hunt a particular situation or a particular game has been raging for many years. It seems like

everybody has a different opinion about the question. And the truth is; they are all right!

It does not matter which gun you favor. What matters; is knowing the particular characteristics of the gun and ballistics of the round you are using. In other words, knowing where the bullet is going to end up when you pull the trigger. A guy I know uses a .270 for everything – Moose to mice. Of course he was a Marine sniper in Vietnam and tends to hit everything in the heart or ear hole, if necessary. But then, that is the point. Accuracy is the single most important aspect of hunting - not Caliber, not load, not bullet weight, not muzzle velocity – accuracy!

TIP - Guns: One evening, Tom terrific and I snuck up over a little knoll on a posse of Elk feeding on the slope below. Tom had his brand new 7mm magnum. filled with brand new ammo. A good bull stood in some short willows and looked on as the others fed.

"If he comes out into the clearing," Tom whispered, "I'm going to take him."

"Good. I'll watch," I said.

He quietly slipped down the slope a few feet and found a good shooting position. I got into position with my binoculars. We were only a hundred yards away, but the wind was in our favor, and the Elk had no idea we were there.

I kept my glasses on the bull as he stepped out. Tom fired. I actually saw the fur ruffle where the bullet hit – through the rib cage just behind the heart. I heard the slap as the round hit. Certainly a lethal hit by any reckoning.

The Elk brought all four feet together, pointed his toes and leapt about three feet in the air like a ballet dancer. He came down running and disappeared into the Oak scrub of the hillside.

"You got him," I said. "Nice shot."

"Yeah it looked like I rocked him good. "

Tom beamed as we walked down the hillside in the fading light. It was a good bull and he had wanted a nice trophy. The herd stampeded when he fired – nothing but asses and elbows as they disappeared, but we were sure the bull would be paws up in the thicket not far away.

We couldn't find any blood at the site when we got there – peculiar. Usually with a shot like that, the exit wound is quite large and downstream a ways, you can usually find a fairly good splot of blood, sometimes some bone and maybe even some fur. We found nothing. Not even a drop. We picked up his tracks easily enough and followed them into the highway of tracks made by the rest of the herd – but nothing. Not even the slightest trace of red.

By then the light was fading fast, but we were certain the bull hadn't gotten far. We whipped out our flashlights and began making search rings in the general direction where I had watched him run. Still nothing. We came back to the scene of the kill and repeated our search. We redid it ten times. Then we went back to camp and rousted up the rest of the hunters, the guides, the camp cook, even the cat and went back to the scene of the crime. We looked long into the night. We looked again the next morning. None among us wanted to leave a wounded or dead animal in the wilds. Yet, despite our best efforts, we found nothing – no blood, no fur, no dead Elk.

"You sure you hit him," the guides asked."

"Yeah, I'm sure," Tom said. "It was a clean shot."

"I know he hit him," I said. " I saw it clear through my binoculars. "

Later that afternoon, we all went off by ourselves to sit on stands and wait for deer. I knew generally where Tom was and sure enough, about mid-afternoon, I heard shooting coming from his direction – one shot, followed by three hurried ones. He came into camp late after dark. We all waited to hear about his kill, but unfortunately, it was a repeat of the night before. He was certain he had hit a deer on his first shot. "Knocked it right off its feet."

But, it got up and ran away, and he could find nothing to tell it had ever been hit. By his recollection, he figured he followed it for over two miles, without seeing the slightest sign of blood. By my recollection he had spent over four hours tracking that deer – to no avail. Tom had a full count against him. One more pitch and he would be out.

We awoke the next morning to a light dusting of snow – about a quarter inch – just perfect for tracking. We found three cows with three calves feeding in a small open meadow up wind of us about two hundred yards out, and moved in close to take a stand in case there was a bull waiting in the trees.

"There he is Tom," I said, after spotting some movement about forty yards into a thick stand of Popples.

Tom had spotted him too, and had begun moving into position for a shot. I took my position behind him with my binoculars like I had two nights before. The bull took his time coming into the clearing. Six or seven other Elk, slithered out next to him and joined the group feeding in the open meadow. After what seemed like forever, the bull moved into position and gave Tom a perfect broadside.

Boom! Tom's shot caught me a little off guard, and I lost the bull in the binoculars for a split second. But, it didn't matter. The shot knocked the animal down and back about ten feet. It lay there on the ground in plain view.

"Got that one for sure," Tom said, looking back at me with a grin as big as Montana

"Good shot," I said, reaching out to shake his hand.

Then, the unbelievable happened. The bull stood, shook himself, and then took off at full stride after his bolting comrades.

Tom dropped to one knee and started flinging lead. I saw every shot miss the running animal and splatter into a hillside. The Elk, all dozen or so, including the big bull disappeared over the top of a small ridge a quarter mile away.

"Damn damn damn triple damn blitsoflix," Tom said. "I can't flaporating believe this flipperationink gun. What the bee eee jeeborating flaps is going on here?"

"Don't worry," I said. "You got him. We shouldn't have too much trouble finding him with the snow and all. Let's give him a few minutes. I think he is going to be pretty sick and we should be able to catch up to him and then you'll finish him off. "

"Ratsoflatso, consuppum trebblesip,"

Tom can be such a wordsmith. I picked his gun up from where he had thrown it, and we headed down to check for a blood trail. To my everlasting surprise, there was almost nothing. We had a highway of tracks heading off through a fresh snow, and the best we could find was a pin prick here and there of blood. Hard to believe. Even if he hadn't hit anything vital, the bullet had hit hard enough to knock a fully-grown Elk off his wheels, yet a Beagle would have a tough time following this blood trail. Go figger!.

We found him paws-up dead over the crest of the ridge, almost a half mile from where Tom had blasted him. But, like something out of some kind of Twilight Zone alien encounter sort-of thing, there was no blood! This big dead Elk was lying in the snow, with nothing more than a few drops of blood surrounding him. He was on his side and the exit wound was pointing straight up. However, instead of being a massive crater, like most exit wounds, this one was just a tiny red circle, all but hidden in fur. It looked more like a tiny stick poke than a bullet hole.

"What kind of bullet you shooting," one of the guides asked.

"7mm. 135 grain, ballistic tip," Tom said.

Then, it hit us, like a brick refrigerator falling out of a two-story window. We rolled the Elk over and found an identical hole on the entrance side – a perfectly round 7mm hole. We took care when we gutted this Elk. We wanted to see if we could track the bullet's path. It was not too difficult once we drained the blood out of the chest cavity. That powerful gun, had zipped that tiny bullet through a rib on the right side of the chest, cracking it, but essentially causing little damage other than a small hole. It nicked the superior portion of the liver, then passed through the right lung, then slid through a small hole in the bottom of the heart distorting this critical organ very little. From the heart, it passed through the left lung and out through a space between two of the left ribs.

Because the hard ballistic tip had distorted very little passing through the animal, the massive damage a softer bullet would have caused did not occur. The light-weight of the bullet and the high speed of that particular gun had not caused the hydraulic shock a heavier bullet would have, which of course, liquefies everything in its path. The hole in the heart killed the Elk. The double lung and liver perforations would have killed it too. Unfortunately, it may have taken a long time, and the chances of our recovering it might have been diminished.

Clearly this is what happened to the other two animals, Tom had hit on that trip. He has since switched to a heavier bullet and dropped the ballistic tip, and has not had any problems.

TIP - Bullets You want to have a bullet that splashes a bit when it hits - but not too much. Our friend Roger in Colorado has banned partition bullets in his camp. Here's why.

We were hunting one week at his place, with a rather large group. We had two in our party and were matched with a group of six from Pennsylvania and two more from Ohio. At some point, someone took an angled shot at a bull and hit it fairly close to the left shoulder as it quartered away from him. The bull did not go down, but was clearly hurt. It limped off leaving a substantial blood trail. The hunter did not hit it again as it ran.

The hunter and one of the guides spent the entire day tracking the wounded Elk, but never caught up with it. Almost every body in camp spotted that Elk at some time during the next week, but none of us were ever in a position to bring it down. On the last day Roger and the hunter he was with finally killed it with a poorly placed gut shot.

I arrived on the scene just in time to help with the field dressing - my luck.

"Ah, gut shot," I said, "That's why he never went down."

"I don't think so," Roger said. "We just did that a couple of minutes ago. Probably wouldn't have killed him if he hadn't already been so sick. Let's roll him over."

We did, and sure enough there was another entry hole just behind the shoulder, which had crusted over and was oozing some kind of slime.

"This should have been a kill right here," Roger said. "But the guy was using those goddamn partitions, and they just don't have the killing power."

"Why not? I always heard they dummied pretty well," I said.

"They dummy too well. That's the problem," Roger said. " All the energy is lost as the bullet flattens out, and they just don't get the job done. I've seen more Elk wounded by them things. I'm banning them from the camp."

We followed the bullet track with a little careful dissection. We found the majority of the lead just under the skin in the neck of the animal, at least two feet from where the bullet had hit. The bullet hit the skin and began flattening out immediately by the time it had hit the bones of the upper shoulder it was so flat and its energy was heading sideways so much that all it did was crush them. It was possible that the Elk would have ultimately survived the wound, living as a cripple. The fact that the angle of the shot caused a bigger deflection of bullet's path contributed, but it's hard to get those critters to stand still to get shot, and angles are the best you can do sometimes. In this case a bullet with a little better penetrating capability probably would have gotten the job done.

TIP - .306 Today, with the popularity of the .300 magnum, the .308, the 7mm Magnum, when I tell people I use a .306, it seems they are always surprised. Yet, almost all of those same people have one (or their fathers do) and almost every guide I know uses one in the field to hunt every kind of Cowboy game there is.

But does it do the job?

We were hunting in Wyoming with Mountainman Dick. We had seen a few Elk, but nothing worth taking. Dick decided to put on one of his famous drives.

"Find yourself a good hiding spot around here somewhere and get sat down," he said to me as we stopped in a small meadow on the side of a heavily –timbered ridge. "See that little cut up there."

"Yeah."

"In about fifteen minutes, there's gonna be about two hundred Elk pouring through it, and they're gonna end up right here in this meadow. "

"You're sure about that, Mountainman." I always called him by his first name.

"Yep."

"Two hundred?"

"Yep."

He took my horse. I found a clump of trees got sat in them like he said, and sure as Hell, in fifteen minutes Elk were pouring into the meadow.

I heard them before I saw them - the usual case. At first more of a perception than an actual sound, soon the perception became a low rumbling, punctuated by the clatter of rocks bouncing into one another. Then, Elk started popping out of the trees. Cow, calf, calf, cow, calf, cow, cow, spike bull, calf, ten, twenty, thirty, asses, elbows, tails, hoofs, fifty, sixty, chaos, every where I looked - if you'd have told me three-hundred I would have believed it. And finally, a bull.

I brought the .306 to my shoulder. The bull stopped in the center of the meadow, as though on Que. Bang, one shot. The bullet caught him about six inches under the spine, a foot behind the shoulder. Not the best shot, but it was enough that all four paws came unglued from mother earth and shot straight up toward the sky as the Elk, spun in the air. He made a complete 360 and I believe he would have stuck the landing in Olympic perfection if he hadn't already been dead. Don't tell me a .306 is not enough gun for an Elk.

That bull never moved and inch. I walked up and touched his eye, less than two minutes after he was hit. Curiously, I will never forget, when I looked up after touching that Elk, I was eye to eye with one of the one of the biggest Wyoming Moose I have ever seen. He must have come out with the masses and stood in the shadows during the kill. I wish I would have had a tag for that one.

TIP - Guns: Almost any large bore rifle will do the job on any of the Cowboy species, including huge Elk and Moose or even tiny Antelope. Don't get lathered up worrying about which one for which species. Pick one and spend your energy learning how to use it.

Any large bore rifle? Not quite. Semi-automatic rifles are a poor choice for Cowboy hunting for a couple of reasons. Number one, they simply are not accurate enough. Yes, you can fling a lot of lead to make up for it, but still. Second, they tend to jam up something terrible if it is cold and a little snow gets in the works. If you have a clip magazine, tiny grains of sand and dirt invariably get into the clip and jam everything. You might get the first round off but not the second. A guy I know shrink-wrapped his clips to prevent this, but then couldn't get them out of the wrappers fast enough to be of any value.

TIP - Guns: Pick a bullet with a little splatter power - nothing less than 165 grains. I prefer 180 grains but not for any particular reason. Rather, that is what I started with and I have stuck with it all these years. Consistency and accuracy are critical. Check the manufacturer's ballistic tables for the round you choose. I printed the drops for various distances on a card, and taped it to the bottom of my stock, just in case I get to senile too remember them.

TIP - Guns: Here is a myth I would like to dispel, (or maybe have someone explain to me). I have heard it said that when sighting in a gun, if it is on at 25 yards, it will be on again at 200. I have no idea where that came from. One guy tried to explain it to me by showing me the arc with the little straight line under it, which is drawn on may ballistic tables. He claimed the bullet traveled on an arced path on at 25 then high, then on again at 200. Please! Nothing could be further from the truth. Three forces affect the flight of a bullet. One, the power generated by the explosion of the powder in the cartridge. Two, the rifling of the barrel. And three; (this is important) gravity.

The explosive force hurls the bullet forward against the resistance of the air (actually more of a liquid to a bullet). It is called the muzzle velocity, and is measured in feet per second in Cowboy land. The rifling in the barrel causes the bullet to spin, reducing yaw and roll as the bullet travels - essentially keeping the bullet from gyrating and tumbling too much. Gravity starts working on the bullet the instant it leaves the barrel. Newton proved theoretically that adjusting for wind resistance, all objects are effected equally by gravity. Theoretically, if you dropped a pea out of the end of one leveled gun at the same time a bullet left the barrel of another gun, both held exactly level, after adjusting for the curvature of the earth, both the pea and the bullet would hit the ground at the same time. The bullet, of course, would be considerably down-range depending on its muzzle velocity.

The little arc on the ballistic tables is the angle you would have to hold the gun to get the bullet to hit something at a given distance before it smashed into the earth considerably short of the target. It is called the elevation. I prefer to think of it as drop. If I zero my gun at two hundred yards, the drop at three hundred yards is about nine inches. Elk Tooth's and Tom Terrific's 7mm mag drops about seven inches at 300 yards. I can't even see two inches at three hundred yards, so the difference is negligible.

TIP - Guns: It is a very good idea to put in some range time before you head out to Cowboy land.

We have a nice three-hundred-yard range at the gun club where I am a member. I am amazed by the Geekdom, which sometimes collects at those places. It's worse than a Star trek convention held in the lobby of the Microsoft building. The collections of high-tech, shooting gizmos is overwhelming. And worse, these guys never take the gun out of the bench rest.

I was at the range a while back, sitting next to a shooter in full tech mode. He was poking little holes into a target about the size of a quarter a hundred yards down range. His gun never left the rest, and I reckoned he could have just sat in the car and fired the thing by remote control given the wires and the whistles and bells and whatnot he had laying around.

When he took a break, I walked down to the two-hundred yard backstop, strung up a sheet of 3x6 freezer paper, took out my magic marker, and drew four oblong circles about 10 inches high by about 14 inches long – just about the size of the kill zone on an Elk or a deer. I sat back down rolled up a blanket from the back of my car, rested the barrel on it and took a couple of shots just to make sure the gun was on. I like it zeroed at about 200 yards. Anything I see at 100 yards will get killed by a bullet that is an inch high. Anything at three hundred yards will require a maximum of nine inches of elevation and will still get killed if I only elevate five or so inches. With a gun zeroed at two hundred yards you can just about hold hair on the back of an Elk at 300 yards with your horizontal reticle and get the job done.

My bullet spread on the target with the gun rested on the blanket was about 2-3 inches, but they were all kills. I could see my fanatical partner getting nervous.

"You know," he said finally. "If you got a good rest like the one I have here, you could get that spread a little closer."

"No doubt," I said. "But where I am going, I can't carry one of those, and even if I did, there wouldn't be anywhere to set it up. Even if I did have the time."

"Well, I'm a hunter, and I need accuracy," he said.

"No kidding," I said, flattening the blanket out on the concrete bench. My goal initially was to see if the gun was on. It was. If I hooked it up to his fancy bench it would not have been more accurate., the pattern would have been tighter – that's all.

In an actual hunting situation, you're lucky to have a place where you can squat down on one knee, rest an elbow on it and fire. You might get a tree branch. Maybe a rock. But there ain't no way you will ever get a bench rest.

One time in Wyoming, my friend Old Dead-eye George had to climb out on a swaying tree branch, rest his gun on another swaying branch just to get an angle on a nice buck strolling up a canyon. It was one of the best shots I have ever seen. If you'd have asked me to make a bet, I would have thought he would have missed it given the situation. The point is that rarely in Cowboy hunting do you get a solid bench rest from which to shoot. A more likely scenario is that you end up flying off your horse, snatching your rifle out of the scabbard, dropping to one knee and taking your best free-hand shot.

"I'll let you try my rest if you'd like," the guy at the range said.

"No thanks," I said, lifting the rifle to my shoulder while balancing the barrel with my other arm and elbow. "The gun is on. Any mistakes from here on are operator error. I need to practice."

The guy seemed kind of irritated that I was practicing like that. I thought he was going to bust a head pipe when I stood up and did fifty jumping jacks before blasting my next magazine full.

In Cowboy hunting, not only do you need to be able to make shots from less-than-ideal positions, you need to be able to make them while you are gasping for air. Remember you are going to be in a different world at a different altitude. Cowboy species don't hold still for long. You're likely to have to sneak up a hill or crawl along the side of one for a while before you can get your shot off. In any case, you'll be excited, and you will be breathing heavily. With each breath the barrel of the gun is going to bounce up and down. You need to learn to time your shots at the top or bottom of every barrel oscillation. It ain't easy folks.

I lost the biggest Mulie I have ever seen just that way. Gabriel and I were putting a sneak on him at about eleven-thousand feet one day, up and down some very steep canyons. Near the end of the assault, he spotted us, and broke and ran. I had to scramble up a significant canyon wall to get the shot. When I got there I was panting so hard the best I could do was to send some lead in his general direction. Between each shot, he added fifty or so yards to the difficulty factor. After about nine or ten shots, he was in the next county.

I like using a large piece of paper because if for some reason the gun is actually off, I can catch my mistake easily. (The gun is rarely off, even after the most jarring experiences on horseback, or in trucks and in airports.) If I am not hitting the paper, I have a big problem, and I will immediately move my target back to the 25 yard mark. That is probably the only time I see a need for using a target that close – that is, if you have no idea where a gun is going to shoot. Safety dictates that you be prudent in a situation like that.

TIP - Guns: Never have a bullet in your barrel when you get on a horse. Bullets in the magazine are okay, but sliding a gun into a scabbard can cause an unwanted discharged. Shooting another hunter or shooting yourself, would be a tragedy. Killing a horse in Cowboy land, could get you hung.

Never have a bullet in your barrel when you are in a truck. IN many states, Colorado, Michigan, having bullets in your magazine is illegal. In Wyoming it's okay to keep the gun fully loaded. It just isn't safe.

TIP - Guns: Never under any circumstances fire a gun while on horseback. In fact, if anyone else in your party is thinking about firing one, get off your horse as fast as you can. If not, I guarantee you will be airborne in a hurry. Probably wouldn't be a bad idea not to even stand in the vicinity of the horses if someone is going to be shooting.

TIP – Guns: Never take a loaded gun into your tent or into any building.

TIP – Guns: A scope cover is a very good idea. However, the fancy plastic pop-up jobs are a pain in the neck. They invariably break or get hung up on the scabbard. The simple little rubber ones are easiest to deal with, and fold up nicely into a pocket when not in use.

TIP - Guns: If your gun does not have a sling, get one. No matter which type of Cowboy hunting you choose, at some point you will be walking. It is very nice to be able to slip the sling over your shoulder. From time to time, you may want to have it on when you are on horseback too. On almost every trip I have been on, at some point we have been aware that we were riding through an area where we might just spook something up and have to act fast. If fast action is required, you don't want to be fumbling around trying to get a gun out of a scabbard. The best Mule Deer I ever harvested was just such a situation.

Wild Bill and I crossed over the top of a grassy ridge at about ten thousand feet. A soon as we reached the crest, the big buck jumped up. He had been sunning himself in the grass about forty yards in front of us. I had my rifle slung over my shoulder, because we were suspicious of the area and figured we might see something. I was glad I had it readily available. I jumped down, scrambled away from the horses and got my first shot off before the deer had gotten out of the 150 yard range. Took three more shots to finally get him killed, but I can guarantee that if I had not had the rifle slung over my shoulder on the horse, he would not be hanging on my wall today.

TIP - Guns: When you put your gun into a scabbard there is a little cutout for the bolt. Get it right. Position the gun so they match up. Be sure to leave as little of the sling hanging out as possible. Tree branches are very adept at plucking a gun out of a scabbard and depositing it in the rocks. I have seen it happen several times. The worse part is that you may not even be aware that it has happened. It's kind of like leaving your pitching wedge on the last green after putting. You won't know it until you need it again.

TIP - Guns: With the exception of Glen Ford, who always strapped one on by the end of the movie, every cowboy wears a side arm. You just ain't a cowboy unless you're packin' iron or prepared to slap leather. Well, in Cowboy hunting, there just ain't no room or need for a pistol.

I know, you've got a big .357 or a .44 that's just itchin to get out of the closet and start cutting grass, but you really won't need it. In fact, they are a huge trouble.

Number one, they are heavy. You will need to minimize your weight in any way you can. Hauling a side arm around is a hassle and extra work for your horse. They catch on stuff, and clatter into the rocks more often than not.

Number two, they nerve the airlines up something fierce. If you are flying, you will put up with enough hassle these days. Toss a handgun into the mix and things will get worse.

Three. You've got enough packing problems. A heavy pistol is just one more thing to account for.

Four. What are you planning to do with it? Target practice? A hunting camp is a place to practice relative silence.

But by far, the single biggest reason not to take a pistol with you, is that it is like branding "rookie" into your forehead. What are you going to do - stand there in your cowboy hat, one foot on a stump, rolling a smoke, polished pistol poised perilously at your side? Oh yeah, it will look good, but please, do it at home in front of the mirror in your bedroom, and come to camp looking right.

FINALLY, YOU'RE THERE

NOW WHAT

You drove or you flew or you walked and now you are there. The next task is to get to the hunting camp. Most outfitters live in a town or on a ranch outside of town somewhere. Occasionally, you may hunt out of the ranch and every morning will start with a truck ride out to the actual hunting area. However, in most cases, the outfitter will have a high camp or a wilderness camp near where you will actually be hunting and you will need to get there before your hunt begins. Most of the time this means a long horse ride at the beginning of your trip and another one at the end. Six or seven hours would not be unusual.

NORMAL CAMPS

Most high country camps follow a similar format. Driving right up to them is not possible. You have to ride there on horse back – especially in the real wilderness areas. It will take a long time, and you will be very tired after that first trip in. You'll ride for hours and then, suddenly you will begin to hear horses whinnying in the distance.

The first thing you will see is some kind of corral for horses. As you approach most camps, your horse will begin chatting with the corralled horses a half mile out.

Near the corral, there will likely be a tent or sometimes an ancient deteriorating cabin of some sort, which will serve as a tack shack for the horses. There will always be a cook tent.

The cook tent is usually the central gathering point of any camp. You'll eat all your meals there and you'll tell all your tales there. Frequently it will be two tents fixed together into one large room. Immediately inside the entrance flaps will be a long table of one kind or another but always large enough to serve ten or more eaters. Thankfully, you'll find a big stove somewhere near the table and during your stay it's virtually guaranteed you will take some comfort there. In most cases a giant pot of Cowboy Coffee will be in continual brew on that stove.

The rear of the tent is the cook's domain – pots pans, griddles, additional stoves, dishwashing gear and food storage. Some camp cooks are more protective of their area than others. Some will allow you to wander around, others will flat out beat you with some utensil if you even come near their world. Tread lightly at first until you figure out the rules.

Near the cook tent, will be the *cook's* tent. The cook is the first one up in the morning – long before the wranglers, the guides, and certainly the hunters. The first sound you will hear in the dark of every morning is the clank of a pot or pan as the cook begins the day. So, their personal tents are usually close to their work.

The wrangler's tent is usually fairly close to the corral. It is the wrangler's job to watch over the horses and all of the horse related gear. They frequently do double duty as packer and may lead mule trains to and from the camp every day or two, on an as needed basis. Chances are that a wrangler will be involved in getting your kill out of the back country and down to the camp in one way or another. And, it is guaranteed that the second sound you will hear in the morning is the clanking of bells as the wrangler wanders around in the wilderness gathering up the horses and mules that have been turned loose to feed during the night.

Wranglers, in first rate camps, frequently share their tents with a camp helper, whose job it is to serve everybody else – the wrangler, the cook, the guides, and, of course the hunters who are footing the bill for everything. A camp helper may show up in your tent in the early morning to start a fire for you. He will be keeping your wood supply current. He will be lighting your lantern and making sure it is full of fuel and functional. He will be gathering the water and helping the cook prepare meals. He will be sweeping up – the cook tent, and even your tent. He will be knocking snow off tents and keeping the trail open to the cook tent.

Guides tents are usually clustered together and may be distanced a little from the hunter's tents. They like to talk about us in the night when we can't hear them.

Hunter's tents are usually two-man tents, although they can hold as many as six or eight depending. The basic format is a stove, two cots or wooden bunks topped with a piece of foam rubber, a small night-stand or table, a stove, and a lantern. Most have a log with nails driven into it hung strategically somewhere for hanging wet clothes. Dirt floors are the norm, although some have an old piece of carpeting running between the cots. It is guaranteed they will be cold and breezy throughout your stay.

The camp will have a latrine somewhere a few hundred feet away from the camp. Usually it is a pit with some form of seating arrangement cobbled together from logs or wood perched precariously above it. The whole mess is usually surrounded by a tent affair of some kind. One struggles to find pleasant words to describe camp latrines. Suffice it to say, they are not for the faint of heart or the delicate of senses. We are talking business only here partner.

Occasionally (seldom) a camp will have a shower tent. If you really need to take shower during a one-week hunt, maybe cowboy hunting is not your thing. Most of us wash up in the stream a ways from camp – if we bother at all. Shower tent is a misnomer. There is no shower in a hunting camp. At best, there might be a small (phone-booth) tent with a cobbled wooden floor and a bucket. Somebody will have to heat the water in the bucket for you (a labor no one is happy about) so you can dip a few cups full out and pour it over yourself while you stand in the tent. It's a promise that if you take a shower in the no-shower tent, during your stay, your name will come up in the guide's tent, the camp helper's tent, the cook's tent and even in the corral among the horses. The good news is that if you wait until you get back to the world, the first shower you take when you arrive will be one of the best of your life!

TIP – Lanterns: Hunter's tents usually have a lantern in them. It will either be a Coleman-style liquid fuel pump model or a newer propane driven model. Either kind can be a problem. They can cause fires. If you are a younger hunter, it is quite possible you may not know how to use the old liquid fuel kind. Rather than fumble around trying to get the thing to work and possibly having a fire in your first night in camp ask for a little demo. These things have mantels in them and mantels are fragile and tricky.

I recently helped a fifty-year veteran outfitter put out a fire which had destroyed the entire rear end of his tent, his sleeping bag, the table next to his cot, the foam rubber mats, on which he slept, even the book he was reading.

The fire started as a result of a faulty connection on his propane lantern. Be careful!

One more thing about lanterns; if you hang one on a hook from the center ridge pole of the tent, which is where they usually hang, it is a promise that you will hit your head on it at least five times a day.

TIP - Stoves: Hunter's tents usually have wood stoves in one corner. Next to the stove will be some kindling wood (if it is a camp with a camp helper) and a coffee can filled with chain-saw shavings soaked in kerosene. There will also be a stack of fire wood. Toss in a handful of the shavings, put some kindling on top and maybe two or three pieces of wood. Hit it with a match, damper it down (the little spring-like thing on the flew pipe) and in minutes your tent will be toasty warm.

Here is the rub. Toasty warm is one thing. The tendency, however, is to jam the stove full of logs just before you crawl into your sleeping bag for the night. Resist this tendency – unless of course you plan to be standing outside the tent flaps in about an hour watching the stars. Wood stoves, filled to their max for the night, are guaranteed to heat your little tent to just one degree below what is the maximum temperature for human existence in about 45 minutes.

TIPS: Cowboy Coffee: You won't be responsible for making the coffee if you go with a reputable outfitter. If not, then maybe you will.

True Grit. Remember that? John Wayne? Tough, tough guy. How about that scene in Lonesome Dove where Robert Duvall takes an arrow in the leg, but still rides and fights and eventually walks out with a broken branch as a crutch? Clint Eastwood, the man with no name. Nasty nasty. "We don't need no stinkin' badges." Remember those guys?

What is it about Cowboys that hardens them so? Punchin' cows? Bustin' broncs? Bull ridin'? If you ask Willie Nelson, he'll tell you it's from being alone too long. If you ask me, it's the coffee.

I chewed my first cup of asphalt black Cowboy coffee on my first hunting trip in Wyoming twenty-five years back. It was like what I imagine

Bungee jumping to be. Almost snapped my neck on the recoil. Sure as hell chased away the agonies from a night in a frozen tent. Forgot all about my damn-near broken ankle and the wicked horse that did it to me.

Here's how you make Cowboy coffee: When you hear the bells clanking on the horses necks, as the wranglers bring them in from their night pasture, take one of those big old cast iron coffee pots down to the creek. The three gallon one ought to be about right. It'll still be an hour or so before sunlight so you might want to take a flashlight. Dip the lip of the pot under the water. You'll likely get a soaker on one foot or the other as you straddle the stream. Don't mind the little sticks and leaves and sand and stuff that'll flow in. They won't affect the taste much and usually get dissolved up anyway. If a bit of tobacco slips out of your shirt pocket when you bend over, and falls in the pot, so be it. You can always offer a reward to whichever Cowboy finds it in his cup.

When you get it full, haul it back up to the cook tent. Get ready, because water will slosh all over Hell when you do this, and you might get something froze that you really didn't even want to get wet at that hour of the day.

The rest is simple. Set the pot on the wood stove. Grab three or four handfuls of coffee grounds (five if you have a small paw), toss them in to the pot and boil the piss out of the whole mess until the first Cowboy pokes his head in through the flaps of the cook tent.

Now here's the trick – and this has been passed down through generations of Cowboy coffee makers. Just before you pour a cup, dump in a little cold water. The thought here is that the cold water will settle the grounds back to the bottom of the pot. I always reckoned that this maneuver drops the temperature just enough so that you don't peel the hide off your first victim's tongue and thins the mix enough so that it will actually pour rather than sort-of clump out into the cups. Take your own read on that one.

Note the reactions of your Cowboys, as they sample the brew. You'll get a few who'll take a sip and almost immediately start yakin' about some

Latte they had in Seattle, or some Mocha they had in Chicago, or maybe some Cappuccino they got out of some vending machine in a rest area along the Interstate. You'll not see them back at the pot.

A few boys, though, will quiver a bit at their first bite, maybe flinch a little. The white part of their eyes might pink up for a second or two, but they won't cry. They might have to jam a hand into a pocket to look for something to hold on to, but dang if they ain't back for a second chunk in a minute, and no doubt, will visit the pot again before the morning is over.

Those are the boys with grit – true grit. They're the ones who'll end up being real Cowboys.

TIP - Food: I do not recall ever having had a bad meal in a Cowboy hunting cook tent. Even a bad hunting cook can usually whip something up, which to a hungry Cowboy, will seem like a King's feast. The problem seems to be with lunches. Some cooks make great ones – two meat sandwiches, some corn bread, a piece of fruit, crackers and cheese, maybe a bag or two of potato chips – others, not so hot – one sandwich and a bag full of candy.

This might not be so bad if you are still young and your metabolism is still tuned to a predominately sugar diet. However, if you are a little older (and we are the ones who can usually afford a Cowboy hunt) or if you already have a little sugar problem going on, the high-carb lunch may not work so well. You can expect to be in the saddle or hiking for anywhere from ten to twelve hours each day. You will be burning a ton of calories either way. I have found it particularly helpful to carry a little protein supplement of my own for later in the day – some hunter's sausage, maybe some jerky. A high carb snack late in the day can cause a high carb crash out and it may come just when you need to be most alert – say when a big Elk happens by.

Again, it might not be necessary, depending on the cook you draw, but it is better to evaluate your own metabolic situation and plan accordingly.

TIP - Personal Hygiene (again):

You are probably going to have to forget most of your personal hygiene regimes.

Shaving will be way more of a hassle than it is worth.

It's a good idea to keep your water bottle filled at night and in your tent. In the morning, you can use it to brush your teeth. If not, you will most likely have to break some ice off some kind of bucket to do it. Move away from the camp area to spit please.

Peri-anal areas can become quite inflamed during a cowboy hunt –particularly without proper cleansing. After using the latrine it is a good idea to have some sort of prepackaged wipe. Tucks is a good name brand.

Riding all day can provoke even the most dormant hemorrhoid into hostility. Think ahead if you are inclined to have problems in that area.

Riding can also cause a lot of general chaffing. Be sure to wear a pair of long-johns under your pants – period! Even in hot weather, a pair of polypros under your hunting pants can be a life-saver. Don't leave camp without them.

I have also heard that some hunters, who shall remain nameless, have learned to keep a small tube of diaper rash cream in their hunting jacket. It'll work wonders on the soft inner parts of a cowboy's thigh if a saddle has scraped the hide off.

TIP - Camp routines: The guides usually determine the wake-up and breakfast schedule. Most will come to your tent and wake you. However, you'll probably be up already. The sound of wranglers driving twenty or more horses back into the corral is hard to ignore.

Breakfast in bed would be nice, but it ain't gonna happen on a cowboy hunt. In fact, just sitting on your bunk with a cup of coffee for a few minutes isn't even a reality. Guides expect you to get up and get moving fast. Besides, unless some wrangler or camp helper has snuck into your tent and started your stove, it is going to be colder than a two-dollar hooker and you will want to get scrambling before something valuable gets froze off.

It's a good idea to get everything you plan to wear for the day stacked up the night before, for easy and systematic dressing in the morning. You don't want to be searching around in duffle bags for a particular garment in the cold – possibly the dark. Plan ahead.

It is quite likely that breakfast will be ready the minute you step into the cook tent. The guides will have notified the cook as to when he plans to leave and the cook will comply. Get in there and get fed.

The guides will stall around for a while after breakfast to give you time to use the latrine and re-fill your water bottles. Check your personal Hygiene items off the list as fast as you can. Don't forget to grab your lunch and your rifle and head to the corral. Chances are your guide will be there with your horse saddled ready to move out. Try not to hold him up too much. If you do, you will be getting up even earlier the next day to compensate.

TIP - Riding out: The actual time you leave camp in the morning can be a subject for intense argument.

Most rookie western hunters think that the same rules for hunting farm-land Whitetails apply to hunting Elk and Mule Deer on horseback. Most experienced western outfitters and guides will disagree. Here's why.

Elk and Deer (Whitetails too) can see perfectly well in almost total darkness. They can hear in any light. Taking a pack-train of hunters or even a single hunter up a mountain trail is a noisy venture. Horse hooves clatter among rocks constantly. The horses themselves huff and puff and fart and snort and generally make a ton of noise. If you ride through your hunting country before light, chances are excellent that you will not see any game in that area until evening. They will have seen you and will be long gone.

However, if you wait long enough to be able to see them at least as soon as they see you or shortly thereafter you just might have an opportunity to get a shot off. Believe it or not, but Elk and Mule deer will give you an unreal amount of time to shoot them. They are not intimidated by horses. To them, a rider on horseback is just another four-legged animal. Elk will stand around and watch you dismount and even load up and take aim before they bolt. Mule Deer will wait even longer. Many a fine wall hanger trophy was taken by a jump-shot taken by a rider seconds after dismounting from his horse. Again, most experienced guides know this and will not ride through prime hunting country in the dark.

That is not to say that you will not be riding in the frozen morning darkness. You will, but only to pass through less desirable country on your way to prime country or to get on top of a potential trophy you saw the night before. If you find yourself riding too early, you will know that your guide is planning to take you on a long trip or that he has some special purpose in mind.

The point is: if you find yourself riding out in the morning far later than you expected, do not be alarmed. Chances are good that you will be seeing some action early.

TIP - Guide naps: By the time your guide has put away the gear and turned down the covers for the horses he will not get to bed until an hour or so after you do. It is a certainty that he will begin the next day well over an hour before you do. You can bet that an afternoon nap will be in the works.

Don't fight it. In fact, join in. There is nothing sweeter than a clear, mountain air siesta in the sun, or even in the snow and rain. If you can't sleep, then just kick back and enjoy the view.

I have seen hunters get very upset because they were not hunting every minute of their trip. Good hunters know that the game is not moving very much in the middle of the day anyway and so it is far better to just hole up somewhere and wait. In any case expect your guide to be sleeping during the day. Bring a book.

UN-NORMAL CAMPS

Tom Terrific, Florida Dave and I glided over the Wasatch Range on a clear crisp mountain morning and dropped into Salt Lake City, just like we had done it before, which, of course we had. We spent the next hour doggedly performing all the standard airport labors of deplaning, scrambling for the first men's room, waiting at the baggage claim, hauling gear, begging for our guns, hauling gear, standing in line at the car rental counter, hauling gear and finally getting the hell out!

We headed north out of the land of too-many-wives and then turned east and started climbing up. We were looking for a deserted two-track that allegedly stumped off into the main road at about the ten mile mark, then terminated about twenty miles up at a camp of some sort, where we were to meet our guides. We found the road, bounced up the twenty miles and bingo, there was the camp as advertised, complete with a corral full of critters and a nice little, two-story log cabin – smoke drifting lazily out of the chimney like in a Hallmark Christmas card. After many years of tent camps, a cabin was going to be a treat.

I was driving and had the window down since it was such a nice morning. Each season has its own scent. I love them all in the mountains, but for some reason the fall scent sparks a planetary hormone release that only hunters appreciate. The air was full of it – full of it at least until we made the last turn into the little valley that held the camp. Then, as if someone had flipped a switch, a new scent, one I really couldn't quite identify, replaced the normal combo of pine, sage, decaying vegetation, dirt and horse shit.

We were used to riding horses into our camps, usually as part of a long pack train of guides, hunters, wranglers and packhorses loaded with gear. We drove right up to the cabin at this one and parked in a little lot next to a stairway leading up to the second floor. Our guides stepped out onto the porch and the usual greetings, handshakes and chatter commenced. That little scent, which greeted us as we entered the valley had by now become…well, the only scent in the neighborhood. It wasn't really unpleasant, just a little strong.

In most camps, the wranglers schlepped our gear off the pack horses and right up to our tents for us. When our guides told us that we had the whole upper floor to ourselves and that we should use the stairway to move in, it became apparent that would not be the plan at this camp. Soon, we were hauling gear again, but this time up a narrow staircase pinned to the outside of the cabin wall.

I was first up. The stairway had a small landing at the top, which led to a simple door with a half widow at the top. I turned the knob and opened the door. "Holey Jamokes," I said to no one. I could not believe my nose. That little scent, which had been smoldering in the background, only barely perceptible in the subconscious, had suddenly become a raging stink that slapped my face, just like Shirley Watson had done thirty years earlier when I suggested we . . . well, never mind.

I lowered my head like a fullback and pushed my way through whatever was hanging in the air and dragged a duffle bag into the dusty room. I turned back toward the door to see Tom forcing his way in.

"What the . . . ," he said, nose twitching like a Beagle with allergies. "What is that?"

"Yeah," I said. "It smells a little musty in here."

"Musty? Jees. There is something dead here."

"That ain't dead. It's something else."

"Yeah, several somethings are dead in here."

The room itself was not that bad, although it was a little hard to see through the smell. It needed a little Martha Stuarting or maybe just someone with a vacuum cleaner, but overall, it would do.

I'd seen dormers before and this was typical. It was one large room, with a scattering of beds, each with an antique mattress and a sheet or covering of some sort stretched lazily across it. We each chose one, with little idea as to criteria. It didn't matter. The idea of sleeping on an actual mattress for the next week had a certain appeal after so many hunting nights on tattered army cots in frozen tents.

It took about ten minutes to move in and organize our bedrolls. We sat on our beds for a minute contemplating our next move. I rubbed my fingers together. They felt oily. Hmmmm? There were pictures of sheep on all the walls – lots of them – momma sheep, daddy sheep, and all kinds of baby sheep. It was an interesting decorating scheme, to say the least. What ever happened to mountain cabins with Moose heads and stuffed fish?

Someone yelled from the floor below that lunch was ready. A narrow, rickety, internal stairway led down to the kitchen-dinning room-living room-master bedroom-only room – combo, which made up the rest of the cabin. We worked our way down in single file, using the grimy walls to steady our balance. They were oily. They had dozens of sheep pictures on them, like the family portraits and graduation pictures you might see on the stairways of suburbia. All the lamps were made from sheep legs. Cute really.

Tom said, "What was this place a sheep herder's cabin or something."

Very good Tom.

"Yeah," one of the guides said. "Was built almost one-hundred-and-fifty years ago. Had something like three or four generations of sheep herder's from South America working it. Ran sheep through this whole country."

"What's that smell?"

Our two guides looked at each other. "What smell," they said in two-part harmony.

For the next week, we shared that cabin with the two guides and that smell. It had become an entity all to itself. It woke us up in the middle of the night to chat and greeted us each morning with its oily smile. It landed on and crawled into everything. Even the horses smelled like sheep.

In the end, the guides were great, the horses better and the hunt a lot of fun. I was reminded of it every time I used any piece of my hunting gear, knife, flashlight, binoculars, boots – you name it – for the next three years. The smell of that camp had entwined itself inextricably into every piece of equipment I had. I actually had to have my camo hunting coat washed. Go figger!

HORSE STORIES

HORSES

THE HEART OF COWBOY HUNTING

There is some controversy as to whom - Will Rogers, Winston Churchill or President Ronald Reagan - said; "There's nothing better for the inside of a man than the outside of horse," but whoever said it was clearly on to something. Take the horse away and you've torn the heart out of any western hunting experience and ripped the soul out of Cowboy Hunting.

NO LAKERS NO DALLAS

On a clear, hot Tuesday, a few million years ago, The Great Plains of America suddenly swelled and gave birth to the Rocky Mountains. If you had been walking in the eastern foothills of the young Rockies, on say Thursday, you might have come across a small Border Collie-sized, five-toed creature called an Eohippus in Greek, or "Dawn Horse."

Those were hot times in the Rockies – tropical in fact. Eohippus made its living munching the leaves of the great varieties of plants along the remains of steamy, shallow seas, which, in prehistory, bathed the west.

Blink – along comes the Ice Age. The broad-leaf plants disappear and are replaced by grasses. Eohippus has to make some changes. He drops off four toes and lets the middle one grow into a big broad hoof – perfect for running in grassy meadows and scaling along rocky outcroppings. He puts on about 1200 pounds and grows five feet in height. His neck grows long and muscular. His cardiovascular system expands to near Lance Armstrong size. His ears sprout so he can hear predators coming and his tail grows to swat away the pesky bugs. Eohippus becomes Black Velvet and every Horse John Wayne ever road.

During the Ice Age the horse migrated to just about everywhere else on the planet. Then, to the unending theories of anthropologists and other "ologists" of various persuasions, the horse totally died off in North America, their ancestral birth place.

Coincidentally, as the horse was dying off, Humans were proliferating. Many researchers are pointing to the bones of over 40,000 horses found outside a settlement in France, which dated back over 25,000 years, as proof that man was responsible for the demise of the horse. Simply put; we were eating them. Regardless, by about 8000 years ago, horses were extinct in Cowboy land.

However, they did not die off in other parts of the world and soon explorers like Cortez, Coronado and Desoto brought bunches of horses back home when they began exploring the deserts of Southwestern United States and Northern Mexico. The horses, of course, proliferated in their natural home. By the year 1600, the Plains Indians had acquired horses and over the next 100 years, the Ute, Apaches and Kiowa Indian tribes helped spread the population of horses far north into Utah and east to the Missouri River. The Nez Perce took them all the way to Canada. Horses and Indian Tribes became inextricably linked in the west until at least 1886 when the white man managed to slaughter the last of the remaining Buffalo and ruin a unique culture.

Meanwhile, in the East, breeders had molded the grandsons of Eohippus into a diverse herd of mounts – Arabians, Barbs, Turkmeres, Thoroughbreds, Morgans, Quarter Horses, Standardbreds Tennessee Walkers, Palominos, Pintos, Paints, Buckskins, Appalosas and more. Anybody who had any work to do, or who wanted to travel anywhere, did so by horse – period. That led to a grinding earthquake change in man's conquest of the land.

Soon malcontent farmers, visionary pioneers, miners and fortune seekers of all feathers began what would become a monstrous, horse-driven stream of guiltless humanity, blind industrialism and relentless civilization, which seemingly flowed mercilessly into every mouse hole of land, clean to the California shore. Without the horse, the westernizing of the country could not have been accomplished in anywhere near the time frame in which it was. With that in mind then, it is not hard to imagine that without the horse, to push it into reality, the wonderment of Los Angeles would probably have come too late to have caught the likes of Kareem Magic and The Shaq. Indeed, it is likely that without the horse, we would never have had the Lakers at all. And, without the horse, there certainly would have been no Cowboys – Dallas or otherwise.

TIP - Cowboy Hunting: Cowboy hunting means horses! The lure might be the visual – a silhouetted man on a horse, outlined against the sunset, a hat, chaps, two hands resting on a saddle horn. Maybe it's something more subtle, like the creaky sound the saddle makes when you step into it, or the steam wafting up off the horse's rump. Maybe it's their sounds – the foot-stomping, the snorting. Maybe it's the smell.

COWBOY GYMNASTICS

Five of us were standing next to our mounts one day, out on a knife ridge, with pristine valleys trailing away hundreds of feet below – a normal place for Cowboy hunters to be. It was so steep the horses had their hooves dug in up to the first knuckle and could not keep their gawking eyes focused on anything but the steep downhill below. To make things worse, a powerful and relentless wind threatened to throw us into eternity.

"When did you start riding horses, Bobby," Tom shouted, while trying to find a place to stand where he could put his feet next to each other rather than heel to toe.

"I remember better when I first starting falling off," Bobby yelled back with his ever pleasant smile.

"You? No,"

"Oh yeah, many times. I guess I was about three. My dad had a miniature pony. It couldn't have been more than about three hands or so tall, but still, I used to have to stand on my wagon to climb up on him. Anyway, that horse was a smart one, because he knew he could walk under the hitching post and scratch his back on the bottom of it. Every time I'd just get set on him, he'd head for the hitching post and scrape me off. I can remember that as clear as a bell."

And with that, Bobby put both hands upside down on his saddle horn, kicked his feet up into the air out over the precipice and did a back-flip into the saddle. All of our mouths dropped open, including the horse's. Bobby sat in his saddle grinning for a second, then spurred up his horse, dove off the edge and yelled back for us to follow.

Before my first Cowboy hunting trip, I thought I knew how to ride. As a young child, I'd spent hours riding on the arm of my mother's sofa, while Roy Rogers, Gene Autrey sang their way into my psyche on T.V. Later, when I was old enough, my dad would rent a horse and take my brother and me riding for an hour on some flat Michigan trail. When I got older, I carried on the tradition and took a rented horse out for an hour a few times every summer. By the time I was ready for my first Cowboy hunt, hell, I'd probably ridden twenty or thirty hours. I thought it was a significant amount. Boy, was I wrong! Worse, all of that extensive experience, with the exception of a few times when I could afford to take a horse out on one of my western jaunts, was on Michigan's flat, soft, dirt. But hey, riding is riding, right? Wrong again! There's nothing that can prepare you for Cowboy hunting.

On a bright blue-sky Wyoming day many years ago, Bobby led us out on our first Cowboy hunt. He was first in line, then his friend and fellow guide Harry, then Tom Terrific, then me and behind me, on a giant horse named Duke, was our old friend Pork Chop. Pork Chop would tend to overload a horse if he was naked. With his gear, he was way over the limit. That was exactly what Duke was for. Among horses, Duke was legendary. To get on him, you either had to pull him up next to a stump or walk him down into a ditch. Pork Chop looked like something out of a cartoon riding way up high back there in the rear.

We'd lined out from the ranch shortly after breakfast. The trail to the hunting camp was wide well-worn, like Interstate 75 heading down to Florida. The camp was about sixteen miles up in the backcountry. The riding was easy, just like in Michigan. I had it made. But, it's amazing how fast body parts start failing on a long horse ride. Knees go first.

I was beginning to wonder if Bobby and Jerry were ever going to stop to rest. They were 200 hundred yards ahead gliding along, with little movement, very smooth, like models walking down some Ralph Lauren runway. Tom, a.k.a. El Terrifico, was working like a wicked witch's winged monkey to stay caught up. To me, it was obvious he was in distress. He had this peculiar bounce in the saddle, kind of a side-to-side mambo. The look on his face was not good. He has a tendency to grey-up kind of fast. Later, he told me he had been concentrating on distributing his weight to only one cheek at a time, almost had it down, until he felt skin break loose.

Asses go right after the knees do. Ass blisters are unusually troublesome on cowboy hunts – particularly if they are on your first day out.

We almost needed binoculars to find old Pork Chop back there on the trail. He was holding on with both fists clenched tight around the saddle horn. Duke had one eye shut. The other was just a slit. It is not unusual for horses to catch a wink or two while they march along on a slow trail, but old Duke was snoring. That's downright unheard of - and rude I might add. Since Pork Chop wasn't doing it, the wrangler, who had been following behind with a pack string of mules, had taken to snatching pinecones off passing trees tossing them onto Duke's rump, to keep him moving.

"Bobby," I yelled. "Can we take a little break?"

"We just got started," he said, stopping, and turning around in the saddle.

It had been hours. I was afraid he'd say something like that. I didn't know anything on that first trip, but now after many years suffering guide abuse, I've got a few of their little tricks figured out. Smartest thing a guide can do is burn out the Cowboy-wannabe-hunter on day one. It makes the rest of the week so much easier. Instead of hearing; "why don't we do this" or "why don't we climb there," all the guide has to do is mention something halfway strenuous and all the hunters will protest in harmony, like the chorus section of St. Mary's choir - "No Wayayay."

"Yeah, but Bobby," I whined. "I only got a bladder the size of a walnut and look at old Tom Terrifico all greyed up everything and Duke, the poor thing needs a pillow."

"Well, we're gonna turn off just ahead and climb that ridge. We'll stop on top and rest."

"Thank you. Thank you Bwana,"

We climbed the ridge. It only took another fifteen minutes and once on top we did tie up the horses and thankfully, got out of the saddle. Duke passed out immediately, but did so, on a slight rise, so that his right side was up-hill from his downside. It was a long drop down from Duke when he was standing on flat ground. Now, given the rise he was on, the ground on his left side was easily two feet father down than normal.

Pork Chop didn't know squat about riding, but everybody knows you get on and off a horse on its left side -   Not so with mountain trail horses. When pork chop stepped down, the ground was nowhere to be found. In a second he was on his back, looking up. He had made his first accelerated dismount. Worse, his foot was still hooked in the stirrup. It was a damn good thing old Duke was sawing ZZZs. A rider dangling from a stirrup can be very unnerving to a horse. Makes them want to trot off dragging the rider through hell.

Jerry looked at Bobby. "Four point five"," he said.

Bobby nodded in agreement and said, "Sorry Pork, but we can only give you a four pointer on that one. Next time, keep your elbows in and point your toes. You didn't really stick the landing either. Now get out from under that horse, before you get stomped. "

TIP – Horses: Never walk behind a horse, without announcing your presence. A horse can look perfectly alert standing at a hitching rail and be sound asleep. If you walk up behind and startle him, you might find yourself kicked into next week. Make a little noise. Call out his name; say something nice about his mother. Let him know you are there.

If you have to approach a horse from the rear, do so from an angle, where it is tougher for him to get a direct kick at you. Walk up slowly, speak to him, gently place a hand on his rump. No horse really wants to hurt you, but they will if you surprise them.

TIP – Horses: Never let your guard down when you are on a horse. They are unpredictable beasts, prone to making sudden movements causing flat out wrecks without a second's notice. When you are in the saddle sit properly at all times never let go of the reins. Don't throw a leg up over the horse's neck like they do in the movies. Don't sit side-saddle in a western saddle. (Don't sit side-saddle when you are cowboy hunting, period). Don't take your feet out of the stirrups. Be prepared to jump or maybe even fly at all times.

TIP – Horses: Always step off a cowboy horse on the uphill side. It's true, normal horses are trained to allow riders on off on the left, but good mountain trail horses will tolerate either. Let him know you are going to do it, by slowly increasing the weight on your right stirrup. Once he catches on, you should have no problem.

Mountains are dangerous. A few years back, a man stepped off a horse a couple of miles from where we were at the time. He dropped off a steep slope, died when he crashed into the river below. He hit his head and drowned before anyone could get down to him. Broken legs and arms are even more common. Ask the guide ahead of time whether or not your horse is ambidextrous.

TIP – Horses: Let the guide or the outfitter take care of the horses. It doesn't matter how many times you have saddled one, or how much equestrian experience you have. No two people do it the same. It is their job and their responsibility, both professionally legally, to saddle your horse and make sure you are sitting on it properly. Let them take that responsibility, until they get to know you. They'll feel better and that will make them want to do a better job for you. Nobody likes a smart ass know-it-all.

TIP – Horses: Horses are extremely strong. Their cardiovascular systems are huge and incredibly efficient. Their muscles are massive. But, you can over load them and affect their performance to where it can be no fun for them or for you. The maximum load a normal horse can carry on an all-day all-week ride is about 250 pounds. Be careful what all you try to load on one and be mindful, as to how you load it.

The optimal Cowboy hunting configuration is saddle a with scabbard, two saddlebags and rigging in the front to keep the saddle in place on uphill climbs and more rigging in the rear to keep it from falling over the horses head on steep down-hills. That's almost thirty pounds.

Place your rifle in the scabbard and make sure that the shoulder strap is tucked in out of the way where some evil branch can't reach in drag it out (Rifles make a terrible noise when they clatter onto the rocks even worse when a horse steps on them). Put your water in the saddlebag on the opposite side. This will keep the two heaviest items balanced and keep your saddle from slipping sideways. Put your lunch in the opposite saddlebag.

Always take some rain gear and depending on the weather, a jacket of whatever weight seems necessary. Roll the jacket and the rain gear together into a tube and strap it to the rear of the saddle using the leather ties on the rear of the saddle.

Usually, the front of a saddle also has tie strings also. You can tie something small and light there, but remember this might interfere with your ride so be careful.

The first time you step into a saddle rigged like this, remember to swing your leg high and wide to clear all the gear. If not, you will catch your leg and before you know it you will experience an accelerated dismount too. More about those later.

TIP – Horses: Stirrup length is critical to surviving long rides. What seems good initially may prove fatal later on. When you stand in a saddle, your butt should lift off no more than an inch if you plan on gentle trail riding, with maybe a light trot from time to time. Stirrups that are too short will sore up a knee in a New York minute.

Peter (Captain Wiz Bang), a young and in-shape friend of ours, rode for two days with a short stirrup. His knees were very sore after the second day.

He didn't think much of it until he stepped in a shallow hole - nothing more than a depression - and ended up needing torn ACL surgery. The doctor said there was little doubt that the long ride had weakened the ligament to where it failed easily.

Long stirrups, on the other hand tend to come off when a horse trots. This can be very dangerous. It is imperative that your feet stay in the stirrups at all times. If you plan on doing a little more trotting or even a little galloping, you might want to shorten the stirrups a little to make it easier to keep your feet in them.

In either case, be sure to put no more than a toe length of your foot into a stirrup. Never put it in so far that the stirrup rests in the little depression before the heel where it looks like it would fit so nicely. If you have to get off that horse fast – a highly likely scenario when Cowboy hunting – you will not be able to and you could get seriously hurt - possibly killed.

As mentioned, one's ass goes right after his knees. There's really nothing to prevent that. You can post for a while if you know how, but that gets tiring. It looks good on a short ride, but after a couple of hours your post turns into a saddle-banging flop that almost tears your fillings out and stiffens your thigh muscles until they ignite.

TIP - Horses: "Lined out," is a cowboy term for getting a horse to ride evenly and smoothly down a trail. Most horses will do this, but it takes practice to get them into their rhythm.

TIP - Horses: You don't need to kick a horse to death. Just a light tap will do it. The trick is to do it regularly. Horses have a specific gait. Each one is different. Some are short and choppy (the worst to my way of thinking) others are long and smooth. After awhile you will begin to feel a horse's rhythm. Try to tap him at exactly the same point in every sequence of steps. Soon, he will get used to the taps and will respond if you begin to increase the frequency. You need to take control, rather than let him figure it out on his own.

TIP - Horses: How you hold the reins are important too. Keep them held a few inches out over his neck, give him slack. Too often, beginners will inadvertently keep the reins too tight. This sends mixed singles to the horse. He gets kicked and the bit in his mouth holds him back, then he gets kicked again and the bit holds him back again. He doesn't know what to do. A confused horse can be dangerous.

TIP - Horses: Don't lazy up along the trail. Nothing says rookie better than a rider who lags far behind the trail and then has to trot to catch up to everybody else. That said though, keep in mind, guides always take the best horses. Why not? Sometimes, there is simply nothing you can do to keep your horse lined out with the guide's. Don't get frustrated and start kicking. You can't change human nature and you sure as hell can't change horse nature!

TIP - Horses: Never let a horse eat along the trail. This will become the dominate thought racing through his little brain and will greatly influence his performance along the trail. If you are hunting, trail eating is particularly bad, because along with every mouthful the horse also inhales a ton of dust from the plants along the way. Invariably this will make him sneeze and cough. Remember, when you are hunting, you want to be quiet. A coughing horse can be heard for a long distance.

AIRBORNE

"This here's Bandit," Bill said, as he held the lead rope of a giant charcoal-black horse, while I got on. "He's a mustang."

"As in Wild Mustang," I said.

"Yep. You betcha. "Old Don Morris caught him and broke him."

Bandit was very tall, but not as long as most other horses, which gave him a compact look. His neck was very thick and muscular with a short-cropped, stiff mane that ran high on the back of his head, giving him a sort-of a crowned look. He held his head high. His ears were sharp and cocked forward. He had a menacing look in his eyes, which apparently old Don had been unable to break out of him. You can take the horse out of the wild, but you can't always take the wild out of the horse. I stepped up gingerly as he cast one of those wild black orbs on me. Everything about him said: back off.

But, he offered no resistance to my climbing aboard and, as it turned out, he was not a bad ride - very fast, very strong and very capable. Old Don, whoever he was, had done a pretty good job. The horse did have a bit of a quirk though.

We left our camp that morning and rode through a heavy, misty fog, which made sightseeing difficult. About an hour out, we were riding on a wide, mossy trail that ran through dense pines. The trail was flat. Ahead, through the mist, I could see a tree had fallen across the trail. It was only eight or ten inches in diameter, so any horse could easily step over it. It had not been cleared nor had the trail been altered to avoid it.

I watched as each horse ahead stepped over the tree without even breaking stride. When Bandit and I approached, I didn't think we would handle the situation any differently. But Bandit had a different view of trail obstructions. Instead of adjusting his stride to step over the log, he planted his front feet a few inches in front of it and jumped.

Okay, I thought. I had never had a horse jump over anything so small before, but whatever.

A short time later, we came upon a small stream that crossed the trail in a ditch a couple of inches deep and maybe a foot or two wide. All of the lead horses either stepped easily over the stream or just walked through it. Bandit planted his feet jumped it. Curious.

He jumped the next log on the trail too, the next stream, a rock pile, a gulley as time went on, anything in his path. Bandit was a jumper. He would much rather jump something than to step over it or walk around it.

I soon learned his pattern. He'd spot the other horses stepping over an obstruction of some type and, with his big eyes bulging and darting around in his head, he'd start maneuvering for a jump. I could feel his stride changing. I could see his head lining up his takeoff and landing zones. I could feel the slight hesitation as he planted for the leap. I could feel his big legs flex and then, zoom, off we'd go.

"Oooh, good one," he'd say when he really stuck a landing.

At one point, we were forced to stop to pick up a hat that had been scraped off by a passing tree branch. When we got back on the trail we were fifty or sixty yards behind the others, up ahead, a big log, maybe eighteen to twenty inches high lay completely across the trail.

"Bandit," I said. "Don't even think about it. "

"Sorry boss, but I gotta do that one."

"No way."

"Hang on." And, with that, he took off.

The trail had been diverted around this big tree. I tried to steer him to the detour. He would have none of it. I pulled back hard on the reins. He almost yanked them out of my hand with is big neck. Before I knew it, we were almost at a full gallop. And then, we were airborne.

"What? Do you guys think you're in some kind of fancy horse jumpin' show," Bill said as we caught up to the group.

"Ask him," I said, nodding toward Bandit. "I've asked him a dozen times to knock that off."

"Well, we don't much get into that kind of stuff around here. We don't want you getting hurt," Bill said.

"See, "I said to Bandit. "I told you, you were going to get us in trouble.

Apparently Bandit didn't care about trouble. Something told me he had been there before. And, as far as getting me hurt, well... whatever. He continued his jumping ways whenever we came to anything taller than a golf ball on the path.

The day smoothed out. The fog lifted. The sky turned blue, the temperature hung in the mid 60's, just perfect for mountain hunting and horse jumping.

We got on some good Elk that day and two of the boys took theirs. I was hoping for a good Mulie, before I got serious about Elk. It didn't happen and before we knew it night had fallen. It was a beauty. A full moon lifted gloriously just after sunset and lit up the sky to the book reading level. Bill and I had broken away from the rest of the tribe and were making our way down from the top in the moonlight. Bandit and I had reached a quasi-truce. I promised that if he would not try to jump every little, tiny, miniscule artifact in the road, I would not hassle him when he jumped the bigger ones. A quasi-truce until… .

I could see Bill up ahead clearly in the moonlight. I could follow his zigs zags easily. I could see the trees as they passed the ground with no problem. I could see whatever it was bandit was jumping. We had been following a good trail down through a stand of dark trees. The moonlight fell in irregular patches everywhere. Suddenly we pulled out into a clearing – a slash more or less through the trees. I could hear the rush of water. Bill pulled up. He and his horse were searching for a good place to cross. The water sounds became louder. Bill and his horse dropped off a bank and were gone.

"Whoa." This was not merely a little creek. This was a river we were crossing. The bank, in front of me, dropped four or five feet to a rocky splash of water eight to ten feet across. The bank on the other side was every bit as tall. I saw Bill and his horse crawl up the opposite wall. "This could be trouble here Bandito," I said.

He did not answer. Apparently his attention was elsewhere. I eased him up to the bank. I could feel his familiar nervousness. His head bobbed back forth as he searched for good footing. I tried to ease him off the edge down the slope. I wanted him to walk through as Bill's horse had done. I knew what he was thinking. I pulled him back walked him down the stream a little looking for another spot where maybe it was not so steep. Maybe I could ease him off on a more gentle descent. He would have no part of it. He paced back forth on the edge of the bank shivering stomping his feet. Then, he calmed and planted both front feet. I felt his muscles tense.

"No waaaaay," I said as I rocketed out of the stirrups. " Bandit, don't you dare."

We were using split reins I had only enough time to grab one as I hit the ground. Bandit's eyes were the size of grapefruit. The moon reflected off his corneas and made them sparkle like giant Obsidian pearls. I tried my best to lead him down the slope, but his mind was made up. I slipped down the bank, losing my balance. I hit a slippery rock, in a split second I was on my back in the river, one hand still holding bandit's rein, his huge bulk still hesitating on the bank above me.

Then, everything was silent. Motion slowed to a crawl. Bandit was airborne.

The lakes of Hell will be frozen hard as rock, and the Pyramids will be worn down to stumps, when I forget the sight of that giant horse sailing over me. The moon lit the sky behind him, silhouetting him in an eerie glow. His black eyes bulging and flickering looked like radar domes on the bottom of a plane. Both stirrups, lighter without my feet in them, stuck out at right angles from his body horizontally like wings. The saddlebags bulged out like jet engine pods along his fuselage. My jacket, tied behind the saddle became aft stabilizers his tail flew straight up like any jet tail completing the picture.

He lowered his head as he flew over and snorted huge clouds of jet vapor my way. Then, he crashed.

Motion returned to hyper speed. I was still holding one rein on bandit. He had misjudged the bank on the other side. Hooves clattered against rocks. He staggered. He fought. He pulled. Clumps of rock dirt flew from beneath his scrambling feet. And, finally he stood gloating on the other side.

I stood, dripping ice water.

"Wouldn't it have been easier to just walk across the damn thing like a normal horse," I asked.

Bandit just stood there, grinning from ear to ear, his big teeth gleaming in the moonlight. Bill rode back to see what was up.

"Decided to walk him across, hey," he said.

"Yep, figured I better."

"Good thinking. That horse usually jumps stuff like that."

Cowboys sometimes go way out of their way to point out the obvious.

TIP - Horses: Give your horse his head. You pick the trail, but let him handle the task of walking along it. Most are far more sure footed than you think. They don't want to fall down any more than you want them too. They walk along on four legs, something like how we are when we crawl on all fours. It is far less likely that you would fall on all fours than if you were standing - so too with a horse.

TIP - Horses: Frequently a horse will choose to jump. Usually it will be when crossing a very steep V-shaped draw. It is cumbersome for him to walk all they way to the bottom then try to make his back bend to conform to the V – so they jump. Lean into the jump. There is some art to it. Don't just sit there and flop back on your saddle, hands scrambling for the horn. Bend your knees, lean into the jump; try to balance your weight to conform to the flow of the horse. After a few practice jumps, you'll get the hang of it – hopefully.

TIP - Horses: Don't be afraid to get off if you are uncomfortable with a situation. You are far better off to walk a horse than to get hurt. Don't worry about appearances – your guide will be glad to see you use common sense.

WHAT WOULD RAY CHARLES DO?

Broadway Joe Willie Namath and the Jets winning the superbowl, Neil Armstrong setting foot on the moon, Keith Richards doing Hamlet – some things just stick in your mind forever. For me, I will never forget my first night, on horseback, hunting Elk in the Rockies.

So far that day, my horse had taken me over the edge of a cliff and straight down on a vertical death drop to the bottom of the valley below. He had mashed me into several trees along the trail in an attempt to get me off his back. He'd stomped kicked snorted and fought me for miles. He'd sored up my butt, made me crazy with constant arguing and name calling. And now, night was falling.

Mountain Dick and I had been out looking for Elk on another beautiful mountain day. I was absolutely giddy with the pure joy of the ordeal, horse problems not withstanding. Dick had managed to put me on a good stand, where a well-planned drive by some otherwise bored wranglers had paid off with a nice Elk. We'd just finished dressing it out and covering it with pine branches for the night, when night did indeed fall.

Out on the plains or on the ocean, night takes a long time to arrive. The light lingers in the sky for hours making it comparatively easy to see for a long time. In the Mountains, when it is lights out, it is lights out! Click and it's dark. Not half-light, or twilight, but dark, mean black, dark, can't see, nighttime. That kind of dark.

I hadn't really considered that fact during the day. The excitement of the proceedings had blotted out such practical matters, but now, while searching on my horse's side with my hands for the stirrup, I suddenly realized that I couldn't even see my feet and we were at least nine miles from camp.

Dick had brought my horse to me and I finally managed to climb aboard, but that made things worse. I couldn't see the ground, the trail, the trees or even the horse. I literally could not see my hand when I held it in front of my horse. There was no moon and a cloud front had obscured the stars.

"Dick? You there?"

"Grunt."

"I've got a problem."

"Grunt grunt."

"Well, I can't see a thing."

"Grunt grunt grunt follow me grunt grunt."

Guides take the best horses. Wouldn't you? But, because they do, you will never be able to completely keep up with them. Dick was gone in seconds. It is difficult to explain how strange it is to be suddenly blind, sitting on a moving horse, lost in an area where you know up down only by how the blood is flowing through your head. Worse, we were moving very fast. Most horses do not have to be coaxed into heading back to the barn.

"Dick?"

If he grunted back, I did not hear it.

"Dick?"

Nothing.

"This is getting serious here folks," I said to no one, not realizing at the time that you could talk to a horse without anyone thinking you were a slice of bread short of a sandwich. "I can't see the ground let alone the trail."

Dick was not listening. The horse was not listening. He took off as soon as I was in the saddle. I tried reining him back a little just to see if I had any control, but he did not stop. He was on his pace back - apparently understanding that I was useless and had absolutely no idea where we were going. If he had taken a notion to jump off a cliff, I would not have known it until we were in the air.

I sat back in the saddle and let the reins hang loosely in my hands. I could do nothing but hope that the horse knew more than I did. Can you imagine? Here was this dumb, stupid animal that I had been calling an idiot all day. I had been belittling him and making comments about his attitude and his personal hygiene habits. And now, I was trusting my very life to him. Go figure!

Within seconds, a Pine tree – the whole thing - hit me in the face, almost knocking me off the horse. I lay flat back in the saddle, with my head resting on his rump. Still, the rough branches scraped across my face, ripping a substantial chunk of ear hide loose. Another hit me in the knee, spearing me like a Knight's lance. We walked on. Suddenly, the horse made a ninety-degree turn to the right. I had no way of knowing we were about to do that and found myself leaning far out into space over the horse's left flank. Then, just as suddenly, we turned back 180 degrees to the left and I went sailing out over the right flank, coming dangerously close to sailing off altogether. Then, boom, straight down. Then, boom, straight up. Then right. Then left. I was bobbing in the saddle like a dashboard hula dancer. Another tree clobbered me in the chest and another stuck me in the arm.

"Diiiiiick?"

Nothing.

I considered getting off and walking, but quickly realized that the only one around who knew, or at least seemed to know, where we were and where we were going was the horse.

"You're my only hope," I whispered in his ear,"

"Wrong," he said. "You're totally hopeless."

And with that, he really took off.

I could do nothing to control that horse. He was going home and I was merely an annoyance, which he could endure. The question was whether I could endure? After an hour of bobbing in the dark, fighting countless trees, which I did not remember having seen on the way up, I was fairly well jellied, beat like a dirty rug.

Then, my horse started trotting.

"Enough," I said, to no avail.

The trotting was bad, but an entirely different terror began working its way into my conscience. I could hear water roaring, far below me to my right. To my left, if I looked up at the sky and strained my eyes, I could occasionally see the top of a high hill, not more that a few feet from me. I recognized this spot. We were side-hilling on a very narrow trail – a few inches across – on the side of a slick rocky hill, thirty or forty feet above a white-capped rapid. If this horse misplaced a single hoof, we would both go hurling out into space and smash mercilessly onto the rocks below. Gulp!

"Whoa, whoa, whoa, whoa," I said yanking back on the reins.

It did no good. Why he continued trotting was a mystery. Did horses have hidden suicidal traits? It didn't matter. I was doomed to sit there and let this insane beast take me home or to Hell.

He took me back to camp. I was never so glad to see the artificial glow of Coleman lanterns. To this day, unless the moon is shinning enough to light up the trail, I hate riding at night. Unfortunately, it is a mandatory part of Cowboy hunting.

TIP - Horses If you cowboy hunt, you will want to stay out through dusk - the prime time for spotting game. It will be necessary, therefore, to ride back to camp in the dark. Losing your sense of vision and your control in the total darkness of mountain night, is a difficult thing to get used to. But, get used to it you must. You will not fully understand the difficulty involved here until you do it.

TIP – Horses: Let the horse take control. Horses are amazing creatures. They are far more capable than you would think. Most horses need to walk a trail just once to memorize it forever. If you don't know where you are going let the horse lead you where he wants. Invariably he will take the shortest route back to camp.

Keep in mind; horses see very well on even the darkest of nights. They have the same reflective membranes on the retinas of their eyes that Deer, Elk, Cats, Dogs most mammals other than humans have. They can always see the trail.

Further, horses see everything in 25% magnification when compared to humans. So, even small details on the trail appear large to them. This can be a problem at times, because they frequently see "boogeymen."

From time to time, a horse will pull up with a start and frequently jump several feet away. Who knows what it is that startles them so. It might be a rock, a clump of brush even a stump they've walked past a dozen times before. But, for some reason, it looks different to them at that particular time of that particular day and off they will go. They see boogeymen a lot at night, so be prepared.

Pay attention. Even though the horse will be calling the shots, don't get sloppy in the saddle. He might stumble, or just plain freak out at the sight of a stump and in either instance you could find yourself suddenly airborne in Ray Charles' world.

WILD STRAWWBERRIES

A reddish brown horse with white hairs intermingled is called a Strawberry Roan. I rode one appropriately named Strawberry on an Elk Deer trip in the Wyoming range. He was, for the most part, a great horse, tall and strong with an easy gate. Like most horses, he had a little quirk.

Sometimes when a group of riders gets lined out on a trail, considerable spaces can develop between animals. Everyone tries to avoid that, but it happens. I was riding drag (last in line) the first day out. The rider in front of me was an inexperienced hunter/rider named Jeff. He was having a difficult time keeping up with the rest of the string. I constantly had to wait for him. Each time I did, I noticed Strawberry becoming progressively more anxious. When we came to turns in the trail, and for a second or two, could not see the other horses, Strawberry would break into a nervous whiney and almost crash into the horse in front of him.

This went on for the entire morning, until Strawberry was beside himself with worry that we were going to somehow become separated from the main group. When we tied up for lunch, I chose a tree a few paces away from the rest, because all the others were taken by the time we approached – a few paces, maybe thirty yards. Strawberry spent the break, stomping his feet whinnying even though he could easily see the rest of the group.

We split up after lunch. The wranglers took the pack string into camp, while our guide Bobby, Jeff and I headed up to the top of the ridge. Strawberry pitched a small fit when the wranglers and the majority of the horses disappeared, but soon settled down when he realized that he would be with two other horses not – God forbid – left alone.

"Shut up Strawberry," Bobby said. "That dang horse."

"Is he always so noisy," I asked.

"No. Normally he's a pretty good ride."

"He's a good ride, but it seems like he doesn't like getting separated from the group."

"Yeah, some horses are like that."

Bobby said nothing more about Strawberry's particular quirk and apparently Strawberry himself had gotten over it, because he was silent for the remainder of the day and a very good ride.

We had seen nothing all day – a couple of lone Elk on a sidehill far off in the distance and a single doe Deer. We pulled up at the top of a long narrow draw, which Booby said, ran from here, at the top of the ridge all the way to the bottom on the trail a few miles above camp. We could go no higher. The sun would be setting in an hour or two.

Bobby sat in silence for a long time. He looked at the sun and back at his watch. He turned in the saddle and scanned the valley in all directions. Clearly he was plotting something.

"You got a vision, boss," I said.

"Well, this draw runs all the way down to the main trail. It's a short cut, but it's steeper than hell and almost impossible to hunt. Once you start down, you gotta just slide your way all the way to the bottom. It's a good two miles, then it cliffs up big time at the bottom. Old Charlie McCafferty and I did it one time, and burnt the hide off the bottom of our shoes. We'da took a rest, if we coulda got stopped. "

The new guy Jeff, gulped and paled a little.

"But every time I ever went down it, Bobby went on. "I scared something up. Both Elk and Deer. It's a good hiding place. The problem is that they just peel off down the draw so fast, that I could never get a shot at them."

"Could we get somebody down at the bottom to ambush them when you came down," I asked.

"Well, I always thought that'd be a good plan, but I have never been able to get it together. "

It is an unwritten rule in the guiding business: Never let a hunter go off by himself - especially on horseback.

"Do you know where this draw comes out on the main trail above camp?"

By asking me this question, I could sense that Bobby, a very experienced guide and part owner of the entire operation was about to break a major camp rule.

"Well, I know where two skinny draws like this one come down on the right."

"This one is the first. Do you know where the main trail meets this one we're on?"

"Yes."

"Well, why don't you ride down the main trail to where that second draw is. Just ride right past this one. Tie your horse at the second one, and then hike back up to this one and get ready. We'll wait until just before dark and then come busting down this thing. If anything is feeding out, we'll get it running and maybe you'll get a chance. If not, we'll see you at camp."

I saluted said, "Yes sir. Should I wait for you at the bottom?"

"No. We won't go all the way down. Gets too steep down there. I don't want old Jeff here to get killed before he gets his first Elk."

Jeff perked up a little. Some of the terror left his face.

"There's a side trail," Bobby went on. "'Bout halfway down. We'll take it and come out just above camp and then drop down. We'll see you in camp, unless we hear a lot of shootin'."

I turned Strawberry around and headed out. I'd been in the area many times before, and knew the trails well – probably the reason Bobby let me go on ahead. I had no problem finding the bottom of the draw. I rode past it, tied Strawberry to a good pine tree. He had only whinnied once when we left the other two horses. He must have sensed that we were going back toward camp and going back to the corral always trumps any fears a horse might have. After a half-mile hike back, I found a downed tree at the bottom of the draw, huddled in behind its trunk in a cluster of dried branches and waited. The temperature began to drop. The shadows of the trees began to lengthen and night began to fall.

It was another beautiful evening in the mountains. I sat there, quite content just to breath the sweet smells of evening, and listen to the songs of the birds gathering a last snack before hiding away in their holes. After a while, I heard a single "click" from the direction of the draw. Sometimes a single "click" is all you'll hear before almost getting trampled by a herd of Elk. A few seconds later I heard another one. Something was definitely coming down that draw.

I lifted the rifle and propped it well on the log. I glanced through the scope to make sure the view was clear. I didn't have to wait long. Cow, calf, calf, cow, cow, spike bull, cow, cow, calf, all sprinting down into the meadow in front of me - no horns other than the spike. I waited. More clicks. Something was still coming – maybe a nice bull. They tend to come out last. It was a bull alright, directly on the heels of the Elk. Unfortunately, it was a moose. He was young, shovels only the size of shovels. Nice to watch, but I had no Moose tag. He was too small anyway. Bobby was right that draw did hold game, but nothing I was interested in at the time.

I waited until almost dark before hiking back to Strawberry. I wished I had never left him.

The half-mile between the two draws was not a flat run. In fact, the trail crossed over a substantial hill. I really hadn't noticed it in my haste to get back to where I intended to make my stand. From where I had been hiding, I could neither see nor hear Strawberry. Unfortunately to his utter horror, neither could he. As soon as I crested the ridge, I began to hear his frantic cries. By the time I got to him, I was the one who felt like crying.

Never before or since have I seen a horse look that bad. He had more lather on him than a Playboy Bunny in a bubble bath. His nostrils were as big as tennis balls, his eyes glowed in the semi-dark like red hot charcoal Briquettes. Wispy feathers of steam rose from his back. Locomotive vents of steam roared from his nose. His ears flattened against the back of his head, then jutted straight, cocking from side to side frantically searching the air for salvation. Long red streams of blood trailed from multiple stabs along his neck, back and rump. This horse was a mess. And, he was in my care.

Strawberry stood facing the stout six-inch spruce to which I had tied him. My knot held. I wished it hadn't the poor thing would have been able to slip away run back to camp and to the camaraderie, which he craved. He stood now, intent on facilitating his own escape by destroying the tree. He had thus far, removed all of the remaining branches both above and below his height by ramming them with his head neck flank and snapping them off - cutting his hide in the process. He'd excavated the ground in a doughnut circle around the tree to a depth of a foot. He'd strained the rope into a tight knot against the tree, by constantly revolving around it looking for an escape, he'd girdled the bark off to a depth of an inch. It seemed his next gambit would be to literally pull the tree out of the ground by the roots and drag it to safety with him.

He barely noticed me when I approached. When he finally did, he jerked his head up with a start and glared at me as intently as he had been at the tree. Something told me this was not going to be a gentle ride back to camp. I wasn't sure I even wanted to go back to camp. I could not imagine explaining to Bobby about how it had happened that one of his best riding horses was standing out in the corral bleeding, lathered, frantic after a short ride with me in charge. No thanks.

I had a bigger problem. I had to get this horse untied and calmed down before either of us could go anywhere.

I moved forward. He growled at me. I backed off. I tried again. He growled and pounded the ground.

"I'm here to help."

"You are the one who tied me like this."

"Don't growl."

"Go to hell."

"Hey – that's enough. These woods are full of mountain lions. You know what their favorite food is? That's right Strawberries. I could leave you here in the dark, by yourself, you know."

Old Strawberry hadn't thought about that. He looked sheepishly from side to side, and then, stepped back while I untied the lead rope. But, the instant I did, he snapped his head up as hard as he could in a futile attempt to snatch the rope from my hand. He did it again and again, constantly stepping backwards, trying to free himself from me.

"No way, big boy. No way I can let you go now. You go back into that camp all tore up like you are, sweating and all, with no me, and those guys are going to freak out. This valley will be filled with helicopters and swat teams and hostage negotiators and sirens and whistles, and news anchors. Maybe even some cheerleaders, who knows what."

"Yeah, yeah, yeah, the more the merrier. I hate being alone."

"No kidding. I think you've made that quite clear. Just calm down, and I'll get you home, I promise I won't ever leave you alone again."

"You promise?"

"I promise."

"Can I have some oats?"

"Can I have a ride?"

Strawberry and I walked for a mile or so, talking idly. We still had three or four miles before we would get back to camp. I wanted to walk him for a while to cool him down. Besides, I tried twice to remount him, and the S.O.B. would have none of it. However, I was determined. If it took all night I was going to get back on that horse and ride him into camp. And, I did. After almost thirty minutes of sweet-talk he let me back on and I rode him in, under a starry sky.

I still had to explain to Bobby about the blood and the puncture wounds.

Bobby was not around when I got back to the corral. One of the wranglers put Strawberry away while I stowed my gear and headed for the cook tent for dinner. In a minute, Bobby bust through the tent flaps bigger than life, his broad Jo Menji shoulders scraping the sides as he moved toward me. Gulp.

He sat down. "What happened to Strawberry," he asked softly. "He's bleeding."

We were Cowboys. Cowboys don't cower behind puny excuses. They don't whimp-out over a little horse trouble. They face their responsibilities like men and let the consequences fall where they may.

"He got a little out of line. I had to stab him a few times with my pocket knife."

"Whew," Bobby said, wiping at his forehead. "We were worried that he was back to his old tricks. Used to be that horse would freak out any time you tied him by himself. Tear up the tree. Tear up the ground. Tear up himself. Get all lathered up whine like a baby. But I reckon we got him broke of all that stuff. "

"Strawberry did that? Naw. Not Strawberry."

TIP - Horses Just about every horse has a quirk of some kind.

They had one at the ranch in Wyoming who was by all standards an excellent trail horse - good rider, easy going, fast, responsive, the whole bit.

But you could not tie that horse to a horizontal hitching rail - no matter what. If you did, he would totally lose control and do just about anything to get unhooked, including tearing the hitching rail out of the ground. I learned that the hard way one day and almost got my head stomped. The reason? simple. One day the horse stood quietly sleeping while tied to a hitching rail next to a barn. A barn Swallow nest suddenly broke loose from the peak just under the roof, and landed smack on the horse's head. Possessing nothing more than horse sense the poor critter associated the accident with the hitching rail rather than with the barn, or the birds and refused to ever stand tied to one again.

You will never be able to cure a horse of a habit like that - especially in a week or two. The best you can do is to learn to work around it.

TIP - Horses: Movie Cowboys ride up to the hitching post, wrap their reins around the horizontal piece a couple of times and strut into the bar. Never tie your horse to anything by the reins for more than a second or two. If you do, you can bet, you'll be working some kind of a leather punch in hopes of welding two pieces of leather back together again. A horse can turn his head and snap a rein easily.

A horse wears two types of gear on his head. The reins are part of the bridle assembly. They are historically made of leather, but today, all kinds of nylon and neoprene contraptions can be found. The reins are attached to the bit, the metal part that fits in the horse's mouth. The bit then is attached to the rest of the leather pieces that fit around the horses head, called the headstall. The bit, bridle and reins are the steering wheel and are only used to drive the horse around.

Beneath the bridle is the halter. This is a rope or heavy nylon affair that wraps securely around the horses head. The lead rope is attached to the halter.

Bridles are weak. Halters are strong. If you have to lead a horse very far or if you want to tie him to something, use the lead rope and a slip knot.

TIP - Horses: Some horses won't lead if you look at them. Turn around. Grab the lead rope a foot from their chin and start walking. Most of the time, they will follow. Occasionally a horse might need a little incentive. A light tap on the rump usually works.

TIP - Horses: Never walk under the lead rope when the horse is tied. This can spook a horse. He can rear back, tear the cross member of a fence off and club you in the head with it. Or, he might come forward and when he reaches the end, land on top of you. You have no where to run when you are in this very vulnerable position.

When you walk around a horse, keep a hand on him as you slide down his side toward his rump. Keep it on him as you move quickly around his rump. Stay close to the horse. If he decides to kick, his maximum power will be three to for feet out. If you are close you may not get tagged too badly.

Remember, never approach a horse, or put a hand on one without speaking to him first. If you startle him, you might get hurt.

TIP - Horses: Keep your face and fingers away from the horses mouth. You might see some movie Cowgirl hugging her horses muzzle playing a little kissy face with him, but that's the movies. Some horses bite – especially strangers. A woman in Wyoming we have known for years, had her lower lip and chin removed by a good horse with whom she had been friends for years. She kissed him. He kissed her back. She spent hours in the operating room having cosmetic surgery to repair the damage. He went back to eating oats, not realizing he had done anything wrong.

TIP - Horses: When you tie a horse, look for a live tree four to six inches in diameter. Get a dead one and he will snap it off. You will want to tie the horse at about **his** eye level so try to find one that has few if any branches at that level that would hinder his movement or poke him in the eyes. Leave enough slack – 18 inches or so – enough for him to be able to move his head some, but not enough for him to be able to lower his head far enough to feed. If you do, he will, and you can bet that you'll come back to a horse wreck of some kind. If you leave him too much slack, he might just decide to lay down and take a roll. When this happens with your saddle gear still on board, you will definitely have a mess.

Never tie a horse to a fallen log. He just might decide to take the log back to camp with him when you ain't lookin'.

TIP - Horses: It's perfectly okay to talk to your horse. Cowboys have been doing that since the dawn of Cowboyism. In the olden days, they had no one else to talk to. These days, the pressures of trying to be a cowboy in our modern society would drive anyone to horse talk. Most horses make good sense. You can learn a thing or two by talking to one every now then.

WHAT KIND OF GOOFY HORSE IS THAT?

"Which one of you is the most experienced rider?"

Tom Terrific, Captain Florida and I were hunting with an outfitter in Utah. It was our first time out with him, he did not know us. He had an old sheep cabin in a nice canyon in the Northern Wasatch Range, not too far from Ogden. We drove right up to it - the plan being to take the horses out from there each morning and bring them back at night . As I drove up, I saw only two horses and several mules.

Jim and Albert, two professional packers, had been getting things ready for the better part of an hour, before Al turned to us and asked the question.

Actually, Jim and Albert were two retired school teachers from Salt Lake. They had been best buddies for years. When they retired from teaching, they took up the dubious trade of mule packing together. Not only did they become wilderness hunting guides and pack-trip commandos, they went on tour around the west, plying their craft at shows and rodeos.

Yes folks, they actually have packing tournaments at certain rodeos and theses two boys were defending champs for the last ump-t-ump years.

What is a packing tournament? Simple. You take your rodeo arena, and make a piles of every conceivable kind of junk at one end – a pile for each two-man team you have in the competition. You want to try to make each junk pile equally challenging to the packers. That is, if you put a refrigerator in one pile, you ought to put something as big in the other piles, like a hide-a-bed sofa or a coffin. If you put some awkward stuff in a pile like laundry sinks, you want to puts some toilets or two-seat bicycles in the other piles. Anyway, once you get your piles built, you turn your competitors loose. Their task is to load their mules with your piles and take a trip around the arena, negotiating logs and ditches and whatever kind of obstacle you can think of to place in their path. Then, return to the starting line and get the junk unloaded before any of the other teams finish. If they lose something along the way, you add time to their ticket and make them repack it. Our guys were the champs.

"Who's the best rider, "Al asked again.

I looked over at Tom and the Captain. They were both pointing at me. Florida had only ever ridden once before. Tom? Well, Tom is an excellent photographer.

I gulped. There were still only two horses. Both were saddled along with three mules. One each for Jim and Albert, and, well, I guessed one for me.

I had never ridden a mule, but I had heard plenty of horror stories.

We used to watch an old cowboy, across the road from the ranch in Wyoming where I hang out, just try to catch his mule. Sometimes it would take all day would and end with him pinning the ornery creature against the canyon wall with his truck.

My lore bucket was full of bad mule stories and I was more than a little nervous.

Albert was helping Florida and Terrific get their saddles set. Jim, eyes down, kind-of snuck up to me dragging a giant mule with him.

"This is the best horse in the county," he whispered, seeming almost embarrassed.

"It's a mule."

"Still, it's the best riding animal in all of Utah," he said, as if trying to convince me.

"I never road a mule before," I said, checking the chinch.

"You're going to love him. He's the best horse in the entire United States."

"He's kind of tall," I said, lifting foot for the stirrup.

Jim had been holding a small step stool behind his back. With a deft, gunslinger motion, he whipped it down at my feet.

"What's that?"

"A helper."

"Am I supposed to carry it in my pocket or something?"

"Naw, you'll figure something else out on the trail."

"I don't know about this mule thing,"

"Smooth ride," Jim said with a big smile. "Best horse in the entire world."

I had just sat down on the saddle when Jim said: "He's kind of stubborn though."

"What do you mean by that?"

"Well, you'll figure that out too."

Great. I was on the biggest animal I had ever ridden - one who had an entire species worth of bad legacies as a reputation – and the guy who put me on him said I was going to find out some terrible bone breaking secret at some time in the near, probably momentary future.

"What's his name? Ball Buster or something like that?"

"Cadillac."

Cowboys are notorious for their wry sense of humor. Naming an animal Cadillac could mean only one thing. I was in for the ride of my life.

Jim dropped his hold on Cadillac's halter, when I looked like I was ready. The mule took off immediately. It only took a second to find out that he did not neck rein. You had to pull his head around to turn him.

"He doesn't neck rein," Jim said. "You have to pull his head around."

"No kidding," I said as I tried to keep the big animal within the area in front of the corral. I leaned back putting all my weight on the reins in a futile effort to get him to stop walking.

"He's hard to stop," Jim said.

"What do you mean? He won't stop at all."

"Yeah. That's what I mean. Just try to keep him walking in a circle until we all get ready, then we'll turn him loose. "

"Turn him loose?"

Jim walked away and mounted his mule – a seemingly much more docile creature. I kept spinning Cadillac around and around in front of the corral. Jim led the way down the trail. Tom and the Captain fell in behind. Al motioned for me to fall in the line in front of him. He led a pack horse, which he intended to use to bring any thing we might shoot that morning back and wanted to stay in the rear.

Within seconds, Cadillac had passed both Tom and the Captain and had pushed his way into the string just behind Jim. I had a feeling that situation would not last. I tried my best to hold him back, but to no avail. Not only did he walk with his head virtually on the rear flank of Jim's mule, but I could see that from time to time, he would actually take a little bite out of its hide. Jim's mule would jump ahead a few feet and Cadillac would catch him and bite him again.

"Damn," I said to Jim. "I'm sorry, I can't stop him from doing that."

"Yeah, he's kind of stubborn, but how's he riding? Smooth huh?"

"I ah, really, don't ah. . . Whoa."

Cadillac had had enough. He'd been on a trail for five minutes walking second in line. That was, in his view, intolerable. We'd come to an area where the trail had expanded a little and the big creature was taking advantage. He pulled out next to Jim's mule despite my best efforts to hold him back and took the lead in a matter of seconds.

"Sorry about that," I said."

"No problem, "Jim said. "You held him back longer than we thought you would. He always does that. Congratulations, you've got the record. How's he riding?"

"Well, now that I've been on him a while, I'll have to admit, he is pretty smooth."

"Best horse in the universe."

I became a believer on that trip. Cadillac was the best horse in the universe. He was the smoothest walker I have ever ridden. A day in the saddle on him was indeed like a day in a Cadillac. He was the strongest, fastest mount I have ever been on. No horse, mule or probably motorcycle could beat him to the top of a mountain. He never quit. And, when it came to riding back to camp at night, you can bet he was in the feed bag long before any of the other horses even broke down onto the flats. But, he was one stubborn son-of-a-bitch!

He was okay in the morning. He'd let you put a bridle and a saddle on him all right. That kind of activity did not bother him. But then he'd stand there. I mean right there. Most horses, will allow you to push them around a little if they are not standing exactly where you want them. If they are too big to mount they will allow you to lead them into a ditch or a low spot or next to a stump or any where you can get on them easier. Not the Cadillac. If you wanted to mount him, in the stable or out on the trail, you'll have to do it wherever he chose to stand. And, when it came to a trail, he knew no boundaries. If our desire was to get from point A to Point B, you could bet he'd get to B first, but it may not be by following along the trail like any ordinary horse. The Cad stepped where he wanted to and that was that – cliff edge, mud bog, rock pile not withstanding. I learned to turn him, but after a solid week of riding him, I never did learn how to get him to come to a complete stop without jumping off and tying him to something. I did learn to get on while he was walking away though.

But hey, those are minor things, right? If you can Cowboy your way around things like that in a horse, you can get along just fine.

TIP - Horses: If you cross a female horse with a male donkey, you'll get a mule. They are usually bigger, stronger, more durable, and far less delicate than a horse.

George Washington introduced the mule to American culture in 1787 after having received two of them from the King of Spain. They soon caught on and became the main work animal of the South. Both sides used them extensively during the Civil War and over thirty thousand of them were used by the American Army during World War One.

If some one wants you to ride one, do not be afraid. They can have some annoying behavioral quirks, like an unwillingness to back up or walk on ice or through water, but over all, they can be fine trail animals.

TIP - Horses: No matter who puts the saddle on (even you), before you put your foot in the stirrup, slide your flat hand between the cinch and the horse's belly. The cinch is the big cloth strap, which holds the saddle in place. Your hand should slide in, but with little play. If you can't get your hand in easily, you'll sore the horse badly in that spot and he will not be of much use after a couple of days. If your hand slides in too easily and bangs around in there, somebody forgot to tighten the cinch and you'll be the one getting sore the minute you put any weight in the stirrup.

Often wranglers or guides will saddle the horses for the day's, ride and not tighten the cinches until just before the riders are ready to mount up. It is likely in the morning's activities that someone could forget to tighten one.

TIP - Horses: Never get on a horse without holding the reins in your hand. It does not matter if the horse is tied or if someone is holding it for you. You would not sit in the driver's seat of a car without having your hands on the wheel and you should never get on a horse without a firm grip on the reins. You take your life in your hands when you climb on a horse. All kinds of bad things can happen. You need to be prepared.

TIP - Horses: Never jump on a horse. I know. Movie cowboys do. But then, movies do ask us to suspend reality. Easily, seventy-five percent of the horse wrecks that happen, happen during mounting and dismounting the animal. If you try to jump up into a high stirrup, you are guaranteed to nerve up horse to where a big-time wreck will be staring you straight in the face. Even if you have to bend your leg at a weird angle to get your foot into the stirrup, you are asking for trouble. Your weight will be way off and you will have a difficult time dragging your self into the saddle.

Unless Sitting Bull himself is chasing you, you've got time. Walk the horse into a low spot or next to a rock or a log where you step up and get on easily. Take the reins in your left hand, place it on the neck of the horse and put your right hand on the saddle horn. Put your foot into the stirrup and step up. Swing your leg over the horse's rear and stick your foot into the stirrup on the other side. Remember, if you have tied gear to the back of the horse, you will have to swing your leg much higher than you think to keep it from getting hung up.

TIP - Horses: The cantle is the broad brim behind the seat on the saddle. It is considered poor form, by horse fanatics, to grab the cantle when you climb aboard. A horse can handle more weight on his front legs than on his rear legs. Mounting too far back throws more weight rearward. Forget that. Go for safety ease. Grab the cantle if you need to. The best horsemen I know do.

TIP - Horses: Drop lightly into the saddle. This is not a fence you are sitting on or the arm of your mother's sofa, for that matter. It is a living creature. True, a tough creature, but a sudden drop of a couple a hundred pounds square into the middle of the back is not good for them. And, what is not good for them is not good for you when you are a million miles from nowhere.

TIP - Horses: Most horses can be trained to back up, but they won't like it. They can't see in reverse and it makes them nervous. The configuration of their legs muscles makes it more natural for them to go forward.

If you need to make a horse step back, while you are getting on or moving him around in a stall, try pushing back on the lead rope with your left hand, pushing back with your right hand on his shoulder and tapping him gently on the shins with your foot. If that doesn't work, move to his rump, while holding the lead rope. Push his rump over to the side drag his head around, turning him totally around, then do whatever it was you wanted to do. They can be stubborn and it is you who may have to adapt.

A mule won't do it – period. Try something else!

SMARTER THAN THEY LOOK – HORSES THAT IS

Mountainman Dick and four hunters lit out one glass-cracking cold morning, face into an angry wind, to get set for an Elk drive, which he had arranged with two of his packers, who were supposed to be heading up to the high camp to fetch down some gear. The idea was that the two packers would divert from their normal route up the main trail to camp and head instead up through a giant stand of timber on the wet side of a long high ridge, then drop down the dry valley on the other side. Dick planned to set the four of us spaced out along the bottom, beneath the dry ridge, where we could intercept anything his boys drove out over the top. He hadn't planned on the weather going corn flakes quite so fast. Twenty minutes up the trail and it began to half rain and half snow, which of course, all turned to ice almost immediately when it hit any shady spot along the trail

We had about a four mile trip – maybe an hour – to get into position. With each minute the weather worsened, turning from light snow and brutal wind to freezing rain and brutal wind. Dick didn't let on that he was a little concerned, but he knew the trail ahead and knew that we would have to negotiate a couple of bad spots to get where he wanted to be.

Mountain trails in the summer are dusty, spider-web strings that wind up and down the ridges along the streams singing merrily as they go - tra, la, la. When it rains a bunch they turn to sloppy, slippery, greasy screaming meanness. Add ice and you've got Yoko Ono harmonizing with a Peterbilt truck and a dental drill. On an ice trail , no hunting boot or horse hoof can take a step up without sliding back two. The hour ride was crowding two. The worse was yet to come.

The winding trail followed the creek up from the bottom, headed vertically for a greasy, sloppy, killer mile, then flattened out in the valley in which we had intended to hunt. On each side of the trail the sage-strewn mountain walls rose at a wicked angle to the top. The trail itself was a narrow shelf, notched into one side-wall of the valley, several hundred feet above the rocky river-bed below. "Narrow shelf" means a foot, maybe eighteen inches wide, almost too narrow for a horse – a sane horse at least. Dick seriously considered turning back, but we had almost reached the first hunter drop spot and the weather seemed to be clearing slightly. In fact, the sun had begun shooting piercing shafts down through tiny breaks in the cloud cover.

The big problem came a few hundred yards farther up the trail, where the river made a sudden sharp bend. Here, the trail, which clung so tenuously to the stark mountain wall, wrapped around a giant bulge formed where the wall of the valley stuck out into the river bend. Each degree of turn, around the big bend, exposed the trail and the treeless valley walls to more of the wind and sleet, turning everything into a giant punch-bowl ice dragon. The poor little trail had no chance of surviving. With each degree of turn, it shrunk more and more, until finally, it became totally obscured under a thick sheet of glass ice that hung, glittering in the intermittent sun, from the top of the ridge to the creek bottom far below. It was here that Dick stopped - the string behind him piling into each other, nose to rump.

Unless he is a well-trained show animal, your average horse does not like to back up. He can't see where he's stepping and he gets nerved up. If he's being piloted by a less-than-experienced rider he really gets riled. If he is standing on a go-straight-to-hell, ice block, toehold, forget about it.

Cowboys tend to get into spots like this from time to time. It kind-of goes with the hat. Dick a very experienced and normally extra cautious guide and outfitter found himself a little short on options. He couldn't go forward out onto the iceberg. He couldn't get five horses to agree to back up in unison, under these circumstances. Turning around would have become one bat-swift flight to Neverland. He sat there for a second contemplating.

"End of the line boys," he said finally. "Must have been ice raining all night up here."

The downhill hoof of my horse kept slipping out from under him - as did all the downhill hooves of all the horses – making it feel like we were heading over the edge immediately. Side-hilling a horse is spooky enough without ice, but this was downright terrifying.

"Dick, I'm a little nervous here," I said.

"Me too. Like a frog in a warm pan."

I hate it when guides admit fear and turn poetic. "You got a plan, Dick? Cause we need one quick," I said, as my horse slipped again.

Dick figured the horses were doomed, but he sure as hell didn't want four hurt or dead hunters on his hands. "Not much we can do boys," he said. "I want everybody to be very careful and get off on the uphill side. Then get your guns out and get away from the horses. "

I stole a quick glance back over my shoulder. Everybody was doing the same thing I was – looking from side to side for a safe place to put a foot. The ground was a glittering field of ice, with tiny islands of rock poking through the surface every so often. I lifted my downhill foot out of the stirrup and gingerly swung it over the horse's back. The instant it hit the ground, it slid out from under me I was on my ass under the horse. Boom – that quick! Fortunately, I was able to grab a stalk of sage and hold myself stable on the trail. The horse stood, rock solid, ears, flat back on his head, never moving a muscle. It was as if he knew that now would not be a good time to let me panic. Behind me, three other hunters sat on the trail under their motionless horses. To my other side Dick sat staring up at his horse, every bit as amazed as we were. The horses had frozen in place, but not because they were cold.

Finally, we were able to find purchase points for our feet among the rocks and sage, and stand. "Get your guns," Dick said, apparently resolved to lose the horses.

After several falls and considerable cussing, we were able to move back on the trail a hundred yards or so to where the footing was adequate. We stood there staring back at the still motionless horses standing in a line on the frozen trail. "What now boss," I said to Dick.

"Don't know. I really don't want to lose them horses. I never lost any before, but I ain't going back out there to fetch 'em either. "

Then, after several minutes, as we stood there watching, the horses lifted their ears, cocking them back forth as if listening to each other. Their heads turned from side to side as they looked first down the canyon toward the river then back up the, icy ridge. Finally, as if responding to some off-stage choreographer, all five horses, in unison, lifted their front legs into the air, spun on their back legs and jammed their butts into the uphill slope. Then, they pounded their front hooves into the downhill slope and sat there, facing down the slope, staring at their front feet. Then, again in unison, they lifted their front legs out of their toeholds and jammed their sharp hooves into the ice ahead of them, sliding on their rumps a few feet down the slope. After a second's rest, they looked at each other as if saying, "now we got it guys." Then, without so much as an "aw shucks" the five horses, repeated the slide and stick process over and over until they were safely down to the flats along the river, where they shook themselves off and got busy munching grass as if nothing had happened.

We all stood there mouths agape.

"Damn," Dick said.

"Damn, damn, damn, damn," the rest of us echoed, in turn.

"I thought they were bear bait," Dick said.

"I didn't think they were that smart," another guy said.

By now, the sun had poked giant holes in the cloud cover; cast a hot light on everything below. The wind gave up its assault on the day and except for a lingering chill, things became quite nice. So goes it in the mountains.

We found a spot where we could climb down to the river flats then hike back up to the horses, who stood there saddled feeding, as content as butterflies on a bagel.

You should have heard those horses talking under their breath as we approached - the names they called us, you would not believe.

TIP – Horses: If your horse tells you he can do something, believe him. He probably can. They are a whole lot smarter than you think, many times a whole lot smarter than you. Mules are Albert Einstein compared to horses. Which when compared to cowboys… well, you figure it out.

DANGER

DANGER

HUNTERS BEWARE

Cowboy hunts are dangerous? You bet they are! It is a question of degrees. Can I get hurt? Same answer. In fact it is almost guaranteed

BLIND MAN WALKING

.
Gabriel and I were slowly making our way up to our high camp in Wyoming. We'd been on the trail for about two hours. The sun was making its appearance above the tops of the ridges and we were beginning to shed layers. The trail was steep and rocky and we rode in relative silence, the hooves of the horses, clattering against the rocks, the only sound.

Suddenly, up ahead, we heard small rocks skittering down the trail. First thought: Elk. Second thought: Horses. Then we heard a lone voice. Third thought: A rider. We're fast thinkers.

Actually it turned out to be two riders. But, only one was talking. Both were on mules. The talker was leading the other rider – pulling his mule along by a lead rope and coaxing the other rider along. "Goin' down a little steep here. Lean back. Come on. You can do it. Not much farther now."

I have seen some miserable looking Cowboys over the years. I've been a miserable looking Cowboy. Usually it's knees and backs that fail. Riding a horse for several days up and down mountains can take the cheer out of even the most enthusiastic wannabe Cowboy, but this guy sticks out as the number one don't-want-to-be-here-guy I have ever seen. The closer they got, the worse he looked. He was riding without a hat. Instead, he had a torn piece of shirt tied around his head, with a large bulging piece of material pushed into one eye socket. The other eye was partially visible, but a constant waterfall of tears made it seem useless. He was in obvious pain, holding on to the saddle horn, trying to squint through his tears. The material over the covered eye was caked in dried blood.

Gabriel knew the guide bringing the injured Cowboy down. "Mornin' Jimmy John," he said.

"Mornin'. Gotta get him down," he said nodding back toward the crying guy. "Caught a branch in the eye last night coming down the trail. Did some serious damage."

The inured guy chimed in, "Its got the other eye watering so bad, I can't see. "

Gabriel and I pulled our horses off the trail making them stumble into the rocks a little on the side of the mountain so that they could pass us easily. That Cowboy was really in bad shape and they really did need to get him down – and fast. Not only was his eye seriously hurt but he had some other rather serious looking gashes on his face and neck. It was obvious he had done a little more than catch a passing branch – a fairly common event while Cowboy hunting.

We heard later that something had spooked his mule the night before – another common event – and the animal had lurched part way off the side of the trail in the black of night, ramming the Cowboy into a dead tree. He hadn't even known what hit him, but clearly it was a bunch of branches not just one. The point is, in one second, he was a happy Cowboy heading back to camp after a day of chasing game around in the high country. The very next second he was blind. We heard later that he lost the eye.

I myself carry a scar over my right eye from a similar but far less devastating Cowboy hunting injury. I was trying to convince a horse I was leading down a pitch dark trail to walk off the edge of a cliff. I was convinced the trail took a sharp turn to the right at one particular point in the journey and he, being far smarter than the Cowboy leading him, knew it did not. (In all fairness, he could see, and I could not. He wasn't all that much smarter than me. Just a little).

The horse had a small, silver, star on the side of his bridle. Cute. He had stopped dead on the trail when I made the right turn and would not budge. I took a step back, stood next to his neck and tried to push him where he knew neither of us should be going. He flinched and in a split second hammered that tiny star into the bony ridge just at the corner of my right eye. I heard a train for a second, then telephones ringing, then The Who, live at the Filmore West, then nothing.

I think the horse nudged me with his nose. I think that is what woke me up. All I knew was that I was face down in the rocks and everything was dark. Remarkably, I still had the reigns in my hand. Had I not, I am certain I would have been horseless too. He was heading back to camp and really did not have time to walk off cliffs much less wait for a dumbbell Cowboy.

I brought my hand to the side of my face. I could sense that blood was streaming down from my forehead. It was dripping into my eye – warm, sticky. Jack hammers were pounding at the side of my head like giant Woodpeckers. I found my flashlight under my chest, shining away. Yes, it was blood.

Back at the camp, it was the unanimous opinion of all the Cowboy doctors present that I really needed stitches. We stuck a Bandaid on it instead. If I weren't so ugly already, I'd have a plastic surgeon work a little magic on that star scar.

HYPOTHERMIA
MOVING TO JAMAICA

Cold. Hunting season generally brings plenty of that. If you hunt in the mountains you'll get more than your share. Sure, you can get shirt-sleeve sun-tanning weather for your trip, but if you do it long enough sooner or later you'll get a dose of sleet, ice-rain, snow, and plenty of little monsters that we call Coldons (like Klingons except they're no where near as cute).

Coldons climb in under your tent edge, slip into your sleeping bag, collect around your feet, and nestle against your spine, where they bury their icey claws until your lips quiver and your teeth chatter. From time to time, Coldons gather in huge armies and raid the day with snow bombs and ice bullets. Alaska Mike (a.k.a. Muskrat Mike) and I found ourselves in a major skirmish in the ongoing Coldon war on a forced march we made one day to the top of the Wyoming range.

The war began two days earlier when we awoke in the morning to a new snowfall of about eight inches. I had gotten up during the night, to step outside for a minute and realized it was snowing but I really didn't think it was going to be that bad. By dawn the tent flaps were held shut by a two-foot drift. What did I know?

Mike, two other guides, two wranglers, a cook, three other hunters and I ate breakfast in the cook tent taking turns stepping outside to comment on the rapidly deteriorating weather. By the time we had finished, three additional inches had fallen and the wind had picked up making vision virtually impossible. The horses had moved into a large cluster, taking turns standing on the outer fringes of the group, and making comments about the hunters, guides, and definitely the wranglers. Other than a pissed-off wife, there's nothing worse than a pissed-off horse.

Soon, it became clear that we were not going anywhere. In fact, it was beginning to look doubtful that we would even be getting out of there before spring. Of course none of us Cowboys would succumb to thoughts of the Donner party or anything like that. No.

We went back to bed. Then played cards. Then took a nap. Then ate lunch. Then read. Then took another nap. Then ate dinner. Then went to bed.

The snow stopped the next day at around noon, but not before dropping over twenty-four inches on our hunt. The Coldons were delighted, and scampered everywhere unrestricted in their glee. We spent the rest of the day, chasing them, and cutting paths to our gear and horses.

The next morning was beautiful. As bad as snowstorms are, when the sun finally comes out, the beauty of the mountains, will about poke your eye out. There is nothing like the clean green of pines outlined against the clear blue of mountain sky. When the pines are draped with heavy, white snow, it is like something out of a fairy tale.

"You up for a little ride," Mike asked.

"Absolutely," I said.

"Well then, let's get saddled up and take a look around. We just might catch something making tracks in all this fresh stuff. "

The best we could do was about an hour. The snow was too deep for the horses, and they were struggling. Despite the bright sun, the Coldons were managing to crawl into every exposed weakness – shirt sleeves, pant cuffs, down our necks - and propelled by a wicked wind were smashing into our faces like crazed Kamikazes.

We stopped at the base of a long, high, knife-like ridge, which ran up a mile or two to the top of the mountain range. We could see a Dinosaur back of wind stripped rocks running along the entire crest all the way to the top.

"You feel like walking a ways," Mike asked. "The snow probably won't be too deep there where the wind has blown it off the rocks."

I was cold. I did need to warm up. I had been sitting around the camp for two days. The view from the top would be spectacular and I knew that we would be able to see anything that moved from up there.

"Yes he does," my horse said, dropping down to one knee so I could slide off easy.

We began marching. One step at a time, I felt like Sir Edmund Hilary. The snow was only ankle deep along the ridge and we made good time. After about an hour I was no longer cold. In fact, I was sweating.

When we reached a flatter saddle, near the top, I looked to my left, and on the valley wall on the other side was a long string of fresh tracks in the snow. Through my binoculars, there were dozens of different track strings running between two large stands of timber and others coming from over the top on that side. I could not tell which way they were heading, but likely, there was a substantial herd of deer or elk in one of the two stands. And, after two days of storm, it was a good bet that they would be moving out to feed soon or possibly start their annual snow migration down to lower elevations.

"Check that out," I said, pointing toward the tracks. "I think maybe I'll stop here for a while and scope that out. Maybe something will step out. That's only about three hundred or so and I can make that shot from here."

I found a good spot in the rocks where I could sit without sky-lining myself. Mike squatted down next to me, but never really got settled. He had his eye on the summit, another quarter mile ahead. Despite the fact that he was my guide, he had not spent as much time in this country as I had. This particular ridge was new to me, but I had been to the top in this area many times before and had a good idea what was beyond that peak. Mike did not.

"You're thinking of going up," I said.

"Yeah. I'd like to see it up there and get my bearings, since we came this far and all."

"Go ahead. I'll be right here."

"If I see something up there I'll signal."

"If you see a Cappuccino machine up there, bring me a large."

Mike dropped off the side a little and began side-hilling his way to the top, so as not to spook anything that might step out in front of me. Soon I was alone again in the mountains. Alone except for an ever-increasing number of particularly virulent Coldons. A wicked wind was whipping them up from the frozen valley floor and sending them under my jacket to freeze my sweat-soaked undershirt. Sweating and then sitting in cold conditions can lead to problems.

After a while, I saw Mike sitting in the rocks at the summit, peering out at the universe on the other side. I was starting to get cold. The wind was terrible. I figured it was probably worse up where he was. An hour later, I was shivering – the first sign of hypothermia. An alarm bell sounded softly in my head.

I had been scanning the two stands of timber for any signs of movement while periodically peeking up at Mike to see if he was still there. Suddenly, he wasn't. I figured he was probably on his way back down to me. Good thing, because I was really starting to freeze. Soon, I would need to start moving again whether any game moved out or not. My fingers and toes were starting to freeze. The alarm in my head was sounding louder.

Over the next hour, the wind picked up dramatically, as did the cold. Mike still had not come back. I had been staring off in the distance for quite some time without blinking or even thinking. I was very cold. No animals had shown themselves. Apparently they had much more common sense than I and knew to stay away from cold exposed places. It suddenly occurred to me that sitting, staring, was a good sign that the effects of hypothermia were beginning to set in, and that if I didn't get moving soon, I would be in trouble. Mike may have already been in trouble.

With considerable effort, I stood on my numb feet, and began walking down the ridge, toward a stand of pines on the side of the valley wall opposite from where I had been watching. I am not sure why – seeking shelter I suppose. When you start thinking without reason, it is a good sign you are slipping into deeper hypothermia. I was shivering uncontrollably, my feet and fingers were totally numb and I was having difficulty with my coordination.

As I walked, my thoughts began to clear. I was still in trouble, but at least I knew it. I did not want to walk all the way back down to the horses, without making some contact with Mike. I did not want to have to walk all the way back up there, to help him in case he was in as much trouble as I was. I noticed the temperature seemed to have dropped significantly.

Once in the trees, I found an ancient, giant pine with hanging branches, which I thought might act as a windshield. I climbed under the branches and found that the big tree was actually two trees, and there was a convenient pocket between their big trunks, which would act as an even better wind block. I squeezed in and began kicking snow until I had made a small fort, which blocked almost all of the killer wind. After resting a minute, I scooted around until I found some small sticks and within a few minutes working clumsily with my frozen fingers had a small fire blazing in the make-shift shelter. The pine trees provided plenty of dead wood to keep it going easily between my feet.

Admittedly, even though I am never far from it, I do not always take my day-pack on small excursions like this one. Fortunately I had it on this trip and in it, I had the one thing I needed most – a small tin cup. By small, I mean only about two inches in diameter. My canteen had not frozen, and I filled the cup with water. Holding it over the small fire, I warmed the water almost to the boiling point and began to sip. Within minutes, the cold had left my fingers and toes and I was back to normal. I immediately started seriously worrying about Mike. He had gone higher than I, to where it was no doubt colder (if that was possible), and as I recalled, it didn't look to me like he was wearing a very heavy jacket.

I had three options. I could wait there and hope that he would come across my tracks and find me in the woods. I could go back down to the horses and get a new fire going down there. Or, I could try to find him. Each solution had it's own set of problems. I sat there contemplating the situation, soaking in the heat of the fire, when suddenly Mike's head popped under the pine limbs into my smoky little lair. He did not look good.

"GGGGGGod DDDDDDDamn," he stuttered. His teeth clattering like griddle- fried grapes. "It's ccccccccold."

His skin had a peculiar Grey color and he was shivering uncontrollably. He said he couldn't feel his toes or his fingers and he had fallen asleep. Like me, the intense Coldons had snuck in on him, and he was in trouble before he knew it. The sleeping was particularly dangerous under the circumstances. It was fortunate that he awoke at all.

I moved back so he could sit and kicked at the snow until I had enlarged the little hiding hole so that both of us could sit close to the fire. Within a few minutes, I had a cup of warm water ready for Mike. A few minutes after that, and he was feeling much better. We were both cold, but we were no longer in danger of hypothermia.

After a rest, we were able to make it back down to the horses. They had clustered together as well as their tethered lead ropes would allow. The trees around them held porcupine bundles of icicles, which had been molded by the wind until they were horizontal spears, each about six inches long. I had witnessed that phenomenon before during a nasty blizzard that passed through our camp several years before. I knew instantly that just such a whipper-wind had passed by those ponies while we were gone. I tried to smile at them, but the look on their faces said it all.

"Yes," I said as I approached the obviously disgusted animals. "That was dumb."

"No, we're fine here, tied to these trees. We love sideways icicles."

And then, I heard one of them say, sort-of under his breath, "We are moving to Jamaica as soon as we get back! Gonna give tourists rides on the beach."

TIP - Hypothermia: Lots of stuff can kill you in the wilderness. Lions Tigers, Bears? Sure, but those are really long shots. Starvation? People probably fret about that more than anything, but it's a real long shot. Falling off a cliff? Happens all the time. But, by far, the most frequent cause of death in the wilderness (about 85%) is something far more insidious. Hypothermia is the biggest threat to outdoor survival, and even in todays,

Gore-tex, Thermofil, Polypropolene, world it accounts for hundreds of deaths each year.

TIP - Hypothermia: Hypothermia can kill you even in relatively mild temperatures. Wilderness hikers have been known to die from Hypothermia in temperatures of 32-50 degrees Fahrenheit. They call it "exposure" in the media. In 1963, The Greek ship Lakonia sunk, pitching 125 people into balmy, 65 degree water. They all died of hypothermia. And of course, we are all aware of the most famous mass hypothermia incident, the sinking of the Titanic, in which over 1500 people died.

TIP - Hypothermia: The human body can survive only if it maintains a constant internal temperature of 98.6 degrees Fahrenheit. A shift of only a few degrees below that, and we die. In fact, we begin to shiver in air at 82 degrees, if we are not clothed, and shivering is the first sign of hypothermia.

TIP - Hypothermia: When we talk about the human body maintaining a constant temperature, we are really talking about just the core. That is, the head, trunk and internal organs. Extremities such as feet and legs can tolerate much colder temperatures. When the core temperature drops as little as one degree F., the body begins to shiver. Shivering is an attempt by the body to re-warm itself by forcing spasmodic contractions of large muscle groups, which in turn produces heat through metabolism. Shivering usually becomes violent as the core temperature drops to about 91 degrees F. And, at that temperature, the body begins defending itself against further core temperature loss, by diverting blood flow away from non-vital organs such as hands and feet. A person who is shivering intensely and has cold or frozen fingers and toes is demonstrating the first signs of severe hypothermia. Further, after only a slight drop in temperature, just five degrees, the mind begins to misfire. Mental miscalculations and cold can be a murderous mix. Accidents are likely at this stage.

As the core temperature drops to between 86 and 91 degrees F., shivering begins to slow and is replaced by muscle rigidity. Mobility can be seriously affected at this point compounding the situation. Severe mental failure begins around these temperatures and often brings on irrational behavior, like actually removing clothing, rather than putting more on. If someone has been shivering and suddenly stops and becomes motionless and stiff, be very careful. This person is in need of help soon.

As the core cools to around 86 degrees F., internal organs begin to fail. Respiration and heart rate slow. At this point recovery from the effects of hypothermia may not be possible. Most people lose consciousness at around 80 degrees F. and die at around 78 degrees F.

TIP - Hypothermia: The best treatment for hypothermia is to prevent it altogether.

The body creates body heat by converting food into energy and by using muscle groups to produce heat. If you are expecting to subject yourself to cold temperatures, make certain you eat enough to maintain your heat level. While actual starvation in the wilderness is rare, the effects of an inadequate diet coupled with cold can bring on hypothermia.

Lack of physical movement in cold conditions can promote hypothermia simply because the body is not producing enough heat while sitting, to maintain the good core temperature. If you are getting cold, get moving!

TIP - Hypothermia: The body loses heat by several means. In any temperature less than 98.6 degrees F., the body radiates heat into the air. If it is windy, heat loss is much more rapid. Other mammals prevent this loss of heat to the air, by growing fur coats. Lacking that ability, (in most cases) humans need to wear clothing. Don't be casual about this. Dress properly. Wear plenty of layers. It is far better to strip off a few things and stash them in your saddle bags or in a cache somewhere if the weather improves, than it is to neglect to bring them and find yourself froze to death!

TIP - Hypothermia: Don't forget a hat. As much as 50% to 75% of the body core heat loss can be attributed to a bare head.

TIP - Hypothermia: Heat loss through air is dramatic but heat loss through water can be up to 240 times more dramatic. The reason is simple.

Water conducts heat 240 times faster than air. So, if you are wet and cold, you are in far more trouble than if you are dry and cold. Strip off wet clothing as soon as possible. Build a fire and get dry fast.

Remember, perspiration counts here. If you have been over exerting yourself, in cold conditions and begin to perspire, when you finally stop to rest, you might find yourself getting cold quick because of the increased loss of heat through sweat soaked clothing. Panting expels a lot of moisture, and again, conducts heat away from the body. Temper your exercise to balance both heat production and heat loss through over-effort.

TIP - Hypothermia: If your prevention steps have failed and you find yourself or one of your less-prepared friends in a hypothermia situation, you need to get yourself or them warm fast.

Step one is to prevent further heat loss. Find shelter. Wrap up in something – a blanket, a canvas packing tarp from one of your rigs, a hollow log – whatever. Hug a buddy if you have to, as disgusting as it may (or may not) seem.

Build a fire. Warm the air around you to more than the ideal 98.6 degrees and you will begin to absorb heat rather than lose it to the air.

Drink warm liquids or eat warm food. The idea here is that putting something warm directly into the core will raise body temperature fast. This is a very effective means to reverse hypothermia in the wilderness. Carrying a small tin cup or a metal canteen that you can use to melt snow can save your life in an emergency situation.

TIP - Hypothermia: Avoid alcohol. Booze only fights cold in the movies. It can actually make things worse in a survival situation by dilating surface blood vessels thereby allowing more heat to escape through the skin not to mention making you more stupid in a situation when you need all the smarts you can get.

TIP - Hypothermia: Finally, if it is impossibly cold, forget hunting altogether. Book a flight on Air Jamaica and try your luck at Cowboy sun bathing.

DEHYDRATION

BRAIN STORM

My wife and I were sitting in a very cozy campsite one beautiful summer morning, in the shadow of Long's Peak. Humming birds flitted around us and we could hear the soft gurgle of a mountain stream a few feet away. We were on one of our annual summer camping trips. The kids were still in the tent sleeping.

I had gotten into the habit of using these summer mountain trips as conditioning exercises for my return a few weeks later to go Cowboy hunting. I always tried to incorporate at least one climb of some kind into them as well as whatever smaller hikes I could get in with the kids. The sun line had begun its descent from the highest peaks and was just about on us – always a welcome event on mountain mornings – when I suddenly had this idea.

I had climbed the fourteen thousand foot Long's peak before. It is not a casual climb. In fact, while many do it in one day, it is best accomplished by spending a night in the boulder field just below the summit and scrambling to the top in the early morning. The usual route for summiting Long's peak goes through a notch in the ridge called "The Keyhole." Just down from the Keyhole is a lesser summit called Storm peak. Storm peak is only ten thousand or so feet above sea level, making it only four or five thousand feet above our campsite. "That's just a walk," I said to myself. "Hell, I can probably run it and be back for lunch."

I've had dumber ideas in my life, but I really can't remember when. "What would you think about me running up Storm Peak this morning," I said to my wife.

"Uh huh," she mumbled, sipping at coffee and never lifting her eyes from her book.

You can't get a clearer okay than that. I started packing.

My goal was to pack very light – a backpack, lunch and some water. The Giardia mess had not yet begun. That is, there was little talk about problems with water in the Rockies. I figured I'd take along just one quart water bottle and fill it when I got in the higher altitudes. However, when I got to the higher altitudes, the Forest Service had placed signs along the trail warning about drinking the water.

I was crushed. I had been drinking the cold, clear, mountain spring water right out of Mother Nature's tit for many years. It was something I actually craved and could not wait to enjoy. This was the first time I had ever seen a warning sign like this. Giardia? I had heard horror stories from people who had experienced bouts of it and I certain did not want to go there. I really did not know what to do. Had I been smart, I would have turned around right there and then and headed back to camp. However, I am not particularly smart and I was fairly well determined to prove it.

It had turned out to be a sunny, hot July day. The mountain sky was Colorado blue and totally cloudless. I'd been on the trail for just over two hours. I could see the summit from time to time and figured I was only another hour or so from it. I was just about out of water, but I felt good. Three hours up meant a sprint back down of only an hour or so, maybe a little longer. Who couldn't do that on just a quart of water?

Me!

It takes a while to feel the effects of hypothermia. A savvy outdoorsman knows when he is beginning to be affected by it. Dehydration, on the other hand, will sucker punch you. One minute you are fine and the next you ain't. It's that simple!

The view from the summit was spectacular, as summit views usually are. I was tired from the climb. I'd been pushing myself and exerting a lot of energy. I had also been breathing pretty hard because I was trying to shorten up the trip and get in shape at the same time. I sat on some rocks and rummaged through my pack for the sandwich I had brought. I took a bite and then another. For some reason, I was just not hungry. I finished off the last sip of water I had and sat there for a minute.

The minute turned into a half hour. I suddenly did not have the energy to get up.

I had been sweating pretty heavily on the way up. My hat and shirt were wet, but the dry air at that altitude and the clear hot day had dried them fast. It had also dried my skin. In fact, my skin felt hot. My face felt like it was burning even though I had covered it with sun protector. And, worse yet, I had begun shivering. It was close to seventy degrees up there – probably eighty down below - and I was shivering.

I had not seen another hiker on the trail the entire time. There were none at the top. They all probably had the brains to do something else on a hot day like that one. I started thinking that maybe I should start heading back down, but I really did not have the energy to stand. My mouth was dry and I was starting to feel sick.

I had peed a couple of times on the way up. When I finally forced myself to stand – not easy because of the head rush - I decided to pee one more time before heading back down the trail. I remember thinking how dark my stream was as it headed for the gravel at my feet. I don't think I'd ever seen it that dark. I wondered if I was bleeding somewhere.

If ever someone was exhibiting the classic symptoms of dehydration, it was me. And, I was too dumb to know it. I was about to get a lot dumber.

Walking with gravity is a whole lot better than walking against it. In fact, on most mountain trails, you can just about run downhill. That had been my plan. About ten minutes down the trail and I was barely walking. My heart was racing and I was panting. Putting one foot in front of the other had begun to require concentration. Within half an hour, I was nauseated and my vision had begun to shrink down to just a tunnel. And, talk about headaches. Jees! Somebody was standing inside my head with a blowtorch, while a marching band was doing their thing in there, and somebody else bounced on a trampoline, and…Jees! My skull was about to explode. And, I was moving a whole lot slower than I had planned. It might take two hours to get down and I was really starting to doubt if I could make it.

You're thinking: why not drink from the stream? Maybe you won't get Girardia. Maybe the forest service put those signs there just to cover their own butts. "We told you not to drink the water."

Simple answer: I didn't think of it.

The effects of dehydration come on very quick. The rule is; if you lose 1% of your water you will lose 10% of your strength. You will also lose about 50% of your brain power. I was walking along next to what I needed the most and didn't even think to use it.

I was deteriorating quickly. My gate had become a stumble. I was getting so weak that it had become difficult to keep moving forward. You've seen those Cowboy movies where the guy tries to walk across the desert and ends up stumbling, then falling and then staring up at buzzards? That was me – almost. My vision had really gotten bad. I could barely see. Strange noises were buzzing through my head like far-off fire engines. It was all I could do to keep from vomiting. I felt as though I could not breathe. Or, at least like I wanted to take a few deep breaths but could not. All I could do was more like a fast shallow pant. Worse, my heart was not beating correctly. I could feel it misfiring.

How many times can you be on a popular hiking trail and not come across anybody else? Not often – especially in that area. That's Rocky Mountain National Park. It's tourist central. I was in deep trouble and there was no one anywhere in sight. Go figure.

I was almost crawling when I finally reached the parking lot where my wife had agreed to meet me. I remember bracing myself against the backs of cars – one after the other – until I got to where we had planned to meet. I could barely stand. When I finally got into our car, I was only able to tell my wife to take me to a hospital in Estes Park, about a half an hour away before falling asleep - make that passing out.

My wife is not dumb – thank God. I woke up long enough to realize that she had stopped at a party store and gotten out. I am almost dead and she's going into a party store? She returned with two giant bottles of Gatorade®.

By the time we arrived at the Hospital, I had finished one of the Gatorades and was opening the second. I was sitting up and actually beginning to feel better – that fast.

One of the sneaky things about dehydration is that it depletes your electrolytes. It is the loss of electrolytes that really causes problems. When you are low on those little babies, you have got to replace them fast. Your heart will flat-out stop working if you don't.

We sat in the hospital parking lot, but we never went in. My wife cured me right there by feeding me Gatorade. The real story here? I watched this exact scenario play out with one of our Wyoming guides.

He went by the name of Willy. Of course, we called him Wild Willy. Nobody liked him much. He was loud, cocky and abrasive. He had this macho attitude that got to be a real pain-in-the-ass. Worse, he was unusually harsh and actually cruel to the horses. How he managed to end up working for one of the best outfitters in the area was always a puzzle. When he informed us one hot October day that he'd forgotten his water bottle, both Dead Eye and I offered to share ours with him. He, of course, declined.

"I don't need no water," he said. "I drink my coffee in the morning and then I don't drink again 'til supper."

Okay there Mister Willy. He was not the kind of guy you wanted to argue with. We really didn't care that much anyway. All we could do was watch as he progressively fell into the same situation I was in on Storm Peak. The only difference was that he had a horse to carry him so he was not expending the same energy I was when I was when I was alone on the trail. Nonetheless, he was almost tipping out of the saddle by the end of the day. He was so stubborn that not only would he not share some of our filtered water he wouldn't even drink out of the stream.

"You need some water," we told him.

"I don't need it," he said. "It's just somethin' I ate that's giving me the gripes. I'll be fine."

He smoked about fifty cigarettes that afternoon. He said something about the nicotine would get him better. It always did. He's lucky he didn't have a heart attack. He was so sick that he could not go out the next day. It's bad enough being dumb. But, stubborn and dumb can be a lethal combination in the mountains.

TIP - Dehydration: Remember: If you lose 1% of your water, you will lose 10% of your strength.

TIP - Dehydration: Amazingly, we lose more water to breathing than anything else. So, even if you are not sweating and not urinating a lot, you are still losing water every time you exhale.

TIP - Dehydration: In the mountains, you need a quart of water every hour – just to keep the headaches away.

TIP - Dehydration: The first symptoms of dehydration are dry mouth, headache, lightheadedness, dizziness and muscle weakness. Dehydration progresses rapidly from there.

TIP - Dehydration: As strange as this may seem, you should be monitoring the color of your urine when you are in the mountains, on a Cowboy hunt. Clear urine (or only slightly yellow) is a sign that you are probably well hydrated. As the color of your urine darkens it could very well mean you are becoming dehydrated. The body – remarkable machine that it is – senses a loss of water early on and begins to concentrate urine in an attempt to preserve liquid. It can be a good indicator of pending trouble.

TIP - Dehydration: Yes, dehydration can kill you. But, in all honesty, few people actually die of dehydration while on a Cowboy hunting trip. Plenty of them get sick though.

You can feel great while you are Cowboy hunting or you can feel lousy. Feeling great is better. Stay hydrated.

ORIENTATION DISABILITIES

LOST BOYS

If your guide pulls out a map, you are in trouble. If the map is on a napkin or written in crayon, hitch up you're socks, you're in big trouble!

Muskrat Mike and I had been riding for hours. We were in mountains that I was quite familiar, but we were exploring a drainage up which I had never been. We'd come up a long, tortuous trail to a summit somewhere above the tree line at about 11,000 cold, oxygenless, feet. Then, we'd turned and headed back down along a creek into a narrow valley and then back up on the opposite side, along that ridge and then, up higher to another summit at about 12,000 feet. At four in the afternoon, the sun still shone steadily and bright, but a bruising wind stole any heat it provided and dropped it somewhere down in Florida – or at least nowhere near where we were. It was colder than Nanuk's mother-in-law up there. Snow had fallen the day before, and several inches of it clung to the crevices between the rocks and at the base of the trees on the downhill slopes. At one point we'd passed a clump of trees from which horizontal icicles had grown out eight inches from every branch, as though the wind had bent them straight. Even my horse had had enough. He turned his head every step or so, and cast a worried eye up at me. I know they can't speak, but somehow I kept hearing words in my head that had a peculiar horse accent: "What are we crazy or something?" Maybe it was the wind.

From time to time Mike would take a flimsy piece of paper out of his pocket and would try to hold it into the wind up near his squinting eyes. He'd then spin in the saddle and survey the surrounding landscape, stuff the paper and his hands back into his pockets and ride on.

Finally, we dropped off the side of the ridge, and walked into a little pocket under some rocks, out of the wind. Mike dismounted and signaled that I should do the same. We tied the horses. Mike whispered that I should bring my gun, and slowly walked out on a small finger ridge, which overlooked a heavily treed slope. There, we settled into some rocks and began glassing the surrounding area looking for horns.

Darkness comes slowly on the plains. The sun's rays linger and twilight stretches on for a long time. In the mountains light and dark are only a few beats apart. A hunter gets only a couple dozen minutes of good hunting twilight each day.

"Gonna be getting dark soon," Mike said.

"Yeah, prime time is just starting. They'll be coming out to feed soon."

"I was thinking we should be starting down, he said"

"Now, at prime time?" This was a violation of hunting basics 101. You never move during prime time, especially when you've worked hard to gain the high ground.

"Well, we have a little problem."

"Problem?"

"Yeah, " Mike said, unfolding the little piece of paper he'd been fighting with all afternoon. "I'm not sure where the camp is and I don't want to be hauling down off this mountain in the dark, not knowing where we are going.

I stared at him for a minute, my brain suddenly blank. I hadn't been paying all that much attention to the trail. I had a guide after all – one I had paid plenty for.

"Muskrat," I said finally. "You don't mind if I call you by your first name do you? That's not really a problem. It's more like a tragedy."

"That's why I want to get off here before dark. Otherwise we might have to spend the night up here and go down in the morning."

That was certainly an attractive proposition. "I'm a little confused."

"Me too."

"Wait. You can't be confused. You're the guide."

"Well, I have never been here before."

This was the first day that Mike and I had been in the woods together, and the first day of this trip. I didn't know him very well. I certainly didn't know he didn't know diddly

"Let me see your map," I said. Yep, you guessed it – napkin and in crayon too.

"Look," he said. "I am really sorry about this."

"I'm curious. How did you get to be a guide in Wyoming with out knowing where you even are?"

"Well, long story. I'm from Alaska."

"Geees."

"I'm Charlie's cousin. One of his guides bailed out on him, and I'm out of work, so he said I could fill in if I could get here in time. I got here last week."

"You got a license right?"

"Yeah, he got that for me. I do a lot of moose guiding in Alaska. I know all the guiding stuff, you know 'bout the horses and animals and stuff, but I am not sure about the area. And, now I got us lost. I'm really sorry. I don't know where that cut off Charlie drew on the map is. I've been looking for it all day. Probably missed it hours ago."

"No kidding."

"We was supposed to come up to the ridge from camp to something called Clause Peak, then wrap around it and wait, 'cause Charlie and Bo and Tom were going to up old Cabin Creek and thought maybe they'd drive something up to us, or we would drive something down to them. And then we were supposed to drop off the back side of this ridge and follow the bottom back to the main creek and go back up it to camp."

"You sure it was this ridge we were supposed to drop off?"

"Yeah, well pretty sure."

"See that snow capped peak way back there, " I said, gesturing with my head.

"Yeah."

"That's Clause Peak."

"Get out of here. That's pretty near five miles back."

"Yep," I believe that's it. I've been on the other side of it a couple of times. You sure this is the ridge we are supposed to drop off?"

"Well, Charlie pointed this way when he was telling me the plan this morning, and I can't figure which other one it would be," he said scanning the area. "The only other thing I can figure is to back track and try to go back the way we came."

"That'd take hours. You sure you remember the way."

"Well, Not exactly, but I could maybe track us."

"In the dark? On flat rock? This ain't no Cowboy and Indian movie, there Muskrat."

"Then we got no choice. We either spend the night or we use whatever light is left to drop off this ridge."

"I hate to miss prime time, " I said. "But, at least we would be down off this freezing mountain."

"Okay then, " he said. "I just hope it don't cliff up."

"Oh, That's very encouraging."

We scrambled back up to our horses, mounted up and started easing them over the edge, along what appeared to be a fairly well developed game trail. I was hoping that it was an actual horse trail, which had just petered out at the top.

My hopes were short lived. After about thirty minutes, in the failing light of the day, the trail began to disappear in a thick forest of pines, the floor of which was littered heavily with giant dead-fallen trees. Dead-fall is a tricky thing to negotiate on horseback in the light of day. It is particularly treacherous in the dark and even more difficult when every step the horse makes drives a clutch of branches and sharp sticks into the rider's face.

Muskrat Mike and I were struggling. The horses were beginning to whimper and stomp – a sure-fire sign of panic. Their eyes were wild, and they held their ears flat back against their skulls.

We had separated – each of us trying to find a way to clear steering. My horse almost fell, stumbling over a giant dead-fall, which sent a bouquet of sharp branches into his belly. His legs were twisting as he stepped into a pothole and slid off broken branches. He was making a host of grunts and squeals, and I could sense that he was seriously spooked. Suddenly we were half trotting, half falling into a solid wall of pines, through which I could see no opening. And then, before I even had a chance to see it coming, a large branch five or six inches in diameter appeared on a short course directly for my chest.

I considered trying to lean back in the saddle and let it go over my face, but there simply was no room. My best bet was to drop far over to the side and try to slide off the horse, Indian style. Unfortunately, the horse was not in the mood for trick riding, and had somehow concluded that he was in charge – a command, which I incidentally, had not yet relinquished. He gave a little lurch and before I knew what was happening I was engaged in a full-fledged accelerated dismount.

Not all accelerated dismounts (a.k.a. horse-assisted dismounts) are created equal. They range from simple foot-slipped-out-of-the-stirrup ground flops to full-gallup-horse-stopped-suddenly-rider-airborne-over-cliff hoohaws. The one I was involved in on that day was a combo. I was partly trying to get off. The horse was definitely trying to get me off. And, a large tree was quite adamant that I get off. It had the added attractions of darkness and an uneven, dead-fall, strewn landing zone. I hit hard, and to make it worse, the horse tried to follow me. Hooves!

I couldn't move. I couldn't breathe. My left arm felt like it had detached. I couldn't see through the darkness and the tree branches above me. I listened to the horse crashing down the slope until there was only silence. I was on my side, left arm going numb, my face jammed into a mossy pile of rocks. I had dirt in my ear and in my teeth. Sharp things were sticking me. Pain reports were coming in from every body part. I was groaning.

Only one thing a cowboy can do at a time like that.

Oh yes, when pressed, I can swear. I can swear like a drunken sailor. I can swear like Shanghai whore. I can swear like . . . well, suffice it to say, that I launched a Titan cuss missile that won't stop until Captain Kirk finds it some time off in the Klingon filled future.

Mike hadn't done much better. He too had left his horse - suddenly. Not only were we injured and lost and cold and pissed off, we were horseless and a long way from camp.

"Things aren't going well," Mike said.

"You have a gift for understatement," I said, through clenched teeth.

Horses are amazing creatures. They look pretty dumb, standing there eating in a field, but in reality they are extremely capable. They are rarely lost. It is well known among cowboy guides, that you can take a brand new horse on a brand new trail just one time, and that horse will know that trail forever. The bad news was that neither of our horses had ever been there before, likely because nobody had ever been there before. Consequently, they too were lost, and hadn't strayed too far. When we caught up with them, they were standing in a small clearing on the bank of the creek – still wild-eyed, but there nonetheless.

This was hell country in the day light, blocked at every step by giant fallen trees and scraggy boulders. In the dark, it was impossible. The creek banks were a rock and tree wall. Ten to fifteen feet below the water flowed like liquid ice over boulders and rocky islands. We held the horses by their lead ropes and struggled to move them down even a few yards.

"This isn't working," Mike said, after falling face first over a log.

"You're exaggerating again."

"The way I see it, we have two choices."

"I can't wait," I said.

"Well, we either stay here and wait for light, or go back up the way we came."

No one is ever really lost in the mountains. All creeks and streams flow downhill to bigger creeks and streams and eventually find their ways to the ocean. If you follow a creek down, you will eventually come to civilization.

"Well, there is a third choice," I said gesturing toward the stream.

Without a second of hesitation Muskrat Mike scrambled down the bank and stood looking up at me knee-deep in the freezing water. "I was afraid to mention this one," he said. Let's go."

With considerable trepidation, I slowly eased into the water. I figured that if it didn't go over the tops of my boots, I would be okay. It was over my boots on the second step. I felt the horse tug on the lead rope. I looked back and saw a very strange look in his eye. "What, this," I heard on the wind, in that mysterious horse accent. "One of us is crazy, and it ain't me."

The only thing keeping that water from freezing was that it was moving. My feet and legs ached like hell's fire. The creek bed was a collage of uneven rocks and boulders, each one more slippery than the last. We stumbled. Our ankles twisted. Our toes bent in our boots. The horses pulled back on their lead ropes and snorted at the absurdity of the situation. But, we were making progress. More so than when we were on the land.

And then, the moon came out, crystal clear against the black of space. What a pleasant night to be in the mountains. There we were, just a couple of guys taking a moonlight stroll in the river with our ponies. After an hour or so, the screaming pain in our legs turned to blissfully numb, and we hardly even knew we were tearing our ankles off their frozen stumps in the Beirut hodge-podge of broken rocks in the river bed.

But we were right –Ha Ha ! The little river did flow into a bigger one, and when we reached their junction, we crossed a trail, which looked like it headed basically back to where we assumed camp was.

Mounting a horse, or even walking on dry land with no legs is a very weird feeling. It's kind of like being a talking head. It took us a couple of tries to actually remount. The horses were not at all helpful as I recall. Mine said something obscene about frozen legs hanging over his flanks and blah, blah. I was getting tired of his constant complaining. Maybe I was getting cocky, because I knew he couldn't toss me off again. MY boots had frozen to the stirrups. My turn to laugh.

Muskrat Mike and I would share many exploits after that – some were even fun. Some thing about adventures like that, welds its participants into a strange bond. He and I had become good friends, but from then on, I took direct control of all navigational procedures.

TIP – Getting lost : Chances are this will not be a problem if you are with a good guide and outfitter, but you never know.

My old friend and long-time guide Harry and I were on high ridge one day standing next to our horses staring out at the panorama. I did not really know where we were since we had taken a circuitous route to get there in pursuit of a big Buck. It was new country to me. When it was time to leave, Harry grabbed his saddle horn and put a foot in a stirrup like he had done a thousand times before. This time the stirrup broke loose, and Harry fell backwards over the side of the ridge and into a big rock pile. It happened in a split second and it happened to a real pro. He was not badly hurt, but he could have been.

If Harry had been hurt, it would have fallen on me to help him. I would have had to get help and I would have had to do it fast. It occurred to me that I always needed to know where we were and what the fastest route back to camp or help of some kind was. From that moment on, I did. I always do.

TIP – Getting lost: Take the time to study a map of the area. Even if you will have a guide. You just never know.

TIP – Getting lost: Always carry a compass. Check it before you leave the camp so you will have a rough orientation as to where you are.

Check it periodically during the day – especially if the sun is not out. Be aware of your location.

TIP – Getting lost: A hand held GPS is a great gadget to have - if for nothing else, to check your altitude from time to time. They can save your life too.

Again, they are not necessary if you are going with a good guide, but absolutely essential if you are on your own.

TIP – Getting lost: Actually, it amazes me that people ever get lost in the mountains. Lost and not found, that is.

All rivers, even the tiniest trickle, even a dried up non-river flow to the ocean. Even if you can not find your camp or your starting point, you can always get out by following a stream. Chances are that you will be following a stream up-hill when you are going into the mountains. Stay alert to the one you are following as you go up. Be mindful of which ones you cross as you traverse along the slopes.

If the worst has come, follow a stream back to the world.

CLIFFS
ON THE EDGE, AND OFF IT TOO

Whitey, Dead Eye and I were way way way back on the top of Greystone ridge, really too far away from camp at that time of the afternoon. The sun was just an inch from the horizon – prime time. But, if we stayed here to see if anything decided to feed out just before sunset, unless we could take a short-cut somewhere, we would not be riding into camp until ten or eleven o'clock at night. This would certainly piss everyone off – especially the cook. And more importantly the horses.

Whitey was relatively new to the guiding business. He had spent a season packing for our outfitter and he was letting him take hunters out for short day-trips on his own this season. He was a nice kid and good with the horses. He was just a little green in the planning department.

Whitey pulled up on his reigns and dropped out of the saddle. We were in full hunt mode, which meant whispering. "Let's do some glassing," he said.

Dead Eye and I dismounted and pulled out our binoculars. This was a great spot, but because it was so far away, it seldom got hunted by our guys except earlier in the day. But, to get here in the morning, you pretty much had to leave the night before. I'd been here a couple of times before.

I moved in close to Whitey. "We're pretty far away," I whispered.

"Yeah. I know"

"We gotta ride all the way back to Smith's draw to get down to the trail and it's about two hours from there to camp."

"Yeah. I know"

You don't show any signs of fear when you are Cowboy hunting. In fact, you don't show any signs of fear when you are Cowboy anything. It's kind-of a code – dumb as it may be. You've heard about Cowboys getting trampled by some rank bull they were trying to ride. A little fear might have been helpful then. And, I don't think there is anything wrong with a little fear most of the time anyway. It can keep you healthy and maybe even alive.

Whitey pulled his binoculars away from his face and pointed down the ridge. "See that line of trees down there," he said. "There's a deep draw there with a little crick running down to Wilson creek. There's a pretty good trail there and it links up with the Wilson trail. That'll take us back to camp in a hurry."

"You're sure?"

"Yeah. Me and Timmy rode up it one day this summer when we was packing in the camp."

"Did you ever drop down to it from here?"

"No, but I reckon if we just ride down this finger, we'll be able to switch-back our way down to it. We'll be back to camp in time for supper."

One switch-backs when the going is too steep to ride straight up or down a hill. "Switch-backing our way down to it" did not sound like fun. I could feel my knees starting to ache. Fear had started working its way into my every thought. Panic was waiting just off stage.

We stood there glassing for about fifteen minutes. In another fifteen minutes the sun would be down. Fifteen minutes after that and it would be haunted house black. Oh good, I thought. We were going to switch-back down in the dark. This will be lots of fun.

"Whelp," Whitey said. "I guess we ain't gonna see nothin' tonight. Better get ridin'"

We mounted up in the failing light and rode out along the crest of a long finger, which came off the top of the ridge and gradually sloped down toward the valley below. In my mind, I was trying to make calculations about the slope of the finger, and what appeared to be the bottom of the draw where Whitey said there was a creek bed and trail and the other side of the valley. I have a very small computer chip between my ears, so calculations are difficult and frequently flawed. Nonetheless, something did not appear mathematically possible unless our slope angle suddenly began increasing at a rapid pace. Slope angles that increase to suddenly are called CLIFFS!

Whitey dismounted just as our horses began jamming their feet into the ground ahead of them to slow their pace against the mounting forces of gravity.

"We'd better walk it from here," he said.

D'ya think? Our slope angle had increased to at least 50% and from what I could calculate, it was about to jump to 100% - also known as being airborne.

We walked about fifteen yards and sure enough we were now standing on the edge of a cliff. The horses were tossing their heads back, trying to pull their reigns out of our hands. Their mental slope calculators are far better tuned than your average Cowboy's.

Whitey stood at the edge of the precipice with his hands on his hips. "I didn't reckon it was so cliffed up here."

"Yep, pretty cliffed up," I said. "We better get riding. It's a long way back up this finger just to get to the top. Then we got a... ."

Whitey cut me off. He was still calculating. "I reckon it's only about a hundred feet or so to the bottom." He started pointing with his finger. " If we slid down through that little trough right there… and then sidehilled it over to that ledge…we could drop down through that chute… then it would be just a few feet to the flat spot… and it's done." He had actually picked out a route over the edge of a cliff. Cowboys.

"You guys are nuts," my horse said.

"Whitey. I can not climb down there. And I don't think you can either."

He had turned and was looking at Dead Eye and me over his shoulder. "I think we can do it. It'll cut two hours off our trip back. It'd be worth it. "

"It wouldn't be worth getting hurt or killed," Dead Eye said.

A stubborn cowboy look suddenly washed across his face. "I'm gonna do it," he said. "If it turns out to be too hard, I'll just climb back up and we'll start ridin'"

"It is too hard, Whitey. Let's get riding. We're running out of light and I'd at least like to be back up on the ridge where we know there's a good trail." Dead Eye seldom offered opinions about anything, but anybody could see that this was a mistake – anybody but Whitey.

He was not listening. "See you all at the bottom," he said, turning toward the cliff.

He was right about how easy it would be – at least the first two steps anyway. The gravel broke loose from under his foot on the third one, the coefficient of friction having been sufficiently overcome. His horse jerked the reigns out of his hands just as his ass hit the dirt. He slipped about seven or eight feet and then really got moving. He went right past that little sidehill spot he wanted to make and went over the little ledge too. Yes, he was mostly airborne with only an elbow here or a butt cheek there catching in the dust, dislodging rocks, which tumbled along with him in sort of mad cluster of falling debris, part mother earth and part Cowboy.

My horse whispered in my ear, "Totally nuts. And, if you think I am going down there to get him, you're nuts too."

We lost sight of Whitey for a minute, as he slipped over the little ledge, but we knew he was not dead yet because we could hear him. "This is what he was saying: "Aaaaaah. Aaaaaaaah. Aaaaaaaaaah."

Then, there was nothing. I thought I heard a low moan, but I was not really sure.

"Whitey. Whitey," Dead Eye and I shouted, in perfect two-part harmony.

Whitey's horse turned and started walking slowly up the finger toward the top. He was shaking his head in total disbelief as he walked. Dead Eye caught him.

"Whitey," I shouted again trying to peer as far over the edge as I could. Still nothing.

"Jesus," Dead Eye said. "We'd better get ridin'. We're gonna need to get some help up here. "

"Maybe we can find the trail he was talking about that leads back up to where he is."

"In the dark?"

"Right. Let's go. Give me the lead rope off his horse. I'll drag him along. "

"He'll probably just follow us. We need to get moving. I'm not worrying about his horse."

Dead eye had a point. We didn't really need to be dragging another horse. Besides, he was right the horse would just follow us home. Maybe even lead us home.

"Guys."

Dead Eye and I snapped our heads around and strained to see out over the cliff edge to the flat below.

"Come on down," Whitey said, as he hobbled out on the flat. He was holding his left elbow and was limping badly, but he was not dead. "There's nothing to it. Piece of cake."

"Naw, we thought we'd just take a nice ride in the dark," I said.

Whitey slapped at the back of his pants knocking rocks and sticks that had clung to his ass to the ground. "You're a bunch chicken shits," he said. "Can you find the main trail back to camp on your own?"

"Of course we can," the horses answered in perfect three-part harmony.

TIP - Cliffs: Every year somebody falls off a cliff in the mountains. Every year somebody gets killed doing it. Everything seems innocent enough. You're walking along the ground gets too steep, you step on some lose pebbles and in the next second, you're falling. I have done it. Fortunately, some scrapes and bruises were my only injuries. Tom Terrific grabbed a tree branch one time to help him navigate some vertical terrain. That got him airborne. Both old dead eye and even the Gunslinger have done it. Florida Dave took his horse over the edge with him. And, one guy we used to know stepped off the wrong side of his horse and woke up dead in the bottom of a canyon about a hundred feet down. It happens.

TIP - Cliffs: Stick to the trails when you are Cowboy hunting. If you are with a reputable outfitter and guide they can lead you away from the main route based on their experience and knowledge of the area. That is one of the things you are paying them for. But, if you are by yourself, this can be a dangerous practice. Don't fear. You will still have plenty of action by staying on the beaten paths and you'll live to tell about it.

Tips: Cliffs: Don't trust a finger. A finger is a secondary ridge which comes off the main ridge of a mountain. The vast majority of them end in a cliff. Think about it. The valleys and canyons in between the fingers and ridges are carved there by of the flow of water over a bazillion years. Despite how long it takes, this is not a gentle process. The closer you get to the bottom the steeper the cut is and the more likely there will be cliffs. Be very careful. Heading down the wrong finger can get you killed. At the very least, it could end up adding hours and miles to your journey by forcing you to back-track to a trail after having taken some perceived short-cut or followed some game far too long.

LIONS AND TIGERS AND BEARS AND WOLVES TOO

Alright, you can forget about Tigers. You are not going to be seeing any of those or any Zebras either on a Cowboy hunt. You might see a mountain Lion though. Their numbers are on the rise in the west, and their boldness is becoming a little alarming. I am not aware of any Cowboys - say the last guy in a string of riders – getting pounced on by a Lion looking for lunch, but sooner or later... .

Talk about bold, however, and these days you have got to be thinking Bears.

GETTING OUT OF DODGE

Paradise is a log lodge with a cozy fireplace and a broad, panoramic view of the Tetons. Our outfitter, Harry and his chief guide Roberto had called us into the living room of the lodge the night before we were to ride up into the mountains for a week of Elk and deer hunting. It was the pre-hunt briefing.

Meetings like this are not uncommon. Most outfitters use them to outline the rules of the camp, describe the plan, make sure everybody has the required licenses and usually collect any money owed on the trip in advance. Harry did all of the above and then turned the meeting over to Roberto.

"I've got some good news, some bad news and some more bad news and then a little more bad news," he began. "Let's start with the bad news. The weather report ain't good. We're supposed to be getting a little rain and snow tomorrow morning. Our ride in is usually about six hours. Might take a little longer this time, and we're probably going to get wet. So, everybody make sure you have your rain gear handy in the morning."

Everybody in the room, including Roberto craned their necks to look out the large picture window at the sun setting behind the Tetons. What ever tomorrow would bring had not interfered with the spectacle going on over the most photographed piece of real estate in the world.

"The second little bit of bad news I have," Roberto continued. "Is that the migration of Elk out of Yellowstone began a few days ago and I am afraid that it is almost over."

This was bad news as far as I was concerned. I don't care about the weather. I can get my head around most of that and deal with it. But, you wait a year between Elk hunts. That's a long time to fantasize. You sure don't want to hear that there aren't any where you intend to hunt. You certainly don't want to hear it the night before you're supposed to be riding in.

"Whoa," a hunter from Wisconsin, I did not know said. "You mean there aren't any Elk for us to hunt?"

"Well, no. There are still going to be some stragglers and we have a few resident Elk in that area who do not migrate, but not a lot."

Roberto was back-peddling. We had booked this particular hunt to try to catch the annual migration out of Yellowstone National Park to the flats in the Jackson Hole basin and the home of the National Elk Refuge.

Elk are migratory creatures like Caribou. Each summer for millions of years, they have been climbing into the high mountains to avoid insects and feed in the pristine meadows. In the winter, when the snow covers up their food, they migrate back down to the lowlands – sometimes hundreds of miles away. Man has interfered with that natural migration and has been forced to build refuges for the Elk to winter to preserve their numbers. While there are many such refuges in the Rockies, The National Elk Refuge in Jackson is the largest. Even though the refuge contains over twenty-five thousand acres and feeds roughly 8000 Elk each year, The overall number of Elk in the Yellowstone/Teton range is still bigger than what the refuge can handle.

Rather than let the animlas starve, the herd has to be culled each year. That's what we were there to do. The refuge managers do it because they have to. We hunters help them because we like to.

Missing the migration was a big disappointment. You could feel the energy suck out of the room as everyone contemplated Roberto's report. "We'll probably still see a few, but they'll be far and few between."

And then, as if this was not enough, he went on. "The really bad news is that we are having a real problem with Grizzly Bears at our camp. I can promise you that you will see one, and there is a very good chance that you will be challenged by one. Maybe even chased. They have become very aggressive. They are now starting to come to the sound of a gunshot because they know there will be a carcass. It used to be that they'd wait until night to forage on it. But now, they are chasing us off the kill before we get a chance to get it caped out."

Again, a pall fell over the room as each hunter contemplated this little tid-bit of bad news. I have been to many pre-hunt pep talks over the years. This was without question, the least peppy. "What was that good news you said you had," I asked.

"Oh yeah, I almost forgot," he said. "The cook made cherry cobbler for desert. Let's go eat."

The first of Roberto's dire predictions came to fruition in the early morning hours. I was awakened by the sound of ice crystals clicking off the windows of my cabin – not a good sign. The pleasant evening, with its lush mountain sunset had turned evil in a hell of a hurry. A strong north wind whistled against the log walls and splattered everything with rain and ice. It blew my hat off as I walked to the lodge for a cup of coffee.

The six hour ride into camp turned into about eight hours of absolute misery. It was the worst ride-in I have made in 30 years and that includes one in which the icicles were standing sideways from all of the trees. Harry, the outfitter who had been riding up into this camp for over fifty years said it was the worst he had ever made. Despite our rain gear - whatever combination of it any of us had – we were soaked. And cold? You have no idea. It took me two days to stop shivering. If the camp had been just one more mile away, I am not certain I would have made it.

Roberto had been right about the weather, although he understated it a bit. When we dismounted in the corral, I noticed something else, which appeared to confirm another item in his triad of gloom.

Many modern cowboys have replaced the old split rail wooden corral fences with portable battery or solar-powered electric fences. Part of this is because of changes in Forest Service policies which prohibit leaving any man-made structures, including corrals, from being left in place around the calendar. Part of it is because electric fences are just a whole lot easier to deal with. Harry had been using an electric corral fence for years. What was surprising was that he had installed another one around the tents. I had never seen that before. When I asked about it, I was told what I least did not want to hear. "We're tryin' to keep the Bears out."

Jees! Talk about confirmation. These guys had evidently been so plagued by problems that they were trying to fend them off with high-tech electrical gadgets. What was particularly troubling was that the outhouse did not have the same protection as the sleeping tents and the cook tent had. It was at least seventy five yards away from the main camp. I wondered how long it would take a cowboy with his pants half undone to cover that distance.

"Does it work," I asked.

"Don't know."

We found out later what worked best. And remarkably it was not an electric fence.

After dropping a good eight inches of snow on our camp, the weather broke a little the next day - not enough to make things comfortable, but enough to allow us to go out and survey the area in hopes of catching a straggler coming out of the park as a result of the storm.

Every piece of gear I owned was wet including my spare underwear. Every piece of gear my tent mate – a guy named Jimmy from Pennsylvania –

owned was wet. Even our sleeping bags were wet. Apparently the manny covering our stuff had blown loose on the ride up and our gear had been exposed to the weather. Jimmy and I decided to skip the morning hunt opting instead to build a nice fire in our stove and dry out our stuff. We went out later in the day and rode up to the top of one of the nearby peaks, which was socked in by a heavy cloud cover. Roberto thought that maybe if we climbed high enough we could get above the clouds and we'd find some clear weather. Or, maybe if we got up out of the little valley we were in, the weather on the other side would be better. Neither case turned out to be true. The weather was so terrible that we could barely see to ride, let alone hunt. Every now and then, we could come across a clear patch. We decided to ride in early, have some dinner and try again tomorrow. Tomorrow would be better. Everyone agreed on that. It could hardly miss.

Just before dark, we heard a gunshot. And, it was not far off. A few minutes later, we heard another one. We all thought that was a good sign. One shot put the animal down and a second shot a few minutes later to put him out of his misery. The guides and wranglers started formulating a plan to get a couple of mules ready to go out and pack it in. Too late. By the time they had caught a couple of mules, the guide and the hunter he had been with were back in camp. We knew those shots did not sound that far away.

Yes, they'd shot an Elk – a small bull. It was only about a half a mile out – if that.

"Great," Roberto said. "We're getting mules ready to go out and get it."

"We're gonna need a bunch of mules," the guide said. "There's already two Bears on it. We're gonna have to drive 'em off it. We saw five Bears and two Elk today."

The guide and his hunter had jumped two bull Elk in a little meadow as they were riding back into camp. They were able to dismount fast enough to get off one shot. The shot knocked the Elk right off his feet, but he got up and ran out of the meadow and over a ridge. By the time they mounted back up and tracked it over the ridge, the first had gotten to it. It was only a few minutes before the second Grizzly arrived at the kill.

The Grizzlys in the Bridger Teton Wilderness and all of the areas surrounding Yellowstone National Park have learned to come to the sound of a gunshot. This is a new phenomenon. They have lost their fear of man. They are no longer content to find a gut pile left from field dressing a deer or an Elk and are now trying to beat the hunters to the fallen animal. They are actually chasing hunters off the kill and have become very aggressive.

The second shot we heard was not a coup-de-gras. It was the guide trying to scare the Bears off the kill. It didn't work. They tried mounting a charge by riding at the Bears at a fast clip, yelling and shouting in an attempt to scare them off the kill. That didn't work either. The Bears actually rose up on their hind legs in preparation to make a counter-charge of their own. The guide and the hunter opted to return to camp.

The outfitter and all the guides had a major Pow Wow. Finally the decision was made not to attempt to rescue the kill from the Bears in the dark, but rather to have some dinner and a few cocktails instead. It's amazing what monumental decisions can come from a group of Cowboys when they put their minds together and focus on one problem.

What I personally found disturbing about the incident was the fact that it all happened so close to camp.

As we saddled up the next morning in the dark, I could look up from time to time and watch the clouds part enough to let a few stars shine through. This was a good sign.

Jimmy took off with his guide Ralphy. They shot a nice bull around lunch time and with the help of a couple of wranglers called in by radio were able to get it packed back to camp before the Bears got to it.

The hunter and guide who had been involved in the altercation the night before rode out with a couple of wranglers and a bunch of mules right after day break. They were able to retrieve the antlers and one front shoulder of meat. The Bears got the rest.

I had drawn the guide boss, Roberto. He and I left camp just as the sky was beginning to lighten enough to allow us to see the ground from horseback. I am not certain that was good. The snow around our camp was littered with Grizzly tracks the size of pie plates. I looked back at the electrical wire that surrounded the camp. It looked awful skinny to me. If I extrapolated a Bear in my mind based on the size of the tracks I was seeing from the horse, the result was a huge monster that would hardly notice a little snap from a wire like that, especially through six inches of fur. I have seen dogs grit their teeth and run through invisible fences taking the small jolt in exchange for a romp through the neighborhood unabated.

"Cowboy up," my horse said. "We're going Elk huntin'. Stop freaking out about Bears."

"Oh yeah," I said, leaning forward and whispering in his ear. "Let's see how tough you are if we see one. Don't do none of that jumping and lurching stuff. I don't want to fall off and have to outrun your sorry ass."

See, I can be tough if I have to.

We came across our first Bear about forty-five minutes out. He looked like a Volkswagen Beetle standing in the snow watching us from about fifty yards away. I have seen Bear before while hunting, but usually only their ass ends as they bolt away from us. This big boy was not running from anybody. In fact, he was doing this rocking thing, where he dug his front paws into the ground and flexed his massive shoulders forward at us as if to say, "You want a piece of me?"

We rode past him without incident, but having my back to the big brute made me as nervous as a cat pissing razor blades. I kept feeling his presence and knew that at any minute he would rip me out of the saddle and have lunch. And just between you and me, that tough-guy horse never took his eyes off that Bear. He walked along with his neck craned backwards and his ears cocked right at it. He didn't straighten out for at least a mile.

Roberto had been right about the weather. He had been right about the Bears. We saw two more that day. Also at close range, but neither of them seemed as menacing as that first big one. He was not right about the Elk. Everyone in camp got one that day. Roberto and I popped a monster bull later that afternoon. I stood guard with my rifle as Roberto field dressed it. We radioed back to camp for a wrangler who brought us a couple of mules. He hangs on the wall of my cabin in northern Michigan today.

Our troubles were not over for that trip however. Jimmy and I both had deer tags that we had planned on filling too. The next day, we headed out with Roberto to see if we could find a couple. Did we see Bears? You bet we did. Four of them, as a matter of fact. And just one puny 4 x 4 deer, almost at dusk.

I had taken a number of mule deer over the years and was not interested in this one. Jimmy, however, had not and wanted to fill his tag. This little guy seemed more than willing to accommodate him by standing broadside in a little valley about a hundred yards below the ridge we had been riding on. He stood there and watched as we dismounted. He stood there and watched as Jimmy got positioned for the shot. When he got hit, the little son-of-a-bitch did not fall down dead. Instead, he ran down the valley and disappeared into a small island of trees three hundred yards away.

Once again, it was almost dark. We jumped on our horses as fast as we could and started following his trail. It was not hard. By the amount of blood in the snow, we knew he was not coming out of those trees. We stopped on a little mound a few yards above the little clump of pines. I held the horses while Roberto and Jimmy slid down to the trees.

"We got him," Roberto said as their flashlight beams knifed around in the trees like laser swords.

"Yeah, well you had better get him out of there fast because we got company," I said.

It had been less than ten minutes since Jimmy had taken his single shot and already the unmistakable outline of a very big Bear had appeared back above us in the very spot where we had been. He was sky-lined against the snow and was moving toward us - not away, or even standing still, but moving our way in our own tracks, our own blood-filled tracks.

"Guys," I said, jumping on my horse. "I am not kidding, we need to get moving here."

Roberto popped out of the trees and started scrambling up the mound to get a look. "Holy shit," he said.

"No Kidding holy shit," my horse said. "If that Bear gets any closer, I'm tossin' fat boy off for bait and splitting for home."

You have to love a horse with good common sense. I looked over my shoulder, the Bear was still advancing. I still held the reigns of the other two horses. Roberto was fussing with something on his saddle. His horse was pushing into mine. We were about to have a Rodeo. That was all we needed.

Roberto yelled at Jimmy. " Get on your horse."

Meanwhile the Bear was standing on his back legs in the trail, less than a hundred yards away and Roberto was heading back into the trees.

"Roberto! Where are you going. We gotta move man." I was getting a little nervous. Okay, I was starting to panic.

I could hear some chopping sounds. The Bear was back on all fours and moving steadily toward us. He was rocking back and forth zig-zagging on the trail like he was thinking about what to do – planning his next move. In what was probably only a few seconds but what seemed like long long minutes, Roberto appeared out of the trees. It was just about dark. I could see the Bear outlined against the snow, but seeing Roberto against the trees was difficult. He was holding something. It took a bit to figure out that he had a hatchet in one hand and the head of that deer in the other.

Jimmy was on his horse. I tried to steady Roberto's as he jammed the hatchet into one of his saddle bags and climbed on board.

I handed him his reigns and we took off - but, not to our left away from the Bear, rather to our right, straight at it. "Roberto. Wrong way," I yelled.

I could not hear everything he said. He and Jimmy were galloping already. It was something about a cliff. I kicked up my horse, which was hardly necessary. He was already on the move and in a second we were galloping down a big hill right in front of that big Bear. I could see him out of the corner of my eye, way way way closer than I would have liked. I hunched up my shoulders as I rode. I knew that at any second I was going to feel that Bear's claws as he dug them into my back and dragged me off my horse. I will never forget that feeling. I don't think that Bear was more than twenty-five yards away when I crossed in front of him. If it hadn't been for the fact that I was on a horse and that there was the scent of a carcass in the air, I am certain that either me or that Bear would have been dead.

TIP - Bears: Grizzlies are a protected species. Game and Fish officers are under mandate to protect them. If you shoot one, even in self defense, there will be an extensive investigation, complete with crime scene investigators and the yellow police tape. If it is determined that your life was not in acute and immediate danger (read that as a Bear has your leg in its mouth) you will be charged with a felony. In the wilderness, the Bears have rights over those of hunters.

TIP - Bears: Don't think Bears are becoming a problem? Google this: "Hunter killed by Grizzly ." It's just a matter of time.

Wolves have also lost their fear of man. It used to be that they were even more skittish that Bears. Not any more. These days, they do not run away either. We had a number of them trailing us on the trip described above. A hunter was forced to shoot one in self defense in May of 2008.

TIP - Bears (and Wolves): It is against the law to leave a carcass in the field. It's a big no no. We did it twice on that trip. Our outfitter reported both incidents to the authorities. Because he is such a well-known outfitter in the area, they relied on what he said rather than investigating. If you are by yourself and have an incident you must report it and be ready for an investigation.

My old friend Paullywog and I were hunting in Idaho's Frank Church Wilderness when he and his guide shot a nice Mule deer. It was almost dark when they hit it and it ran down into the bottom of a canyon where packing it out in the dark would have been difficult. So, they gutted it out and left the carcass under some pine boughs with the intention of bringing in some mules to pack it out in the morning.

By morning it was too late.

We had seen a number of Wolf tracks around our camp and on the trails where we rode. We heard them howling every night and in the early mornings. When Paullywog and his guide went down to the bottom the next morning to pack out the deer, I rode to the top of a bluff far above them incase they kicked something out on the way in. From our perch, my guide and I heard thirteen different Wolves (or one Wolf running from place to place) howling in the valley below. When we returned to camp that evening, I expected to see some deer quarters hanging from the meat pole. There was nothing. All the wolves had left Paullywog were the antlers and one hoof. We took them with us when we left.

Here's the point: We were stopped just before we crossed over the Idaho border into Wyoming by two Idaho State Troopers and one Idaho Game and Fish officer. Our outfitter had reported the incident, as he should have, but these guys wanted to see the evidence for themselves. They knew who we were and had been watching for us. We had done nothing wrong, but it underscores how serious these guys are about following the rules.

TIP - Guard: Horses, despite the enormous help they are to Cowboys in any situation, can also act as pretty fine security devices too. Savvy Cowboys learn to listen to them. They can tell whenever something at camp is not right – say in the middle of the night. It is not hard to figure out when a Lion, Tiger, Bear or a Tin Man is approaching camp. The horses will tell you.

Mules are even better. In fact Mules can be much more proactive and can provide far better security measures than alarms.

I do not know whose idea is was to put the electrical wire around the Camp up there in the Teton Wilderness, but I for one did not trust it. Those Bears were big. They had a lot of fur on them. I had some serious doubts about how well that little wire would work to keep them out. I've grabbed a few of those wires in my time – or they've grabbed me. Yes, it is unpleasant and certainly something you should avoid, but they are far from lethal. If there was something I wanted on the other side of an electric fence, I can assure you it would not stop me from getting it. I was pretty sure it would not stop a Bear that had similar intentions. Apparently, our outfitter, a very experience Cowboy hunter and one who was old enough to know a thing or two, felt the same way.

We had fresh snow every night on that trip. And with each snow we had a number of fresh Bear tracks surrounding the camp every morning. They were closer and closer to the wire every day. The horses could not make it through the night without having some sort of nervous tantrum and everyone knew why. Finally, old Harry made a bold move. Instead of locking the twenty or so mules up in the coral every night with the horses, he turned them loose. Mules are far smarter and much tougher than horses. Harry knew that they would stay together and not wander far from camp. He also knew that there was no way a pack of Mules would let a Bear or even a group of Bears come any where near them or the camp.

I believe he was right. From inside my dark tent at night, I could still hear the horses freaking out from time to time, but every time I did, It was not long and I would hear the thundering hooves of an small army of protector Mules chasing the demons away.

HORSE WRECKS AND RODEOS

Yes, Cowboy hunting can be a little dangerous. You might catch a little hypothermia. You might get dehydrated. You might fall off a cliff and you might even get into a pissing match with a Bear. But, admittedly the chances of any of those things happening are slim.

However, the chances of you having some sort of problem with a horse and possibly getting hurt are very high. In fact, you can almost count on the fact that on just about every Cowboy hunt you will attend either you or someone in your group will have a problem with a horse – lots of problems with lots of horses.

ROYAL OAK RODEO

I was born and raised in Royal Oak Michigan, a par five away from Detroit – not a place known for much of anything Cowboy.

In the last few minutes of light – a time when most game is bagged – Mountain man Dick and I took a nice elk on a high plateau a couple of horse hours above the ranch in the Wyoming mountains. It was way back when the Royal Oak green behind my ears ran pretty much all the way to my heels.

"Nice Shot," Dick said. "But, take a good luck around. Notice where you are. See that peak over there? We call that the Tits. This here creek next to us called SOB. The trail is a couple a hundred yards to the left there. Got it?"

"Yeah. But what am I, keeping a log book or something," I said, ever the smart-ass.

"I don't know, but I want you to remember where this thing is, because I got something I gotta do in town tomorrow, and I won't be able to come back up here and pack it down and I'm short on manpower and it's going to be too late to get it back tonight and I only have Dan. And... ."

Dick got himself lost in thought and just started rambling there for a minute and thinking and staring off into space. "I am going to have to send you up here with Dan to get it, and he's only been on the job a week ,and I don't know if he can find it, and I never thought you'd actually hit it, and I want you to know where it is so you can show him, and I'll give you a couple of horses, real gentle ones like BB and…no she's up at Pow Wow with Bobby, so it will have to be…I don't know about that one and Dan, well… sending two rookies after an Elk…nuts… who'da thought you'd hit the goddam… ."

Eventually, Dick and I got the Elk field-dressed and covered with a stack of pine boughs. Dick said that would help keep vulltures and coyotes and other things off the carcass until morning.

Other things?

We headed back down to the ranch in coffin-like darkness.

The next morning after the usual confusion it takes to line out a couple of riders and a couple of pack-horses, Dan and I were on the trail to fetch my Elk.

"You're new here, huh Dan," I said.

"Yeah, just starting my second week. "

"Where you from?"

"Michigan"

"Really. So am I."

"No kidding. Where."

"Royal Oak."

"That's where I'm from," Dan said, spinning around in his saddle. Where bout's in Royal Oak."

My guess was that he was not much older than about eighteen or so. It was obvious that he was interested in news from home. "Twelve mile and Connecticut."

"No kidding. I live at Twelve and Wilson."

"I'll be dammed," l said. "We're homies." Wilson was the next street over. Despite the considerable difference in our ages, it was true, we were homies.

The ride up to the Elk was uneventful. It was nothing more than another spectacular day in Wyoming wilderness. I found the Elk with little difficulty. Two Golden Eagles lifted off the stack of pine bows when we rode up. In this case, the "Other things" were not particularly menacing to anything other than gophers.

We tied our horses to a couple of trees and dismounted. Dan tied one of the packhorses to another tree, and then tied the other one to a fallen log about as long as a telephone pole. I didn't think much of it at the time.

An experienced guide could probably quarter an Elk in about a half an hour. Dan and I took almost two to get the job done. But it was a beautiful morning and I could not think of anything I'd rather be doing. When we were done, we sat down and rested on the log to which Dan had tied the pack horse.

Dan looked at his watch. "It's almost noon."

"Yeah," I said. "Time for lunch."

"Yeah, but then I want to get packed up and back down," Dan said a little nervously. "They'll be wondering where we are down there."

"Don't worry Dan. I'll tell them I made you take me on a sight-seeing trip."

We ate quick and repacked our saddle bags. Then, Dan picked up an entire Elk quarter and began walking toward the pack horse tied to the log.

"Hold that panier open for me and I'll drop this in," he said.

I moved toward the horse and spread the leather lip of the panier sack so Dan could drop in the meat. As I did, the horse turned his head back toward us, and cast a giant eye our way.

I can still see the look in that eye. I've seen it dozens of times since. A horse will give you that look in the split second **JUST BEFORE IT IS ABOUT TO TOTALLY FREAK OUT!!!**

If only I had known. Bug eye. Flared nostril. It's a sure sign.

Dan was struggling with the weight of the quarter. It was bloody and the fur was damp. He held it against his chest and arched his back to drop it into the panier. I caught another glimpse of the horse eye. This time the panic registered in my mind. "Dan we might have a problem," I said.

I did not completely get the statement out before the dooky hit the fan.

That horse had no intention of getting anywhere near a bloody stump of Elk leg, let alone actually carry one down a mountain on his back. Not today anyway!

He started with a little buck, then rapidly escalated the entire affair into an Olympic-caliber tumbling routine. The fact that he was tied to a log meant nothing. He picked it up like it wasn't even there and started making his way back home, right now!

I took a giant step back, tripped over the moving log and landed on my back in a pile of sharp sticks. Dan caught the full force of the exploding horse in the chest, catapulting him backwards onto the pile of chopped Elk. A branch from the airborne log slapped the rump of the other packhorse, which immediately launched him into a acrobatic routine of his own. The pandemonium, of course, spread in a second to the other two horses who had been dosing at the hitch. Before we knew it, trees were snapping, and horses were screaming and dancing like Junebugs on a hot griddle.

Dan scrambled to his feet and began running down the mountain after the packhorse who was pretty much making a new trail down the slope with the log in tow. I fought to stand. Sticks had penetrated various parts of my body, and I had just missed being impaled on a large, broken branch, which stuck out of the pile just looking for a likely victim. A dust storm had risen under the hooves of the insane horses and began blotting out the sun. Grasshoppers and flies took flight to avoid the carnage all around them. High above, two Eagles stared down in total disbelief, at the rookies from Royal Oak and their raucous Rodeo.

Dan, the packhorse and the flying, bouncing, tearing log disappeared down the mountain as I battled to calm the other horses. There really wasn't much I could to but say things like: "okay, okay, calm down, take it easy, it's all right, coo-chee-coo." You know, the usual horse stuff. These guys were very agitated, and I did not want to risk getting too near them until they could get a grip. It certainly hadn't taken much to get them so wild. I didn't want rock the boat too much.

Finally, after about five minutes of soft-talk, the three horses stood silently at their posts, chest's heaving, eyes de-bugging, nostrils shrinking back down to only tennis-ball size. But, there was no sign of Dan or the other horse or the log. It took a full hour before he showed, horse in tow, log not present.

"Damn," he said, panting, his shirt soaked in sweat. " I had to chase this guy halfway back to the ranch before I caught him. Look at the cuts on his flank from branches on that log he was towing. Dick is gonna to kill me."

"There, there , it'll be all right, coocheecoo," I said.

The real problem was still ahead. We still needed to get the packhorses to agree to fetch that Elk down to the ranch for us.

We started by separating the horses. Panic is like a virus. It will spread fast to hosts in close proximity to one another.

Then, we gently and carefully loaded the other packhorse with two quarters of Elk. It took a while, because we were going slow.

Going slow, however, did not help with the other packhorse. We started by tying him to a good, strong tree. We softly stroked his neck. We hand-fed him bunches of sweet green grass we plucked from around from the creek bank. We talked lots of "Coo-chi-coo" to him and did everything short of hiring a Geisha girl to satisfy his every desire. Nothing worked. Every time we came anywhere near him with a chunk of Elk, he went nuts.

Dan said they had packed out another Elk for a hunter three days earlier. He was certain they'd used the same packhorse to get the job done. Why he refused to do it today was a mystery. Regardless. We eventually came to the conclusion that if we wanted to get that Elk down the mountain we were either going to have to carry it down ourselves or find a different horse to do it.

Guess whose horse we used? Guess who had to ride that ornery packhorse back down to the ranch? Sometimes it doesn't matter who you are or how much you pay. When it is your turn in the barrel it's your turn.

TIP- HORSES: They say horses have the mentality of a two-year-old child. Who knows what they think from moment to moment or day to day. Best bet: don't trust them. Something they will gladly do today, they will not think of doing tomorrow.

TIP- PACKING THEM OUT: If you can, tie your packhorse to a good tree before you try to get him loaded. Get him away from other horses if possible. Go slow. A dead butchered Elk looks like mayhem to a horse – and it is. Rub a little blood on your hands. Pet his face. Let him get used to the smell. Put some on a manny and gently rub his back with it. Don't make any sudden movements. Don't drop anything heavy like an Elk leg into a pannier. Baby it in. Get someone to hold his halter and keep him from turning his head to see what's going on behind him. Try to not let him see what you're putting on him. And, most importantly, be prepared to get the hell out of Dodge! Something as simple as a flared nostril, a bugged eye, a small whinny can turn ugly fast. If the horse starts to freak you need to stand clear fast. Don't be a hero and try to get the horse calmed down. It won't happen once he starts. Just stand back and let him tire himself out.

ROCK PILE RODEO

Gardner Montana hosts the northern entrance into Yellowstone National Park. It is one of the most scenic areas in the entire world. Climb just about any bluff, look south, and you will be treated to one beautiful natural canvas.

A giant hunter from Texas, who called himself "Tex" (go figger) and I stood on just such a bluff, above a rocky canyon, about ten miles east of the Gardner entrance, on a warm October morning. We could see about twenty miles into Yellowstone when we looked up, and when we looked down, we could see the fence line of the park itself only about two hundred yards away. We were about as close to the border as we could get - too close in fact.

Our guide was a nice enough guy named William. He claimed to have had considerable experience hunting and packing in the area, but to both Tex and I, he didn't seem all that encumbered by deep thought processes – if you know what I mean.

"You boys stay here for a while," He said, climbing back on his horse. "I'm going to circle around this ridge and get a look from the other side. If something comes up out of the park you'll have a good shot."

"Why don't' one of us go with ya'll, so maybe we might both get one," Tex said.

William stared up at the sky for a second, as if seeking Devine guidance, then said: "Naw."

Tex and I glanced at each other, sharing a moment of logic dissolution acceptance – LDA in hunting parlance.

As William disappeared behind a stand of timber, I said: "Well, maybe we ought to at least spread apart a ways. I'll go around that timber and try to get a different look at this little canyon. We'll have it covered a little better."

" Okay. Ya'll be careful. Hollar out if you need some help."

"You bet," I said.

As I walked away, Tex found himself a nice spot to get settled in hopes of getting a shot of anything coming out of the park and walking up our little patch of mountain – a possibility, but at that time, one I thought was leaning toward the remote side. I walked about a half mile around the rim of the little valley we had been assigned to monitor to a spot where I could see Tex and the area below him where he could not see. When I got settled, Tex waved at me so I knew we had the spot covered. He could see below me and I could see below him and if either of us got a shot, there would be no danger of hitting each other. We sat like that for an hour and watched as the sun molded the colors on the Yellowstone canvas spread magnificently before us.

I must have been lost in the beauty of the morning or daydreaming or maybe sleeping, because I never saw Tex lift his rifle. Suddenly a shot rang out and ricocheted it's way around the canyon to me. I jumped. Tex stood up in his little rock perch, raised his arms in triumph and let out some sort of Texas whooping "hollar."

I still could not see what he had been shooting at, but there wasn't much point in sitting there any longer. I got up and started working my way back around toward the big man. As the angle of my sight changed, I could see the situation. Lying in the rocks a few hundred yards below my perch was a big Elk. Apparently it had been sneaking up the canyon below me where I could not see. Our read of the situation had been good.

As I walked up to Tex, he hollered out: "First one. It's my first one and it's a goodun."

He was right. It was a nice Elk, a six by six with good long brow tines. I'd have shot it in a heartbeat if I had been able to see it. From Tex's perch, it was about a 200 yard shot – just about perfect. However, as we began climbing down to where the animal had fallen, an element of concern began working it's way into my thoughts. Tex was all but running down through the boulders, caught up in the exhilaration of his first trophy. I couldn't blame him, but I was moving a lot slower and thinking about what a tough spot this was. The head of the canyon above us terminated in a difficult collection of Volkswagen-sized boulders, stretching several hundred yards, and gradually rising twenty or thirty feet to the trail above. A man could easily pick his way through the rock and get up that way, but it didn't look like a good place to try to take horses – especially loaded down with Elk. Below, a field of rocks and chair-sized boulders fanned out below the Elk all the way to the Yellowstone fence and beyond. This was going to be one tough pack-out. The Elk lie squarely in the middle of the problem and to make matters worse, he was wedged into a small ravine four or five feet deep.

Tex and I worked our way down to the Elk, took the obligatory photos and then sat down to wait for our guide to show. We hadn't brought any packhorses with us, and so somebody was going to have to ride the two miles back to camp to get a couple. It was a hot day and since Tex would likely want to stay with his Elk and William would likely want to get started quartering it up, I assumed it would be me. Wrong.

It took William almost an hour to get to us. There was no telling where he had been. It was almost ten o'clock already and getting even hotter.

"So William," I said. "Do you want me to ride back to camp and get some packhorses and pack saddles. Randy is there and he can help me get things rigged up. Maybe I can talk him into coming back with me and help out."

William cocked his head up to the sky again for decision help and said: " Naw. I'm gonna cut it up right now."

It was a big Elk. It was lying in a bad spot. It was difficult for us to move efficiently in the rocks. It took the three of us almost another hour to get it field dressed and quartered. At one point or another we all fell into the rocks, or twisted an ankle or wrangled a hand or a wrist or all of the above. But finally, the Elk was ready to be packed out. Of course, we didn't have any packhorses to put it on, but then Cowboy logic survives in very rarefied atmospheres, which are frequently inaccessible to the normal mind.

"Time for lunch," William said, yanking a brown bag out of his saddlebag.

"It's a little early for me William," I said. I'd be willing to go back now and get those packhorses while you guys eat. I'll catch a bite in the saddle. That way we can get this thing back and still have time to get set up for the evening hunt."

William cocked his head skyward, and pulled at his chin whiskers like he was actually thinking. "Naw," he said.

Our horses were still tied at the top of the canyon, so we had to hike back up to get our lunches. "You want us to bring our horses down here," I said.

"William stared up for a second and said: "Naw"

He was the boss. We hiked up, then hiked back down to the Elk. We sat in the rocks and ate lunch, regaling each other with various stories - some even true.

"I reckon we are going to need a packhorse or two," William said as if suddenly coming upon the true meaning of life. "I reckon I'll have to go back and get 'em, unless one of you boys want to do it."

Tex and I looked at each other. "Naw," we said, in perfect two-part harmony, and settled in for an after-lunch nap.

It took old William almost three hours to return with the packhorses. Make that packmules – and one of them very ornery at that. The guides, the wranglers and even the outfitter himself had been having a lot of problems with this particular mule ever since we'd been in camp. Everybody gets a wild hair from time to time. Mules seem to get one a little more often.

The canyon we were in, was bounded on one side by a fairly steep rock wall. Tex had been wedged into a nice hidy-hole on that side when he took his shot. The other side rose gradually to a flat ridge line about a hundred yards or so away. The rocks thinned out on this side of the canyon, and there was a good trail along the ridge. William rode down the trail on that side and brought his horse and the mules up to the Elk. Both animals struggled to get good footing in the rocks and boulders.

"Why don't we heft these quarters over to that flat spot where there ain't so many rocks and load 'em up there." Tex said.

William looked to the sky. "Naw," he said. "We can get it done right here."

He didn't tie his horse to anything. There wasn't anything to tie it to. He merely wrapped his reigns around the horse's neck and let him shift around until he found a little footing to balance on. The mules were having the same difficulty – constantly changing and shifting positions to get good toeholds in the rocks. This was just not a good spot to park animals.

We stuffed the quarters into the panniers and tried to set them up on higher rocks to make it easier to lift up onto the mules.

"Here hold this mule," William said to me, holding out the lead rope of the cantankerous mule. "You take this one," he said to Tex, holding a lead rope for him to grab. "I'll lift the panniers up and we'll have it done.

I could not find a good place to stand. The mule looked like all of his weight was shifted onto his front right leg and that the other three were just hanging balancing in the rocks and I did not like the look in his eye. Worse,

William looked intent on trying to load the first Pannier onto the high side of the horse. He would need to climb up onto a rock carrying the Pannier then press it above his head to drop the straps unto the packsaddle.

I could see the eye of the mule shifting - first toward William as he struggled to accomplish this circus act, then to me, as if to asking if this was really going to happen, then back to William, then back to me. And then I saw it – the telltale look, the slight shifting of the ears, the sudden sense of fear and pending doom. "Hold it William," I said.

But it was too late. William stood on his tiptoes, balanced on top of a boulder, his back arched under the weight of seventy or eighty pounds of Elk, and leaned over toward the mule. He was able to land just one strap over a strut on the packsaddle before disaster struck.

The mule's nostrils flared. His eyes bugged. He let out a small whinny, and then like the gate had just opened on a bull ride, he took off. His head snapped straight back, jerking the rope all but lose from my hands. He leaned forward, shifting his weight and brought both hind legs up in a snapping double kick, which missed Tex by inches. He then arched his neck down, and launched straight up, bringing all four feet off the rocky ground. When he touched down, he spun almost one-hundred-and-eighty degrees and launched another double back kick. I dropped the lead rope and tried to scramble backwards. My foot caught in a rock and in an instant I was on my back, gasping from a bullet of pain, from a sharp boulder as it speared the flat spot between my shoulder blades. As I fell, the vision of two airborne horseshoes only inches from my face etched themselves permanently into my memory.

From the corner of my eye, I could see Tex, as he made a move similar to mine – dropping the lead rope, and falling into the rocks. His mule – the gentler of the two – seemed every bit as uneasy with the situation as the maniac I had been holding and took off for the trail and home. I saw his back disappear over the ridge top as I scrambled to my feet. William's horse apparently had little loyalty when faced with trouble either. The last I saw him, he was heading for Yellowstone, galloping through the rocks, stirrups flapping like wings.

But it was William and his plight, which was the most troubling. Apparently, William had no fear of hopping mules, freaked-out horses or sharp rocks. For some inexplicable reason, perhaps Devine guidance, he thought he could calm the situation by holding on with one arm to the half-strapped pannier and riding the mule into submission. The wild turns the mule was making had spun William around so that his back rested on the mule's flank and he stared off into space with the cracked look of terror on his weathered face. He looked vaguely like Captain Ahab snagged helplessly in harpoon ropes on the side of the White Whale.

I'll give him credit. He rode several of the mule's wild launches into the hot Montana air before he too was totally airborne, free of any restraints. His return to earth was considerably less than aerobatic, however. He hit hard in the rocks, and I could almost see chunks of flesh being removed from various parts of his anatomy as he clattered thru the granite and quartz. But Cowboys don't give up easily. Those who are intellectually depleted find quitting even harder. While lying in the rocks, face twisted in agony, Wild William of Gardner Montana, had the clarity of thought to make one last grab of the insane mule's lead rope in a gallant and heroic attempt to stop the animal from running off with his cohorts. The result was also less-than-ideal. The mule, apparently not bothered by a flopping chunk of Elk smashing into his ribs with each lurch and not hampered in spirit by a limp Cowboy hanging on to his lead rope, continued to head for Alaska, dragging poor William for several more yards through the gauntlet of concrete.

"Oh my God," Tex said, getting to his feet, and scrambling toward William. "Are you alright boy."

I had no wind. It had left when the rock crushed into my back. I could not speak just yet, but I knew there was no sound coming from William. I was certain he had broken a few bones, I just hoped that none of them were in his head or neck. I stood finally, and though each breath hurt like hell, I was at least breathing. I made my way to Tex, who was on his knees leaning over William. "You dead," he said to the prostrate form in front of him.

There was no response from William. He was breathing and his face was turned skyward. Suddenly, both eyes popped open and he stared straight up at the blue sky for several seconds before he said: "Naw."

I wish I had William's connection to the universe.

He was not dead – half dead maybe. Definitely banged up. He was bleeding from a nasty gash on his right shoulder – a rock had torn his shirt wide open before hacking away at his flesh. He had another cut on his forehead, from which blood had first beaded in large droplets and then began trickling gently down in miniature rivulets. He wiped at it with his sleeve and then looked back up at the sky for a second. I could not find a spot on him that wasn't plastered with dirt and bits of rock – fragments, I assumed, chipped off when his head collided with the boulders.

"Maybe you should just stay down while we go get help," Tex said.

"Naw," William said, rolling over on his side. "This ain't nothing. I get hurt worster than this all the time. I'm fine. Just need a minute to get it together."

He continued his roll until he was face down in the dirt. Then, doing kind-of a pushup, managed to use his right leg to stand. He kept his left leg straight. Obviously it was giving him some problems. When he turned, I could see why. His jeans were torn from his knee almost to his crotch directly over the thigh. He reached down and gently pried the torn fabric open to get a look at the problem. The muscle of his thigh had obviously taken a hard hit. The surface layer of skin was badly scraped. The layer immediately below that was turning purple as we watched. A knot the size of a Pineapple had formed in the muscle and looked to be growing right before our eyes.

"That's what they call a hematoma," Tex said.

"Naw," William said. "It's just a bruise. But it ain't broke, cuz I can stand on it okay."

Hematoma, bruise, whatever, That thing was going to make walking very difficult for old William for quite a while.

"You're bleeding on your forehead, there," I said.

"Naw, That's just a little blood."

"Like I said, there's a little blood on your forehead. Are you hurt anywhere else?"

"Naw, Just my back and my shoulder and my head."

"Well maybe you should sit here while one of us rides back to camp and gets some help."

"Naw, where'd them mules go," he said, scanning the hillsides around us.

"Kansas, I reckon," Tex said.

"Naw, Kansas is that way," William said, pointing a finger generally south. "They probably went back to camp."

"Maybe Alaska," I said, trying to interject some humor into the situation.

"Naw, Alaska is too far," William said, without even the slightest trace of a smile. "They ain't that far yet."

"You sure your head is okay there pardner," Tex said. "Maybe you ought to sit down."

William stared skyward for a minute. "Naw," he said.

"Well, you can't walk with that leg," I said. I'll go up and get our horses. You can ride and Tex and I will take turns walking back to camp. "

"Naw."

William stood there for several minutes staring off into Yellowstone. The suns rays were leaning toward the horizontal. Tex and I had run out of suggestions and words in general. Gratefully William had been thinking while he was staring and came up with a suggestion that would save the day.

"I can't walk with this leg. So why don't one of you boys go up and get your two horses, and bring them down here. Then I am going to have to ride and you boys will have to take turns walking back to camp."

Whew! Our confidence was restored.

The Mules and William's horse were back at camp when we arrived. The ornery one had managed to bring one quarter of Elk back dangling in the half-seated pannier. The outfitter and one of the wranglers had put a new pack train together and were preparing to ride out to rescue us when we rode (and walked) into the corral. They and William went out immediately and returned just in time for supper with the remains of the nice Elk Tex had bagged.

William remained a beacon of intellect, at which we could all marvel. He did limp pretty badly for the next few days, however.

TIP - Hunting: Don't hunt too close to the fence in Yellowstone country. It is tempting and perfectly legal, to hunt game as it comes and goes near the borders of the National Parks. However, be advised that shooting something on the other side of the fence is a violation and punishable with very strict fines and even jail time. In the past, if you shot an animal outside Yellowstone National Park, for example, and it ran into the Park to die, you could call a ranger, who would come out and assess the situation. If he felt that you had legitimately shot the animal outside the Park's jurisdiction, he could at his discretion allow you to go into the park to bring it out. You still would need an entry pass however. Today, that rule has changed. Now, if you shoot an animal outside the park and it runs into the park to die, too bad. Harvesting any animal inside the Park, dead or alive without an in-the-Park tag, is a crime. If you are caught, you will be in very big trouble.

TIP - Packing out: Loading dead meat onto a pack animal is dangerous business. Be smart and be careful!

TWENTY MULE TEAM STOMP

Trouble happens fast in Horseworld.

Florida Dave, Tom terrific and I were hunting Mulies in Northern Utah's Wasatch mountains. We had two very experienced guides named John and John. The Johns had a remuda of animals that contained about twenty mules and a couple of horses. They were very adept at managing them. It was obvious that they had been at the Cowboy hunting game for many years.

They kept the mules in a small corral, made from wooden poles, a hundred or so yards below the camp. Each morning, we hunters would bring our day gear (day pack and rifle) down from the camp and stack it against the fence, where the Johns could pack it up.

The Johns liked to take pack animals out hunting with them each day so that if anybody got anything, they could just pack it up on the spot and bring it in, rather than mount a separate mission to pack the animal out – a prudent plan. Each morning they would assemble their respective pack trains consisting of horses or mules for themselves, horses or mules for the hunters, and pack animals enough to satisfy whatever vision they had had the night before, in the corral and then lead them out for mounting.

We hunters had gotten used to the routine and stood one frosty morning talking softly outside the corral, while the Johns worked, waiting to be given the mount-up signal. When the pack trains were all but assembled, one of the Johns left the corral and walked up to the camp for something he had apparently forgotten, leaving the other John to finish up the work.

None of us ever really knew what happened. I remember hearing a click of sorts and then instantaneously all hell broke lose in the corral. I turned to look over my shoulder and all I saw was jumping, stomping, snorting, kicking, whinnying horseflesh. The entire corral was pandemonium. Mules were everywhere, snapping their lead ropes, straining against one another in tug-a-wars, yanking poles out of the fence, sending panniers and assorted tack flying everywhere. And there, in the center of the chaos, flat on his back, was John, arms over his face, deflecting dozens of blows from sharp angry hooves, rolling from side to side getting mercilessly stomped.

"Holy Guacamoles," Florida said, as all three of us instinctively headed for the gate to attempt a rescue.

Horses and particularly mules have a tendency to bulge their eyes out when they are nervous or scared. They seem to be able to do it much better than most creatures. That corral was nothing but bulged eyes and stomping, kicking feet.

I can still hear John grunting as hoof after hoof slammed into him somewhere. I shifted immediately into emergency mode and began formulating mental plans to get an ambulance up here. Can we call one from up here? We will have to drive down - an hour at least – before we will be able to find one. Probably be better to try to take John with us, if we can get him in a car. Depends on how badly he is hurt. Might not be able to move him. Might need a helicopter. And then, it was over as instantly as it had begun. The mules moved away from their victim and stood blowing great clouds of steam through their flared nostrils.

John scrambled to his feet. He had a little trickle of blood on his forehead and was clutching at his ribs with one hand and his thigh with the other.

The other John appeared just outside the fence. "You got 'em ready yet," he said. "These boys would like to go hunting before the morning's over."

"Yep, all ready," John said, trying to stand straight and catch his breath. "These mules were being difficult and I had to take a little time to teach them a lesson is all."

"Yep, they learn best when you lay on your back in the dirt and yell up at 'em. Good work."

John limped for two days after that and every time he turned to his left, he let out a little grunt. He was lucky.

TIP - Horses : Never let your guard down when you are around horses. They seem so sweet and gentle it is easy to want to treat them like

Kittens, but they can turn nasty in a heart-beat and you can get hurt before you know what happened.

TIP - Horses: Stay on guard while riding them as well. It is easy to get lulled into a dreamy state as you ride along on a long trial. Later that very day, Florida Dave ended up with his leg pinned under a horse after it decided to step off a trail and fall about thirty feet taking him with it. It was just luck that Dave's leg was not broken.

TIP - Horses: If you do find yourself in some kind of rodeo – likely on a Cowboy hunting trip – get away from the action as fast as you can. In the end, despite what we say about them behind their backs, Horses are pretty smart people. The don't want to get hurt. They don't want to fall of a cliff or crash into one another. They'd like to just stand there and munch on grass.

They have very good reflexes and know how to get themselves out of trouble. We get hurt, trying to keep them from getting hurt. If hell breaks loose, it's best to just stand back and watch. Most of the time, the horses will work it out amongst themselves and order will be restored without your intervention.

TRUCK HUNTING

COWBOY LITE

NO HORSE HUNTING – STILL FUN (SORT OF)

Cowboy hunting begs the question: What is a Cowboy? Obviously, a man on a horse, tending cattle, but "Cowboy" is more than that. Cowboy is a frame of mind.

Cowboys don't necessarily have to be tending anything. In fact, they don't necessarily have to be working. Sometimes you have to visually line a cowboy up with a fence post or something to tell if he's even moving. Other times, you be hard pressed to keep your golf cart along side a walkin' Cowboy. It depends on what's caught his fancy at the time. Either way, you'll find something horse-like interwoven in any Cowboy's frame of mind.

Historically, cowboys were tough to separate from their horses. They worked on them, played on them, ate on them, slept on them, sang songs on them, and dreamt on them. For a true cowboy it's not much different today.

Horses are a part of everything cowboy – especially Cowboy hunting. You yank the heart out of Cowboy hunting when you take away the horse. It just ain't the same. It dilutes the adventure. Horses are the ultimate four-wheel-drive vehicle. But, these days, they don't take your Cowboy hat away if they catch you driving a pickup truck, or an ATV. In fact, I can't think of a single Cowboy who doesn't handle a pickup truck as well as he does a horse. And, true-to-form , they work in them, play in them, eat in them, sleep in them, sing songs in them, and dream in them.

So, despite a valid resistance by some of us against the march of time and technology, we are going to have to throw trucks and ATVs into the mix of Cowboy hunting. Truck hunting is, after all, better than not hunting.

ROARIN' ROGER

Tom Terrific, a hunting buddy of mine, and I were out in Colorado one time with a great old Cowboy named Roger, looking for Elk. We'd driven a car from Denver to his hunt camp – a trailer on a beautiful bend of the Yampa River, with a spectacular view of the Flat top wilderness area, in the White Mountains. Tom and I were used to tents, but the trailer was okay – kind of bunky, but okay.

Roger, his wife and all of their staff are the nicest people in Colorado. They treated us to a wonderful home-cooked meal and a lot of laughs that night. The next morning, we jumped in Roger's pickup truck and drove through a beautiful little valley, which opened into a broad flat meadow. The road we'd taken in was flat and easy all the way back to the highway – a simple ride for a hunter of any age. Roger told us that this meadow was known to hold plenty of Elk, who passed through at all times of the day, to feed. All we had to do was to wait.

I wanted to get out and pick some spots around the meadow for cover away from the truck. Roger insisted that waiting in the truck was better. He figured we'd have less of a chance of spooking them. Tom and I looked at each other, but we were still in our "being polite" mode.

After what seemed like only a few minutes a nice little herd of Elk came out of the timber to our left. There were several cows, a bunch of calves, two or three spike bulls, and one nice legal bull, with big white-tipped brow tines and long heavy branches on top.

"Roll the window down, then open the door real slow and slip out," Roger whispered.

I did as he asked.

"Kind of get down on one knee," he whispered leaning across Tom, who was still sitting in the truck. "Stick your gun through the window and use it as a rest."

Again, I did as I was asked, and took up the view through my scope.

"Get ready. Wait." Roger was leaning across Tom's lap, whispering instructions.

The Elk were so close; all I could see through the scope was fur.

"Okay," Roger said, " Take him."

I could see the big bull clearly. It would have been a very clean kill. My bullet would have knocked him off his feet on the spot, but I couldn't pull the trigger.

"Shoot," Roger said, his voice getting a little edgy.

I tightened my finger on the trigger. The elk looked straight at me, sensing danger. I could see Roger and Tom out of the corner of my eye, and the gleaming chrome of the rearview mirror.

"Shoot. He's a good one. Shoot. He'll be gone." Roger sounded a little agitated.

I started exhaling, clicked off the safety, and then held my breathe, ready for the shot, as I had practiced a million times. But hell, I could have hip-shot this one.

"What are you waiting for?"

"Sorry Roger, "I said, pulling the gun back through the window. "I can't do this."

The Elk bolted, and within seconds were out of range back in the timber, from where they had come.

"What the," Roger had leaned back in his position behind the wheel, taken off his hat, and was scratching his head. "You might not get another chance like that one. I thought you wanted an Elk."

"I do Roger. But not like this. I came here to hunt, not just harvest something." I looked at Tom. He nodded and then turned toward Roger.

"I could see the truck," I said. I couldn't shoot anything with a truck fender in my view. Something about that just didn't fit with my sense of what cowboy hunting or any kind of hunting should be.

Roger looked befuddled. He took a smoke out of his shirt pocket and lit up. He'd been hunting Elk like this for years and had taken hundreds of guys like us out into this valley for the "sure thing." I don't think he'd ever had someone not take advantage of an opportunity like that one before. " I can't guarantee you'll get another chance like that one."

The mood had changed. Tom Terrific tried his best to lighten up the tension, but Roger was virtually silent - lost in thought apparently. We drove around aimlessly for several hours, finally ending up back at the trailer for lunch.

Tom and I weren't used to eating lunch back at a trailer. We'd always taken a sack lunch in our saddle bags and ate it on mother earth's dirt. We were starting to wonder if maybe we had misread these guys.

"I guess I misread you guys," Roger said as soon we sat down at the table. He'd been conferring with a couple of his other guides. "We're used to a different crowd around here. A little older crowd maybe. We thought you were," he paused for a minute. "Well, hell, you know, city boys. We got another plan for you boys after lunch."

Tom and I looked at each other. Hmmmm. "Plan B" can sometimes be a son-of-a-bitch.

On the other side of the trailer, Roger had another truck we hadn't seen – a big truck. And, it had been specially modified with irrigation sprayer tires that looked more like rotary paddles than tires.

"We figured maybe you boys would like to see a little more of this country around here," Roger said, as he led us around back. "We got us a little baby here that'll go anywhere."

Tom and I did not know what to expect. We thought maybe we'd be driving up to another camp or maybe up on some ridge to walk down, or still hunt, or something. The only part we were right about, was that we were going up.

Roger was right, that little baby would go anywhere. We started out on a gradual rise a mile or so behind the trailer, but then, turned a corner, and found ourselves staring at a couple of ruts that ran straight up on a knife edge ridge and an angle that defied even the least strict laws of gravity. Roger's foot never moved an inch off the accelerator.

"Whoa, Dude," I said, "Where you going?"

Tom was white as rice, and speechless.

"Up there, you want to see some Elk don't ya?"

"Yeah, but. . . . "

"Don't worry about it," he said. "This little baby will go anywhere." With that, Roger grabbed the shifter, which Tom had pinched between his legs like a cold pillow and slammed it into another gear. "Hang on boys," he said.

You can stick him in a truck, but you can't really take the cowboy out of a cowboy, and cowboy was just oozing out of Roger's pores, even though we were miles from the nearest horse. I guess it was the couple hundred horses under the hood that had gotten him going.

"But, Roger it's muddy and . . . "

"Yahoo!"

Have you seen those pictures where the astronauts are strapped flat on their backs, looking up at space, waiting for their rocket to catch? When you see nothing but blue sky out of the windshield, and cigars start slipping out of your breast pocket and land in your ears, you'll think those space men have it easy. At one point I could sense the truck was angled back to where I knew we were going tip over. I felt the front wheels lift, and I knew Roger could no longer steer.

"Rooooggggerrrrrrr," I screamed.

"Yaaahhhoooo,"

"Rooooggggerrrrrr!"

"Yaaahhhooooooo!"

You wouldn't think a nice guy like that would have a death wish.

Finally, his little baby settled down. We climbed like that, a tire slipping from time to time, the front wheels coming off from time to time, until finally I began to see the tips of trees again in the window. Then more trees, and then we were back to relatively flat. We'd made it to the top.

"I told ya," he said. " I told ya this little baby can go anywhere."

"Yeah," I said, trying to sound kind-of nonchalant "I figured since there were tracks in the ruts that you had done that a few times before. "

"Those were down tracks. We generally just come back down that way. That was the first time up as far as I know. You boys were on the first flight of Roger's Rocket. Congratulations."

"How long have you had this place," I asked.

"Oh about twenty years," he said.

"And you waited until today to run up that ridge?"

"You're welcome," he said.

Tom and I had learned a whole new way of cowboy hunting – and actually, we kind of liked it. Roger took us to the top of several ridges after that each with it's own set of terrors. He'd either let us out to walk down on our own, or spiked us out to sit and wait. Even though we had gotten to our posts by truck, when we were alone, we did feel like we were cowboy hunting again.

TIP - HUNTING: It depends on what you want. My friend Dead Eye likes to sit in trees. He flies each year out to a place in Montana, rides a four-wheeler out to a tree stand, and then sits in it for fourteen or fifteen hours, before riding the ATV back to the cabin. He stares at the same stand of trees for hour after hour, day after day. Forget the ATV and you've got my mom on a weekend Bingo binge (excuse me Dead Eye). Still, this is way different than pickup truck hunting or horse hunting but it is what he likes.

You should definitely do what you like - within limits, of course.

I have had guys who weigh three hundred pounds and are hopelessly out of shape question me about deer hunts, in wilderness areas, where many trophies are known to hang out. This is not a realistic possibility for them. Wilderness areas are what they are because of their difficult access. It keeps most people at bay. Money, time, skill are not factors in the equation here. Most outfitters won't let you on one of their horses if you weigh over 240 or so. If they did, the horse, the ride, the mountains, the sheer physical exertion would very likely kill the hunter - or worse, kill the horse. In either event, all involved would have had a bad time. That is a far greater sin. If you are one of those guys, consider one of the easier hunts for your first time. A truck hunt might be what you need.

TIP - Hunts: Before you sign on with an outfitter for a hunt. Tell them what you expect, and definitely tell them what you can do. Don't try to impress him. If you are out of shape tell him. If you are older, tell him. If you have never been on a horse, tell him. If you are young and wild and want to jump off a cliff or two, tell him. If an outfitter doesn't think he can accommodate your style of hunting, he will tell you. He does not want you to get hurt or have a bad time. That's bad for business.

TIP - Pickups: It's worth repeating. While there is nothing wrong with hunting with a pickup truck, substituting one for a horse kind-of tears the heart out of the experience.

TIP – Pickups: If you have to pull a guy's fingers out of a dashboard, like I had to do with Tom's, try squirting a little WD-40 in around the first knuckle.

GETTING THEM OUT

REALITY

You have been thinking about this minute for the better part of a year – your whole life in some instances. You've filled out forms, dealt with airline schedules, automobile logistics, packing dilemmas, whining hunting partners, surly guides and outfitters, totally antisocial horses, aches, pains, disappointments. Now, your life has boiled itself down to this tiny moment in the entire history of planet earth. You lift your gun, peer though the scope, select just the right patch of fur, align the crosshairs – and BOOM!

Buckle your seatbelt. Your troubles have just begun. You now have to get whatever you killed out of the wilderness.

LIQUID SHEEP

Bronco Bobby and a rookie hunter named Al were sheep hunting one day. Yes, a rookie hunter scored a sheep tag. It is almost impossible folks, but like the Wyoming game and Fish department maintains; it is possible. There is no justice.

Anyway, good sheep are very hard to find. They tend to hang out in areas, which are almost unreachable by astronauts let alone cowboys. It took them days to locate a trophy. Unfortunately, it stood on a rock outcropping miles above the rest of the rocky world far below.

Al thought he could hit it from where they were. Bobby worried that if they wounded it, it would fall off the cliff into an absolute hell hole and they would never get it out. He thought maybe they could circle around behind it and get a better shot – a sure kill shot, in a location where retrieval would be far easier. He left Al on stand to watch the ram while he went around scouting out a better location. Fifteen minutes later, he heard a shot and managed to scramble over to a vantage point just in time to see the big ram topple over the rock edge.

Al said he thought the Sheep was getting ready to walk off. It gave him a good side shot and rather than lose it, he decided to try his luck. He hit it square on the first shot. It went down close to the edge, got up, staggered and the next thing he knew it was airborne.

Bobby watched helplessly as the ram hit first on his left full-curl horn shattering it to pieces. Then, the real bouncing began. He figured it crashed into the rocks no less than ten times before finally coming to rest in a bloody heap on the valley floor. All he could do was sigh.

It took them hours to work their way down form their perch and back up again, to where the sheep lie. Buzzards had found the corpse by the time they got there. However, there was little left for them to share. The left horn was completely gone, presumably left somewhere up above in the rock scrabble. The right hung in tattered shards like a battle field flag. In the fall, most of the bones had broken and all of the internal organs had turned to jelly.

The meat was mostly ruined. Essentially, the ram had been reduced to a Swiss cheese bag of skin with some pulverized goop inside.

No question Al had made a good shot – just behind the left shoulder, caught both lungs, a definite kill. But, to what end?

TIP – Hunting: Take a good hard look at where the trophy you intend to bag is before you shoot. In the fever of the hunt, it is easy to get caught up in the moment and pay a huge price later. What good is a dead trophy if you can't get him out?

Unless you can hook Roger's pickup winch to an animal you will have to take it out with a horse or on foot. It takes a minimum of two packhorses to bring out an elk. Usually a deer is about the same; although there is a way, you can sling a single deer over a good riding hose and bring it out in one piece. Gabriel and I did it one time. Took most of the afternoon to get the horse to agree to it, and then we had to walk eight miles back to camp in the dark – not fun. And for those of you who think you are going to quarter an elk and walk each piece out individually, good luck.

DEAD DEER WALKING

The sun had just crossed below the 45-degree mark on another blue-sky Colorado afternoon. The temperature was in the mid fifties – a nice afternoon for walking.

Tom Terrific and I had been bouncing around in Roger's modified mountain truck most of the day, trying to figure a good plan. The two-rut road was absolutely terrible – nonexistent in some spots. Roger was never shy about giving the truck gas and actually seemed to give it a little extra shot just before we went over any bump larger than a grape. Whenever he did, Tom and I would actually hit our heads on the roof of the truck. If we ducked down to avoid contact, it was more than likely that we would hit our faces on the dashboard. After one blaster of a bounce, and a big "Yahoo", from Roger, Tom reached quickly for his mouth and started rubbing his front teeth.

"Dammit!" he said. " I think I broke a tooth on that one. Look Roger, we haven't seen diddlysquat all day, why don't we pull this thing over for a few minutes and just glass around?"

Tom is normally a fairly tolerant guy, but I could sense that he had just about enough cowboy truck hunting for one day, and we had two choices: either get him out on his feet, or start a Jose Quervo I.V. drip on him immediately.

"Yeah, it's been a little slow," Roger nodded without letting up on the peddle. "But you see that ridge up ahead there?"

Tom nodded.

"Well there's another one on the other side running parallel to it. There's usually a few deer in the valley between them, and old Harold was over there a few days ago and said he seen a passel of elk about halfway up."

"Well, let's go over there then and wait for them to feed out," Tom said.

He didn't say it, but I knew he was a second or two from self-destructing and had to get out of that truck. I could not have agreed more, but the way I saw it, there was no trail heading that way, which we could navigate with a truck.

"So what, are going to just walk over there?" I asked.

"Naw."

Dumb question. We had hunted with Roger many times and as I recalled, he had never walked anywhere. In fact, he rarely got out of his truck. He was a "drop-you-off" kind of guy.

As the words were leaving my mouth, he turned off onto a set of barely discernable tire tracks, which made the rutty mess we had been on all day look kind- of freeway like.

"Holy shittoly," Tom said. (He can be so poetic sometimes.)

Even if all you can see through the front windshield of a pickup is blue sky, your sense of spatial relation tells you when you have reach a vertical angle that defies all the normal laws of physics – the simplest of which is gravity. You can even sense when the front tires are making little, if any, contact with the ground. Apparently our old friend Roger is disabled with regards to these senses. He is likely deaf as well, since he obviously couldn't hear the avalanche of rocks tearing at the wheel wells as our tires spun almost uselessly against the mountain. He's clearly blind.

Tom and I leaned as far forward over the dashboard as we could, in a futile but natural reaction designed to throw a little more weight forward over the wheels. Roger leaned back, elbows locked, stiff-armed against the steering wheel. He was in full Neil Armstrong mode – a rocket man heading off into galaxies unknown. A gleeful grin slashed across his face as he ignored both our screams and the red-lined tachometer. The engine roared. Rocks smashed against the metal truck bed with loud, unnerving clangs. Heart rates thumped up to flat out panic levels. And then, suddenly, we were weightless. We - the entire truck, with us in it – were airborne. Pickup truck flying – a new and fantastic sport - get ready Wide World of Sports. I almost puked.

Funny how stupid we can be at times, and then at others how capable we are of assimilating millions of unrelated thoughts within a mere microsecond. In that tiny instant, the wild whistling engine went silent. Roger's insane "Yaaaaahooooo" was only an expression on his open mouth. The rocks thumped in slow motion only slightly more audible than my heart. And I? I had begun searching through the clutter of my mind desperately looking for some skill or some shred of previous experience that would get me out of this fix. I saw myself bowling. No, that would not do. Making snowmen in my mother's front yard? No, No, No, that wouldn't help. Eating chocolate cake at my sixth birthday? Sorry. Thumb? Yes! Thumb sucking. I was an excellent thumb sucker as a child, and I could be again dammit!

Then, with a kidney jarring crash, we landed – sort of. We were, at least, relatively horizontal again. Roger let up on the gas and I think I heard the sigh of relief whistle though his teeth. I know I heard the roar of relief screech through Tom's.

I looked around. We were back on a well-used two track.

"Roger," I said. "We're on a road again. "

"Yep. I thought we could do that."

"Why didn't we just come up here on the road in the first place?"

"We'd have had to go back the same way we came and then we'da had to drive all they way around the ranch to the other side, and then come up this road from that side. Would'a took forever and I was thinking. . . ."

I cut him off. "We asked you not to do that."

"What? Take short-cuts?"

"No, think!"

"Oh yeah, but, I was thinking. I got a couple of new boys back at the ranch. They're supposed to be doing a few things back there and I got this feeling like they ain't. I really need to check up on them. And I was thinking that if I was to drop one of you boys off up here and let you get staked out, then I would drive the other guy down to the bottom of the valley and he could walk slowly back up here to the top and maybe he'd get a shot at one of those elks or maybe he might drive them up to the other guy. Meanwhile, I'd go back down to the ranch and check things out and then come back up here at dark and pick you boys up."

Roger stared at both Tom and I with a strange kind of "Ya-wanna" look on his face.

I knew Tom would be up for that offer. "Sounds good to us."

"Good. Which one of you boys wants to do the walking?"

I never saw Tom take quicker advantage of a situation.

"He does." He said, as he opened the truck door and jumped out. (Well, sort of fell out, and then kind of crab-walked away from the truck like it was on fire).

"Okay, well then," Roger said, leaning over me. "Just walk over there a few yards and get yourself fixed so you can see down the whole valley and wait. I'll be back up here just after dark to pick you up."

I don't think Tom heard a word. Never before have I seen a man turn grey the way he does. Anyway, he walked off, mumbling.

Tom and I had both elk and deer tags, so either way Roger's plan seemed workable. I was excited.

I really do not mind walking in the mountains, so even if Tom hadn't been so willing to sit, I would have suggested that he be. Just about any moron could walk up this particular valley, and I was certainly moron plenty enough for the task, so Roger had no problem turning me loose, to head up on my own.

By the time I had adjusted my day-pack, hitched up my rifle and got my walking brain online, I could no longer hear Roger's truck. In fact, at that particular moment, there were no planes in the air, so I could not hear anything man-made – a rare silence that is both beautiful and numbing at the same time. The mountains have their own "hum", which can only be heard in total silence and by those with active imaginations or by compulsive liars. Either way, a noisy grasshopper finally buzzed away like a miniature helicopter, breaking my trance, and I began walking. I hadn't taken a hundred steps when I heard a shot far up the valley, where I thought Tom was sitting. Prime time was just about to begin for me in the bottom of the valley, but I figured it would be a while yet before Tom, up on top would be running out of light. Maybe he was taking a practice shot? Naw.

The valley was only a few hundred yards across at its widest - narrower in some spots. It was a garden salad of vegetation. The shade side, the cool side, was heavily treed with tall fragrant pines. At their base a carpet of soft needles caressed clusters of mossy rocks and soft green plants. The sunny side was a collage of open brushy areas punctuated with islands of tough scraggy pin oak ten to twelve feet high. Around their base a broken parking lot of sharp rocks held snags of dried plants like those in a Martha Stewart vase. A small stream struggled along in the central trough – sometimes only a wetness among the willows. Next to the stream, a fairly good horse trail allowed me to stroll along like a Saturday morning mall walker.

When you are trying to drive game out of a particular area, you move fast, deliberately trying to make noise in hopes of pushing the critters up ahead of you. When you are trying to put on a stalk drive like I was, you walk very slow, a few steps at a time, stopping frequently to listen and scout the territory ahead. I had only traveled a couple of hundred yards when I saw the first deer – a nice four-by-four, standing on a rock outcropping watching me from above. I put my binoculars on him and lit him up instantly. He was a good buck, but still within his ears, so I passed. I was glad I did, because it wasn't two minutes later, that I came upon two others – both a little bigger but still not what I was looking for. We had been looking for elk in this valley, but damn, it was just full of deer. I forgot all about the elk, right quick. Good mulies are generally harder to find than elk, and with clumps of does and small bucks running across the valley every thirty yards or so, I started focusing my efforts on this opportunity.

Most guys would not be on a cowboy hunt without wanting to take home a trophy. I am no different, but I have a weakness. I find it difficult to pass on an atypical buck. In a half-mile on this tiny trail no less than forty deer walked, ran, or streaked in front of me. They stood broadside on the hillside watching me pass. It had been a virtual shooting gallery, but I had resisted. Then, suddenly, a cluster of does moved across a little bench, two hundred and fifty yards above me. Four nice bucks and one very nice buck followed them. With my eye, I could see he had an overturned table sitting on his head. Through my binoculars, there were points everywhere jutting out from this nice rack. Not only was this a good buck, but he was an atypical too.

A split second later, the butt of the gun was on my shoulder. A split second after that, and I had found him in the scope. A split second after that and he was no longer visible - anywhere. I dropped the rifle barrel down and scanned the hillside. Deer ran everywhere – both bucks and does, like pool balls scattering after a break shot. The echo from the shot, bounced its way back and forth up the canyon. I put my binoculars up, searching for Mr. Atypical, but he was not among the runners. I did not know if I had hit him or not.

Hmmm. Problem. Whenever you shoot at something, problems begin. The sun had all but disappeared from the bottom of the valley. I did not have much time to find a wounded deer, and much less to complete my assignment – driving elk and deer up to Tom. I hoped that he had already gotten something with that lone shot I heard earlier.

I thought the hillside on both sides of this valley looked steep. I didn't realize just how steep, until I started climbing up to look for a blood trail. The deer could negotiate this vertical rocky terrain easily, but I was having a lot of difficulty.

This hillside was a series of giant steps made from huge blocks of rock like the Egyptians had stacked up to build the pyramids. Each was waist high, too tall for me simply to step up on. I had to find small water draws between them, then grab rocks and oak scrub with both hands, and virtually pull myself up to the next one. I was climbing on my hands and knees at some points, sliding back on loose rock at others, expending vast amounts of energy all along.

Step, slide, gravel in hand, step slide, gravel in knee, step slide, gravel on forehead. Pant Pant. Picker in hand, slide, cactus, slide, step, pickers picker pickers, rock in knee. Pant pant. Skin off elbow, skin off knee, skin off forehead. And so on, until I reached the level at which I thought I had last seen the buck. I was exhausted. It took until the last few minutes of twilight and the last ounce of energy I had to find him. When I finally did, I was not happy to see that he had managed to wedge himself down between a clump of oaks half on a ledge and half off – a very difficult location. I've said it before and I will say it again. As hard as locating a good trophy is, the real problems begin as soon as you pull the trigger. I could not leave that deer there over night without at least, field dressing him, but for the minute, all I could do was to sit there and pant.

To make it worse, this buck was not the atypical trophy I thought it was. He was a good trophy mule deer, well outside his ears, and welcome on any hunter's wall, but the atypical part of his rack turned out to be a stout, multi-forked scrub oak branch that he had managed to trap between the forks on his real rack. It's hard to be unhappy when you've bagged a big boy like that, but I did feel a slight twinge of disappointment.

When my head stopped pounding, I started thinking. I assumed Roger would be coming from the ranch on the trail where he had dropped me. He would pick me up first and then we would go back up and fetch Tom. From there, who knew?

The only sound was the beating of my heart, and the chirping of the night birds, who were beginning to dart back and forth looking for dinner. There were no tell-tale shafts of light from truck lights cutting through the shadowy mountains. Roger was going to be late and it looked like I would have to dress this one out myself.

Knife work on a dead deer is not a particular challenge. Getting this deer positioned so I could get the knife on him was like Twiggy taking on the Hulkster at a Wrestlemania festival. He was really stuck!

Finally, after pushing, pulling, roping, levering with big sticks, holding a flashlight in my teeth till my jaw ached, swearing a bunch, and taking off just about everything I had on to let the sweat out, I got him laid flat, and gutted out. I flopped back on the rocks and stared at the darkening sky - for a second that is, because no sooner had I laid back when I heard Roger's truck and saw his lights, stabbing at the night. Perfect timing – I really could have used his help.

I scrambled down the mountain as fast as I could, part on my ass, and part on my feet, until I could feel the heat building up on the soles of my shoes and the seat of my pants. I didn't want Roger to miss me and assume I was already up the valley sitting with Tom. I met him at the end of the trail just as it came out on the two-track road. He had his two new ranch hands with him, Jake and Jeff, about 18 and 19 respectively, but both built like young, red, fireplugs.

"You ain't s'posed to be here," he said. "What happened?"

I recounted my short-lived hike up the canyon with both arms propped stiff against Roger's truck, in an effort to remain vertical.

"We reckoned you'd got something up there. We seen your flashlight bobbin' around up there from way far off."

"I left my orange hat hanging in a tree so we could find it, but I don't think I can go back up there tonight to help get it down. Tomorrow maybe."

"No problem," Roger said. "Boys run up there and fetch that deer down here."

Jake and Jeff did literally that. They flew out of the truck, ran up the mountain, and "fetched" that deer back in what seemed like about five minutes. Have I mentioned how nice it is to have a guide? Have I mentioned how nice it is to have two muscle boys along – both too young to recognize pain?

We piled back into the truck - me in the front with Roger, the two J's in the bed with the deer - and headed up to fetch Tom.

Tom does not like being alone in the dark. Years of over-taxing his liver have left his brain capable of conjuring horrific visuals. We tell him over and over that there are no Vampires in this part of Colorado anymore, but nonetheless, he worries. His eyes were wild when we found him, standing in the middle of the road, rifle locked and loaded, held high across his chest – ready.

"Where have you guys been," he asked.

I repeated the story to him in short form.

"Was that you shooting, "I said.

"Yeah, I got a nice buck right after you guys left. Saw maybe ten more, but no elk. "

"Where is he," Roger asked.

"He's lying right out in the open in a small clearing about five feet from where I shot him."

"Did you gut him?"

"Nope. Went down there to make sure he was dead and came right back up here. I figured you guys would be coming a lot sooner than this. It's been like two hours since I shot him."
"Closer to three," I said.

"No problem," Roger said. "The boys will go down there and fetch him up."

"I don't think they'll have to," Tom said. "You can drive this truck right up to it."

"Better yet," Roger said way too enthusiastically. "Hop in."

Tom was right. We were able to bounce the back of the truck almost to the deer, but it lay just over the top of a small rock drop-off, which amazingly Roger didn't want to cross. The two J's probably could have tossed the deer over the rocks right into the back of the truck, but Roger had an electric winch rigged to the top of his truck, and insisted on using it to drag the deer into the bed. I guess he wanted to impress us with his mechanical prowess.

He reversed the switch and played out the cable. J and J wrapped it around the deer's neck, and within seconds, Roger had snaked it along the ground and into the back of the pickup. He stood there in the truck grinning.

"Slicker n Pomade on a pompadour, hey boys?"

Tom and I had been standing at the side of the truck watching, flashlights trained on the scene. Roger jumped down, Jake and Jeff joined us and the five of us stood for a minute next to the truck dazzled by the clear Mountain night and the trillions of Colorado stars, which had blinked on while we were working. For a couple of seconds, there was silence and peace in the world.

It was a quick couple of seconds. The peace quickly shattered and rained down chaos upon us. Why? Because that damn deer suddenly stood up. Oh yeah, hooves pounding on the bed of the truck, clattering, banging, smashing, horns tearing into the rear window of the cab, head butt after head butt, glass shattering, horns denting the rear of the cab.

Five jaws hit the ground, then five men jumped back at least ten feet like Olympic broad jumpers in reverse. That deer had been dead for almost three hours - neck shot clean and simple. Like I have always said: Once you shoot an animal, your troubles really begin.

Meanwhile the deer was tearing the beans out of Roger's truck.

"Shoot the son-of-a-bitch, "Jeff said, snatching Tom's rifle out of his hands.

"No," Roger yelled. "You'll blow a hole in my truck."

I thought my heart was racing after climbing up the pyramid steps. What did I know?

Roger stepped gingerly on the running board of the truck, and reached up for the switch on the winch. This action did not have a calming effect on the deer. It started using its front feet like hammers at the back of the cab and at Roger himself. Finally he was able to snug the winch up tight so the deer's head was tight against the drum and its antlers were unable to do more damage. It did not stop him from running, back and forth, feet pounding the bed of the truck, head stuck in the noose.

Jake, drew his knife – a three-inch folder. He needed a sword. Roger drew his. Jeff handed Tom his rifle, and followed suit. I don't mind shooting game. I wouldn't be a hunter if I did. You would not be reading this if you did. But, I have to tell you, something about a stab festival is a little unnerving. Rather than try to describe it, suffice it to say, the deer finally succumbed.

TIP – Hunting: The point here is (for the fourth time) hunting, tracking, stalking, shooting big game is really the easy part. The real difficulties begin once you pull the trigger.

TIP - Packing: Whether you intend to cowboy hunt on a horse, in a cowboy truck, or on cowboy feet, always take a day pack. In any of these situations, you may need it. If you foresee any situation where you might be hiking or sitting by yourself on a stand, you will want a few basic supplies. Toilet paper, matches, a spare knife and a flashlight are bare-minimum basics. Food and water supplies will likely be needed if you plan on spending more than a couple of hours by yourself. A utility survival blanket (space blanket) can be a life saver in an emergency. A length of rope may be helpful as well as a rain coat or a poncho. Things change fast in the mountains. What looks like a benign, friendly situation can turn ugly in a hurry. You are far better off carrying a little extra stuff than to be caught short. The first rule of survival is to be prepared. The Boy Scouts would agree.

TIP - Planning: You have more shot options at the beginning of your trip than you do at the end. Plan ahead. Shooting an Elk that is standing on a well-used trail – one where you can easily get a packhorse is one thing. Shooting one way back in some canyon where travel is limited is another.

Even though it is possible to hack an animal into quarters and carry the individual quarters out on your back, it is not easy and it takes a long time. We saw a guy bring one out on a bicycle one time. He carried the quarters in a big basket on the back of the thing while he walked along side. He must have been a Vietnam vet and got the idea from watching the Vietnamese humping supplies along the Ho Chi Minh Trail. The method worked pretty well, but he still had to make four trips up a long trail and then out along a long ridge to fetch his game. We saw another guy use a wheel barrow to haul a big moose out one time too. The point? It took them both a day and a half and was much more work than they had intended to undertake.

You've got that kind of time on your first day and probably even on your fifth day. However, unless you are willing to pay your outfitter and guide to come back up and get your game after your trip is over, you do not have that kind of time on your last day. If you are hunting on your own, you do not have that option on even your second-to-last day.

So, plan your shot – not only on the likelihood of your making it, but also on the reality of your getting your game out after you do so.

TIP - Getting them out: Don't be surprised to have your car checked at the state line by Game and Fish officials in Cowboy land. They are very serious about not leaving game in the wild. They frequently set up check stations with the help of the State police. <u>Hunters are required to stop.</u> If a car, looks like it might be carrying a hunter or two and it does not stop, the State Troopers will chase it.

If they find the cape and horns of something in your car, you need to be prepared to show a receipt for the processed meat. If not, you better have a damn good explanation for what happened to it.

GOING HOME

BAD DAY

The clanking of the bells dangling from the horse collars, signals the start of the day as usual, but there is something different in the air today. The morning seems less urgent than a normal hunting morning and it is later. We have not been awakened by a visit from our guide, who on a normal morning would have poked his head into our tent long ago. A soft grey glow leaks in around the tent flaps instead of the harsh white light of the cook tent lantern. The suggestion of sunlight is everywhere. We are going home today.

Of course we've known this day was coming since the first day, but that does not make it easier to take. This place, this tent, has become a home of its own over the last week. I suppose that if we had been real Cowboys living in a remote place like this for months at a time, going home or even going to town would have been an event to savor – something to look forward too. For us, it is a return to a life we have been trying to escape.

I look over at Ricardo. I roll the "r" even in my mind's silent voice. He is awake, lying there with his hands behind his head, lost in some contemplation of space, man, God or law. Naw. He's thinking about packing his gear or thinking about nothing at all. Probably the later.

I slide into my clothes waiting there in a heap at the ready where I have learned to leave them. Preparing for the morning cold has become a pre-bedtime ritual, performed thoughtfully the night before.

The tent flap is stiff from frost as usual – the fire in our stove having petered out hours ago. We only worried about keeping it going for the first couple of nights. After that we really didn't need it or were too tired to care.

A gentle steam drifts lazily up from the creek bed. I can see the first drops of sunlight splattering off the far mountain peaks and then reflecting back to the tiny grains of frost clinging to the willows. They glitter and sparkle like bulbs on a Christmas tree. With a swoop, a Jay silently takes his place in a tall pine above the camp – a sentinel to guard us against something – evil spirits perhaps. He's there everyday. Soon he will begin to caw and fight with his comrades over droppings left in the corral.

I walk behind the tent to pee. We usually just pee right in front, in the middle of the night when no one can see. I love to look at the stars then. For some reason they always seem to be a little brighter in the asphalt dark of a clear mountain night. It's way too late for them now. The sky is peculiar just before the sun rises – colorless, but with the promise that soon the sun will tease gentle hues out of everything. Today will be a beauty. It's easy to tell. The vibrant green of the pines will contrast against the severe blue of the Wyoming sky and raise everyone's spirits – even those who will soon be leaving this amazing place.

The overnight horses – the ones we leave in the camp at night – pay me no attention as I make my way to the cook tent for a cup of coffee. They are busy working a bale of hay dropped into their corral. I wonder if they can sense a trip down to the ranch is in the offing today. Probably. They usually know what is going on before anyone else does and they have internal clocks that signal them when it is time to move on.

I am greeted by a cheerful "Good Morning," by the camp cook, as usual. She tells me she will be riding down to the world with us today. She has not been to town in a month and is looking forward to it. The camp will host another group of hunters next week and then the staff will begin disassembling the camp and hauling it down. It will take at least ten, maybe twelve trips to get it all done. It's almost five hours each way. The State of Wyoming requires that everything be removed from the camp area each winter and then brought back up in the spring. Before the government bureaucracy, our outfitter could stash a lot of stuff in an old sheep herder's cabin near the camp and save himself a lot of effort. Things change.

It's breakfast as usual, too – good food and plenty of it. But, there is a different feeling to it. The guides and wranglers are dressed differently. We've become accustomed to their hunting garb. The combinations are different. Perhaps they want to portray a different image as they ride into the ranch. They each have different identities there and are beginning to morph into them. We are changing back too. Soon, we will be "guests," again. Shortly thereafter we will be reduced back to tourists and shortly after that, we will be back in our lives with this trip a memory haphazardly filed in our individual library of memories, where it will be dusted off from time to time and replayed with ever decreasing frequency. The thought brings an internal sigh, which I suppress so that those around me are not charged with my melancholy. I sense they have their own.

The guides and wranglers stand to leave en mass. Clearly, they are on a mission. They instruct us to pile our gear on the canvas mannies that will be waiting outside our tents and disappear. I sit at the table sipping my coffee after everyone has left. The cook advises me that I had better get going. I think she can sense my reluctance. I have hunted here many times. We are old friends. She knows I would prefer to stay. I think back to my first trip to the Rockies, thumbing rides along the freeway in the sixties. I wonder how things would have played out, if back then, when I was just a kid, I had stayed.

It seems that as soon we toss our duffle onto the mannie, someone drags it off to the corral where the pack string is being assembled. Horses always walk a step quicker when they are headed back to camp or to the ranch than when they are heading away from it. Apparently the trait has worn off on the guide and wranglers. I want to ask what; is their hurry, but think better of it. I gather up my on-board horse stuff, make a last check of the tent and walk slowly to the corral. The Jay in the tree caws at me as I pass under him. He wants to say good bye I guess. Maybe he is mocking me. He gets to stay for as long as he wants.

Tiny explosions of light stream from cameras as the other hunters snap their parting pictures of the camp. I have given up on photography long ago, opting for mental memories instead. Like a drowning man grasping at anything floating, a wave of panic washes over me. I could call my office and beg – no, I don't have to beg. I can just tell them I am staying for another week. I can afford it. I'll talk to the outfitter when we get to the ranch. I'll come back up with the next group of hunters. I still have a deer tag. That's plenty of justification in itself. Okay, I don't have to hunt. I'll just ride along and watch. I'll carry the cameras and film for everybody else. I'll help the wranglers. I'll clean the corrals. I'll sweep up.

In the end, I succumb. My horse moves without any prodding by me. He is part of the conspiracy. He knows the real world is waiting. It needs me to fill some little void in its ongoing puzzle. Resistance is futile.

The real problem with Cowboy hunting? It comes only once a year.

TIP - Packing out : If you are with a reputable outfitter, chances are that he will be hauling your game out periodically during your stay. So, if you shoot a Deer on the first day of the trip, it will probably be waiting in some cooler in town by the time you are ready to leave. Most outfitters have made previous arrangements with meat processors to collect what they bring out of the mountains as spoon as possible. The outfitter will have forms from the processor for delineating just how you would like the processing handled – how many steaks, how many chops and roasts, how much hamburger, how you want it mixed, how you want it packaged, etc.. He will essentially take your order in the wilderness and pass it on to the processor so it will be ready for you to pick up on your way out.

If you happen to take your game late in the hunt, it may be that it will be still in camp when you are ready to leave. You will be hauling it down in the pack string with you on your way out. This will cause a few difficulties when you get back to the world. For example, if you have to catch plane the very next day after you get back, your meat many not ready to make the trip with you. Or, even if you are driving back to your home, you may have to wait until your meat has been processed and packaged before you can leave.

Game processors usually work seven days a week during hunting season. Depending on the number of carcasses they take in on a particular day, they can usually completely process an animal within twenty four hours – sometimes faster. The problem comes with freezing it. Many processors have the capability to flash freeze your meat. That will speed the process up, but may not necessarily solve your problem.

So, you have a dilemma. If your meat will not be ready for you to take back with you, you will either have to wait around until it is or have the processor ship it to you – gulp!

Be sure to buckle your seat belt before you ask a processor what it will cost to ship your meat back to you. Those Elk steaks you will be eating will be some of the most precious delicacies you will ever indulge yourself in.

TIP - Airplanes: Back in the day, the airlines were very lenient with regards to how much baggage you carried with you. Those days are long gone. Today, they charge you for every bit of excess baggage you have – everything over one checked piece and one carry-on. Some charge for everything. They also charge for baggage which comes in over the weight limit, like a box of frozen Elk very well might.

If you plan to take your meat home with you on a plane get ready to haul out some cash.

TIP - Airplanes: As if shipping charges weren't enough Airlines consider dry ice to be a hazardous substance and will charge you a surcharge for carrying it. The baggage checkers at say the Denver airport know a hunter when they see one. They will know what is in those cold cardboard boxes you have wheeled up to the check-in counter. Don't try to tell them there is no dry ice in them. You might find yourself sitting in a room with a bunch of TSA guys explaining why you tried to smuggle hazardous materials on to a plane.

I tried arguing that dry ice is not a hazardous material because in the end, it is just carbon dioxide and carbon dioxide is used in fire extinguishers to put out fires not to start them. It did not work.

The bottom line? In either case, whether you ship your meet home or carry it with you on a plane, it will be an expensive proposition. When you are figuring the cost of your trip, plan for it in advance.

TIP - Packing out : You do not necessarily have to keep your meat if you do not want it. Sometimes your outfitter will want it or he will know of a family who might. You can donate it, but in most cases you will still have to pay for the processing charges.

Some meat processors participate in meat donation programs to needy families in the area. They will take care of distributing it, but you will still have to pay for the processing.

TIP - Taxidermy : We are not finished talking about the logistics of getting yourself and your game out of the mountains. Let's face it, you go on a Cowboy Hunting trip with the hope of bagging a trophy – something you can mount on a wall. And, there is a very good chance that you just might succeed.

A reputable outfitter will have no problem caping out your trophy and getting it packed out of the mountains. The problem then becomes what do you do with it after that?

Most reputable Outfitter will also have a deal with a local taxidermist to pick your trophy up when you get down and take it to their shop. The outfitter may transport it there for you as part of his service. All you will have to do is to visit him and tell him how you want the mount configured – head up, head down, sneak mount, right turn, left turn, full turn or partial turn, etc..

The next problem will be getting the damn thing back to your home. Think the shipping charges for a load of Elk meat are heavy? Wait till you get the shipping bill for a shoulder-mount Elk. There are no boxes that you can stick one in – not even a refrigerator box. Special cartons have to be made by the taxidermist, which are about the size of a Volkswagen Beetle. Wooden restraints have to be build to support it in the carton so that it will not be damaged. A commercial carrier like Yellow Freight or ABF or Conway has to be used to haul it to your door. Do you think that is going to be cheap? Think again. You will need to take these charges into account when planning your trip.

TIP - Taxidermy: Perhaps you have a good taxidermist near your home and would like to have him do your work. No problem – if you have driven out to your hunt. If however, you have flown out, you will have to have your horns and your cape shipped.

If you drive, keep in mind that a cape needs to be frozen fast. Letting on sit around warm is not a good idea. You may find that your taxidermist will not be able to use it or if he does, the quality may not be as good. Most meat processors will freeze your cape along with your meat, but of course, they will charge you for the service. They will also ship it for you, but because a cape can be quite heavy, the shipping charges will accumulate fast.

Your antlers are another problem altogether. They are awkward items that do not package well. A reputable outfitter will ship them for you, but be prepared to pay an additional fee. Unless he has a packaging store near him, he will have to dig up a suitable box and some packing materials. He'll have to then get it to the post office or to a shipper of some sort. You may want to pay him for his efforts if you intend to come back and hunt again.

You can take a set of antlers home on a plane, but get ready to jump through a whole new set of hoops.

To take antlers on a plane, every point over one inch long must be covered with a rubber tip. Rubber tip? Do they make rubber tips for Elk antlers? Makes you wonder sometimes, who writes these rules.

Western Outfitters have learned to work around the problem by using short lengths of garden hose wrapped in duct tape to cover the tips. A good outfitter will provide some hose for you – unless you have pissed him off for some reason. If so, you will have to stop at a store somewhere on your way to the airport to buy some garden hose and some duct tape. You might want to plan for such a stop when you are making flight arrangements or check with your outfitter before you go to see if he will provide this service for you.

Keep in mind, if your antlers turn out to be big ones, there is no way they will fit into an overhead bin on a plane. So, you will have two options. Either find a box and some padding material, get them packaged and then check them as extra luggage or carry them past the check in point just before boarding the plane and let them stash the horns at the last minute for you.

You might want to call the airlines in advance and ask them what they suggest. Either way, you will probably have to pay.

TIP - Taxidermy: If you are planning to use an outfitter near your home in say, Michigan, you might want to ask him in advance if he has any experience mounting western game. There is a difference. Just because he has done a good job for you on a Michigan Whitetail, does not mean he will be able to do the same quality of work on a Wyoming elk.

TIP - Packing out: When we are talking about packing out, we are not only talking about your gear and your game. We are talking about getting you out – not only of the wilderness but out of the area too.

Many wannabe cowboy hunters do a good job of planning the front end of their trip – choosing an area choosing an outfitter, making travel arrangements, etc., but forget to plan the other end of the trip. As you can see, there are a lot of things that will need attention before you can get back to your world. Booking a flight home at six in the morning the day after you are supposed to ride out of the bush is probably not a good idea. If the outfitter's base is not close to an airport, he will have to make arrangements to transport you at what might be an inconvenient time. Or, you might have to make those arrangements yourself. Either way; if you can afford to hang around until the next day or at least until the afternoon of that day, you will take a lot of pressure off your outfitter and off yourself.

TIP - Tips: You will need to do one more thing before you leave your outfitter. In fact, you might have to do it immediately when you get back to the base camp or ranch or whatever disembarkation point your outfitter uses.

If you check the Forbes list of the country's richest people, you will not find the name of any Cowboy hunting guide. These guys do not make much money. They could never afford to go on a hunting trip themselves. The Outfitters pay them a daily salary, but it is no where near what they need and nowhere near what they deserve. To be blunt these guys work their asses off. They rely on tips to supplement their pay. They hope (expect) to get one from you.

Trying to figure out who to tip and how much is always an awkward problem. Your guide deserves one, of course. But, the wranglers, the camp helpers, and the cooks all feel as though they deserve one too and again, they probably do.

You can tip each one individually or you can make one mass tip and let the outfitter figure out who gets what. Some camps split tips automatically. That is, everyone tosses his tips into a large pot and at the end of a season or at the end of a hunt, they divide it up according to some formula they have reached among themselves.

You can tip individually or you can mass tip – all four members of a hunting party can combine a tip and give it to the outfitter for distribution. Tipping individually may be more appropriate in cases where one guide does an exceptionally good job for one member of your party.

The point here is that you have to tip after your hunt. It is usually done as soon as you get to camp and get your gear unloaded. Many of these guys have wives and families or something else that needs attention and it may very well be that they will be getting just one day off to get it all done, before they have to start humping back into the wilderness. They really do not have time to wait around for you to get it together to give them your tip, so think about it in advance, plan for it and just do it as soon as you can.

The question of how much is a tough one. Most guides get around one hundred dollars a day. They may work ten or twelve hours a day. Do the math. They are not making much. If you ask an outfitter, he'll probably tell you that ten percent of the hunt is a good base figure to use as a starting point. But, extraordinary effort deserves a little more. If your guide ends up scrambling down some cliff and carrying your Elk on his back, he might deserve a little more. If a guide ends up caping out your trophy, while you stand around and watch, he might deserve a little more. If he performs some other feat of heroism that makes your life easier or even livable, he might deserve a little more. Tips should be customized and, if you think that you might want to come back to the same place to hunt again, they should be generous. They will remember who treated them well and who did not the year before.

So, figure a minimum of ten percent of the hunt and add to it as you see fit based on your perception of individual effort. Three, four, or even five hundred dollars is not unreasonable for a good guide. Another fifty or seventy five for wranglers and cooks is not unreasonable either.

TIP - Tips: It is a good idea to throw a few plain white envelopes into your gear so that you can be prepared to fill them and dole them out at the end of your trip. It makes things clean and smooth and adds a nice punctuation mark to the end of your trip.

FINAL TIP

Cowboy hunting is an adventure, not a harvest. Wall mounts are stories, not just heads hanging on a wall. The bad part about Cowboy hunting is that it comes just once a year.

www.ingramcontent.com/pod-product-compliance
Lightning Source LLC
Chambersburg PA
CBHW031642170426
43195CB00035B/254